# THE STRUCTURE OF PSALMS 93–100

BIBLICAL AND JUDAIC STUDIES FROM THE UNIVERSITY OF CALIFORNIA, SAN DIEGO

Volume 5

edited by
William Henry Propp

Previously published in the series:

1. *The Hebrew Bible and Its Interpreters*, edited by William Henry Propp, Baruch Halpern, and David Noel Freedman (1990).
2. *Studies in Hebrew and Aramaic Orthography*, by David Noel Freedman, A. Dean Forbes, and Francis I. Andersen (1992).
3. *Isaiah 46, 47, and 48: A New Literary-Critical Reading*, by Chris Franke (1994).
4. *The Book around Immanuel: Style and Structure in Isaiah 2–12*, by Andrew H. Bartelt (1996).

# THE STRUCTURE OF PSALMS 93–100

by
David M. Howard, Jr.

EISENBRAUNS
Winona Lake, Indiana
1997

Published for Biblical and Judaic Studies
The University of California, San Diego

by

Eisenbrauns
Winona Lake, Indiana



Library of Congress Cataloging in Publication Data

Howard, David M., Jr.
The structure of Psalms 93–100 / by David M. Howard, Jr.
p. cm. — (Biblical and Judaic studies from the University of California, San Diego ; v. 5)
Revision of the author's thesis (doctoral)—University of Michigan, 1986.
Includes bibliographical references and index.
ISBN 1-57506-009-4 (cloth : alk. paper)
1. Bible. O.T. Psalms XCIII–C—Criticism, Redaction. I. Title.
II. Series: Biblical and Judaic studies ; v. 5.
BS1430.2.H68 1997
223′.2066—dc21 96-49913
CIP

The paper used in this publication meets the minimum requirements of the American National Standard for Information Sciences—Permanence of Paper for Printed Library Materials, ANSI Z39.48-1984.♾™

# CONTENTS

*To my parents*
*David M. Howard, Sr.*
*and*
*Phyllis Gibson Howard*

*sippĕrû baggôyîm kĕbôdô*
(adapted from Psalm 96:3a)

# *Preface*

This work explores the structural relations of a short segment of the Psalter. It is an extensive revision of my doctoral dissertation at The University of Michigan, completed in January 1986 under the direction of David Noel Freedman. The present work is a true revision at almost all levels. Every chapter has undergone extensive rewriting and updating, except for chapter 3, the chapter devoted to translation of the texts themselves. There, the revisions and updating are minor.

In chapter 1, the core of the literature review remains unchanged, but it has been updated to reflect publications from the past decade. In addition, changes have been made to clarify the focus of the present work. Two updated versions of the original literature review have appeared in print previously (Howard 1989 and Howard 1993a). The present work incorporates both of these updates (which are used by permission; see acknowledgments) and further supplements them.

In chapter 2, an entire section, entitled "Rhetorical Criticism as Structural Analysis," has been deleted and replaced by one entitled "A Synchronic Analysis of the Masoretic Text." The title of the earlier section reveals the origins of this work in 1983 as a "rhetorical" study, that is, one devoted to analysis of the surface structure of the text, focusing on the features of unity in that text. However, in the years since I began the original work, Gerald Wilson's influential dissertation has been published (Wilson 1985a) and Psalms studies have turned very much in the direction of this kind of analysis, rendering a defense of my methodology on "rhetorical-critical" grounds unnecessary. (In addition, I discovered in the process of describing rhetorical criticism in biblical studies that it has generally had a focus different from classical rhetoric in the Aristotelian tradition. I have explored this difference in a separate essay [Howard 1994].)

In chapter 4, the revisions have been the most extensive. This is the heart of the work, presenting the raw data of all the links between every psalm pair in the section. Of necessity, it is an exhaustive treatment; however, the original chapter was at times tedious to read and significant points often were buried in the middle of much that was not so significant. A major effort has been made to clarify this chapter and render it more readable.

The primary revision in chapter five is the addition of the results of research on Psalms 90–94 that I undertook shortly after completion of the dissertation; this material eventually appeared in my essay "A Contextual Reading of Psalms 90–94" (Howard 1993b [used by permission; see acknowledgments]). This helps to place Psalms 93–100 into their context.

In addition, two new appendixes appear. First, the material on ascertaining the dates of psalms originally found in chapter 3 has been relegated to appendix 1, since diachronic work of this sort is of negligible value in a synchronic work. Second, a short section on wisdom editing of the Psalter that appeared in the original work in chapter 1 (pp. 17–18) has been deleted and is now replaced by a more extended discussion in appendix 4, "Wisdom and Royalist/Zion Traditions in the Psalter." This discussion responds to some recent trends in Psalms studies concerning the supposed tension between royal and sapiential outlooks in the Psalter.

Every effort has been made to update the bibliography and to take recent work into account throughout (except in chapter 3). It is encouraging to see this aspect of Psalms studies—namely, that of "the shape and shaping of the Psalter"—receive so much attention in recent years, both in this country and in Europe. Many papers have been read and published, and several doctoral dissertations on some aspect of the Psalter's final form have been completed or are now in progress.

There are two primary contributions that this volume makes to the field of Psalms study. First, and most important, is its contribution to the above-mentioned new emphasis in Psalms studies by means of (1) its extensive review of the literature and (2) its elucidation of the shape of the Psalms 93–100 corpus. My method is distinct from most, in that my work here is exhaustive, making use of the entire lexicon of the psalms under study. In this way, I approach the problem of the editing of the Psalter from the ground level, moving upward. I am convinced that some form of this method—refined and revised wherever needed—is essential in our efforts to identify the contours of the Psalter in a more established way than we have done in the early stages of this avenue of Psalms research.

A second contribution of this work is its nature as a commentary of sorts on Psalms 93–100. The translation, text notes, and notes on poetic structure in chapter 3 can be consulted with profit even by those uninterested in questions of editorial activity.[1]

In what follows, the standard Psalms commentaries are cited only by author in most cases; the references in these cases are to the commentary's treatment of the verse or section under discussion. Where this is not the case, the citations include date of publication and page number(s).

1. This is the nature of most of Tate's (1990) citations of my dissertation in his *Psalms 51–100* commentary.

# *Acknowledgments*

It is a pleasure to acknowledge the contributions of many to this work. Originating as it did as a doctoral dissertation, pride of place must go to my *Doktorvater* at The University of Michigan, David Noel Freedman. Freedman was the ideal dissertation supervisor, and he has been an interested friend and encouragement in the decade since completion of the original work. His learned, copious, and rapid responses to materials sent to him are legendary among those who have worked with him, and these were most helpful to me throughout the original thesis process. In addition, he has been a persistent voice urging me to publish this quickly, without major revision or expansion. I have not heeded his words about timeliness (nor even about revision), but his advice about waiting for another time to expand the work (to include Psalms 90–106) was appreciated, providing the needed constraints that allowed me actually to finish the project.

The two departmental readers of my original work, Charles R. Krahmalkov and H. Van Dyke Parunak, likewise were very helpful in my formation as a student and have been cordial and affirming in the time since graduation.

Special thanks are due to Bethel Theological Seminary, the institution where I wrote the dissertation while teaching full time. Bethel provided generous secretarial help in 1984–86 and various funds that assisted me in completing the work. In addition, my colleagues there were very supportive, especially Marvin Anderson, Daniel Block, George Cannon, and John Sailhamer (a colleague at Bethel and, later, at Trinity). Thanks also are due to my present institution, Trinity Evangelical Divinity School, for granting a sabbatical leave in the Winter quarter of 1995, during which the revision was completed.

I also wish to thank Dean Billy K. Smith and his staff at the New Orleans Baptist Theological Seminary, where I resided during the sabbatical and completed the revision. The Seminary's generous provision of an apartment, a study room with computer, and access to the library were very conducive to writing, and my contacts with many of the seminary faculty were stimulating and refreshing.

The list of professional colleagues to acknowledge must begin with J. Kenneth Kuntz. It was his paper on Psalms 20 and 21 at the SBL meetings in Dallas in 1983 (see now Kuntz 1986) that gave rise to the idea of the original dissertation, specifically, that connections between psalms could be profitably explored. This idea matched my conviction (then and now) that the Bible can and should be read holistically, not just atomistically. Ken has become a friend and encouragement in the years since. Chris Franke, a fellow Freedman student (although in a different time and place), has likewise been a friend and an encouragement in publishing; it is an honor to have this work appear in the same series as her dissertation. Among Psalms scholars, it has been a pleasure to get to know many of the members of the SBL's Book of Psalms Section, which only began as a "Consultation" in 1989. The atmosphere there is warm and congenial; many important topics are being explored, including "the shape and shaping of the Psalter."

Portions of chapter 1 have already appeared in print, as Howard 1989 (copyright Luther-Northwestern Theological Seminary) and Howard 1993a (copyright Sheffield Academic Press, Ltd.). They are used here by permission of *Word and World* and Sheffield Academic Press, respectively. In addition, portions of this work dealing with links among Psalms 90–94 (see relevant sections of chapters 4 and 5) also have been published (as Howard 1993b); this material too is used by permission of Sheffield Academic Press. My thanks go to both publishing organs for these permissions.

My thanks go to Bill Propp and his editorial board for accepting this work into the University of California, San Diego Biblical and Judaic Series. Special thanks also go to Jim Eisenbraun and his staff. Jim has been a source of wise words and encouragement to me ever since he preceded me at The University of Michigan many years ago, and his and his staff's careful shepherding of this manuscript through the publication process has improved it in many ways.

My wife, Jan, deserves a special acknowledgment, as one who stood with me through the ups and downs of my graduate program and the writing of the original dissertation. She has been especially affirming of my writing endeavors in recent years, including this revision. It is a joy to do my work in companionship with her. Our two daughters, Christina and Melody, have been cheerfully dismissive about Dad's work; one of them told a friend once: "Yeah, Dad's a 'Doctor,' but he can't help anybody." Nevertheless, they are a priceless gift to us from the God spoken of so eloquently in these psalms. I write these words on a bright, sunny Saturday, eleven years to the day after another (dreary) Saturday on which I toiled on the original dissertation. I did not know, until two months later, that Christina was on that very day being born and that Jan and I were the parents of choice of her birth mother.

The original work was dedicated to my parents, and so it remains here. My father and mother early in life introduced me to the God who reigns, and this fact has shaped my life ever since. Their lives have consistently been models of faithful service and dedication to him. Their active interest in my graduate studies and subsequent academic career has been a continuing source of affirmation and stimulus. The dedication reads as follows (modified by a single vowel point from Ps 96:3a): "They have declared among the nations his glory." In their case, because of a lifetime of missionary service, this is literally true.

October 5, 1996
Lindenhurst, Illinois

# *Abbreviations*

| | |
|---|---|
| BDB | F. Brown, S. R. Driver, and C. A. Briggs, *Hebrew and English Lexicon of the Old Testament* |
| BH | Biblical Hebrew |
| BHK | R. Kittel, *Biblia Hebraica* |
| BHS | *Biblia Hebraica Stuttgartensia* |
| *GAG* | W. von Soden, *Grundriss der Akkadischen Grammatik, Samt Ergänzungsheft* |
| GKC | *Gesenius' Hebrew Grammar* (ed. E. Kautzsch, trans. A. E. Cowley) |
| JB | Jerusalem Bible |
| $KB^3$ | L. Koehler and W. Baumgartner, *Lexicon in Veteris Testamenti libros* |
| MT | Masoretic Text |
| NAB | New American Bible |
| NASB | New American Standard Bible |
| NEB | New English Bible |
| NIV | New International Version |
| NJPSV | New Jewish Publication Society Version |
| RSV | Revised Standard Version |

# *Chapter 1*
# *A Contextual and Structural Approach to Psalms 93–100*

## Modern Critical Approaches to Psalms Study

The related questions of (1) a single, large, overriding principle of organization behind the book of Psalms and (2) the connections between individual, neighboring psalms, or among groups of psalms, have received varying degrees of attention in the history of Psalms studies. For the most part, these two questions have been ignored in favor of other interests considered to be more pressing. Even when students of the Psalms have been concerned with these issues, their attention has rarely been focused exclusively on them, and the results usually have been meager.

With the rise of critical scholarship in the nineteenth century, scholarly interest in the Bible, the Psalms included, focused on the historical backgrounds of the biblical materials and often included radical reconstruction of the biblical text. Representative of this period and the approach that predominated are the works of Briggs (1906), Cheyne (1891, 1904), Ewald (1880), Perowne (1890), and Wellhausen (1898).

Modern Psalms study was dramatically reshaped by the work of Gunkel (1926, 1933). He focused attention on the literary forms (genres) of individual psalms and paid attention to the *Sitz im Leben* that gave rise to each form. Since the psalms in the biblical canon were not arranged according to literary genre, the work of Gunkel and all indebted to him since has ranged throughout the Psalter, collecting and discussing together the psalms of various genres. At the same time attention continued to be paid, in varying degrees, to matters of authorship and historical reconstruction (the search for the *Sitz im Leben*).

Mowinckel (1922, 1962) followed Gunkel's lead in classifying the psalms by genre, but went beyond Gunkel in emphasizing the cultic background of almost all the psalms (the few "wisdom" psalms excepted [1962: 2.104–25]). Mowinckel's other notable influence has derived from his view that the major festival in Israel was the harvest and new-year festival, the centerpiece of which was the so-called "Enthronement of YHWH" festival (1922; 1962: 1.106–92).

Almost all study since Gunkel and Mowinckel has reflected the influence of these two scholars. Typical of these, modern works which continue to pay attention to forms and (cultic) *Sitz im Leben* and at the same time display a relative lack of interest in the two questions posed at the outset, include the following: Anderson (1972), Buttenwieser (1938), Calès (1936), Craigie (1983), Drijvers (1964), Kidner (1973, 1975), Kissane (1954), Kraus (1978, 1988–89), Leslie (1949), McCullough and Taylor (1955), Nötscher (1947), Oesterley (1937, 1939), Sabourin (1969), Schmidt (1934), Weiser (1962), Kraus (1978), and Gerstenberger (1988). Dahood's work (1966–70) represented a major departure from these approaches, because he paid attention to Ugaritic materials, but he likewise had brief sections on forms and showed no real interest in the Psalter's organization.

The most that any of these commentators has done with regard to the organization of the Psalter (or of subsections of it) is found in the introductory sections of the commentaries. Typically, the division into five books (Psalms 1–41, 42–72, 73–89, 90–106, 107–50), marked by the doxologies at the end of the last psalm in each group, is noted, and a comment may be made about some of the various collections or pseudo-collections within (or across) these divisions. Examples of these are the *ma*ᶜ*ălôt* psalms (120–34), the Asaphic (73–83) and Korahite (42–49, 84–85, 87–88) collections, the Elohistic Psalter (42–83), and the *maśkîl* groups (42–45, 52–55). There has been no real interest in the internal structures of these collections, except casual comments that they were probably liturgical collections of one type or another. More specific questions of organization and structure *within* these groupings largely have gone unaddressed.

## Studies Devoted to Contextual and Structural Relationships

### *Pre-1970s*

The rabbis traditionally were more attuned to the second question posed above, that of connections between neighboring psalms, than were Christian scholars. Their works especially reflected attention to key-word links between consecutive psalms ("concatenation"; Brennan 1976: 126). Often, these links involved repetition of key words at the end of one psalm and the beginning of the next.[1]

1. See Cassuto 1947 for a brief but wide-ranging essay on this principle, which he termed "verbal association."

Prior to the rise of modern critical scholarship, interest in the psalms in Christian circles was dominated by allegorical or messianic concerns (Neale and Littledale 1874–79; Waltke 1981: 3–5). This concern addressed the first question above (the principle of organization), but often did so in a way that violated sound canons of interpretation. A traditional commentator of great influence who is representative of the messianic approach and clung to it even after the rise of modern criticism, was Hengstenberg (1860–69).[2]

Numerous studies did show some interest, albeit limited, in the two questions at hand. Most of this interest was limited to noting slight relationships between consecutive psalms, but occasionally an interest in the question of overriding motifs throughout the entire Psalter appears as well.

In the nineteenth century, Delitzsch (1846, 1881) and Alexander (1865) paid the most attention to questions of this sort, especially to connections between consecutive psalms. This concern was the major thrust of Delitzsch's 1846 publication, and it is seen in his commentary on the Psalms, as well. He investigated the connection of ideas between consecutive psalms and thought that these ran topically throughout the Psalter (1881: 1.15–23; and *passim* throughout the commentary proper). He stated (1881: 1.21): "This phenomenon, that psalms with similar prominent thoughts, or even with only markedly similar passages, especially at the beginning and the end, are thus strung together, may be observed throughout the whole collection." He saw in the arrangement of the Davidic psalms the key to the unifying motif of the entire book, namely, a concern with the Davidic covenant and, ultimately, a messianic concern.

Alexander (1865) likewise was sensitive to links between consecutive psalms, and he devoted a major section of his introduction to the coherence of the Psalter (pp. vii–xiv out of a total of 16 pages). He argued that the messianic motif was primary, with the Davidic covenant (2 Samuel 7) given a prominent place (pp. xiv–xv). He discussed several possible principles of arrangement, the most relevant one for this discussion being that juxtaposition of psalms was often due to "resemblance or identity of subject or historical occasion, or in some remarkable coincidence of general form or of particular expressions" (p. ix). He admitted that in some cases the connections are easier to see than in others, but also stated (pp. ix–x):

> Sometimes, particularly in the latter part of the collection, we may trace not only pairs but trilogies and even more extensive systems of connected psalms, each independent of the rest, and yet together forming beautiful and striking combinations, particularly when the nucleus or basis of the series is an ancient psalm, for instance one

2. See also Fischer's essay (1987), showing the Christological emphasis of John Henry Newman in the nineteenth century.

> of David's, to which others have been added, in the way of variation or of imitation, at a later period, such as that of the Captivity.

Alexander's commentary proper shows careful attention to the details of possible connections between psalms, including key words, motifs, and even grammatical constructions.

Since Delitzsch and Alexander, however, very few commentators have pursued these concerns. Kirkpatrick (1901) and two popular Jewish commentators, Cohen (1945) and Hirsch (1960, 1966), were the notable exceptions. The first two observed many key-word connections between psalms, but attempted no significant analysis beyond this observation. Hirsch's comments were limited to telling the "story" of the psalms in terms of Israel's exilic experiences. Niemeyer (1950) did address the specific question of the ordering of the Psalter, but he rejected the approaches of Delitzsch and others who saw a clear ordering. Niemeyer's work was wide-ranging, examining principles of organization in such corpuses as the Mishnah, the Qurʾān, the Book of the Covenant (Exodus 21–23), Proverbs 25–29, and the Book of the Twelve. In the Psalter, Niemeyer saw no overarching editorial hand(s), only standard collections that have been recognized by almost all scholars.

Westermann's article (1962, 1981b) on the formation of the Psalter was a significant exception to the prevailing mood of his day. In this essay, he made seven distinctive observations, several of which anticipated the work of Childs and Wilson (see below). The most significant of these were as follows. First, he noted that the collections of individual laments tend to group early in the Psalter, mainly in Books I and II, and that the great praise collections tend to group toward the end, mainly in Books IV and V. (In this way, the outline of the Psalter as a whole mirrors the outline of the lament itself: both end with movement toward praise.) Second, he noted that certain praise psalms function to close small collections of psalms (e.g., Psalms 18–19, 33–34, 40, 65–66, 100, 117, 134). Third, he noted the function of royal psalms as part of the Psalter's framework.[3]

### *1970s and 1980s*

During the 1970s and 1980s a more steady stream of works concerned with the links, structure, and overall motifs of the Psalter has emerged, and it has become a torrent in the 1990s. Goulder (1975, 1982) has focused

3. Yeivin's article (1969) on the divisions of the Psalter into sections is not truly concerned with original editorial activities per se but rather with rabbinic and Masoretic traditions of dividing into sections (*sedarim*).

on these issues in connection with liturgical aspects of collections in the Psalter. Discussing the tendency to classify psalms according to genre, which has resulted in random study of many psalms, he stated (1982: 8):

> The dazzled student soon suppresses as naive his instinct that it is proper to study [Psalm] 1 before [Psalm] 2, and that there is something curious in beginning a book on the Psalter with the 110th, or 89th psalm. . . . The instinct that the order of the psalms may be important is not however naive, and is far from irrational. . . . [I]t is entirely proper to begin the study of the Psalter with the expectation that it will be an ordered and not an assorted collection; or, at the very least, that it will contain elements that were rationally ordered.

In a similar way Brennan (1976: 126–27) stated the underlying presupposition typical of such efforts:

> [A] careful reading indicates that the Psalter has not developed in a haphazard and arbitrary way, but has been carefully woven together in such a manner that previously independent compositions, or smaller collections of such compositions, now comment upon or respond to one another. Hence, for a proper understanding of the Psalter it is not enough to study each of its 150 components in the historical context from which it originally sprang. They must all be studied in their relationship to each other, since all of them together convey more than they do if looked at separately.

Brennan first treated Book V of the Psalter (Psalms 107–50). He saw the governing principles of the final collection as literary, not liturgical (1976: 128), and his work traced the key-word connections therein. His second treatment (1980), although shorter, was in some ways more ambitious than the first, since here he stated more directly that not only was there an internal coherence in the Psalter, but that there was a unifying motif, wisdom. While the original *Sitz im Leben* of individual psalms and even small collections in the Psalter was the cult and the "I" of many of the psalms was the Davidic king, the reader of the Psalter in its final form was to read it as a book; it was not necessarily to be performed or used as a manual for liturgy. Thus, the "I" was now each individual reader. Brennan concluded (p. 29) that

> Such a reading of the Psalter opens the way to an eschatological and messianic interpretation of many texts which had originally only a limited national and historic setting. The Psalter comes to be seen as a magnificent dramatic struggle between the two ways—that of Yahweh, his anointed king, and the company of the just, and that of the wicked, the sinners, the evil-doers.

In reaching this conclusion, Brennan put much stock in the significance of the content and placement of Psalms 1 and 2. Psalm 1, a Torah psalm, clearly lays out the two ways, thus setting the stage for a reading of the entire book as reflective of the struggle between them. Psalm 2 is a royal psalm, and its placement made clear that the memory of the Davidic king was to be kept alive even after the fall of the monarchy.

We should note that this attention to Psalms 1 and 2, and especially Psalm 1, as the heading for the Psalter, is not unique to Brennan (or any of those below). Most introductions and commentaries note this in passing and note that, while the Masoretic Text of the Psalter carries superscriptions for only 116 psalms, the Old Greek traditions carry superscriptions for all but Psalms 1 and 2, lending credence to this idea. What is new with Brennan and the others is the emphasis on the confluence of placement and content of these two psalms (or at least Psalm 1) as having a determining effect upon reading the rest of the Psalter.[4]

In a similar way, Childs (1979: 504–25) focused on the final form of the Psalter and saw eschatological reinterpretation as the governing motif. He stated (517):

> [A]lthough the royal psalms arose originally in a peculiar historical setting of ancient Israel which had received its form from a common mythopoetic (*sic*) milieu, they were treasured in the Psalter for a different reason, namely as a witness to the messianic hope which looked for the consummation of God's kingship through his Anointed One.

Like Westermann, he saw the royal psalms as the backbone of the Psalter, noting that they were not grouped together, but rather were strategically scattered throughout the collection. Like Brennan, he too emphasized the placement of Psalm 2 (pp. 515–16). The significance of the placement of Psalm 1 is that it is a Torah psalm, functioning as a preface to the book, signaling that everything that follows is, in effect, God's Torah, to be read, studied, and meditated upon.[5] In doing so, the faithful reader would reap the blessings promised in Psalm 1. The words of men to God had now become identified with God's word to his people. Childs commented (pp. 513–14) that

> Israel reflects on the psalms, not merely to find an illustration of how godly men prayed to God in the past, but to learn the 'way of

4. On the question of the original unity or independence of the two psalms, see Willis 1979a.

5. This idea has now been developed in an important full-scale work by McCann (1993b).

righteousness' which comes from obeying the divine law and is now communicated through the prayers of Israel.

Gerald Sheppard, a student of Childs, agreed with him that Psalms 1–2 form the "Preface" to the Psalter (1980: 136–44).[6] After noting some of the specific lexical links between the sapiential Psalm 1 and the royal Psalm 2, he summarized their general relationship (1980: 142):

> The profane nations and rulers in Ps. 2 are identified with those who walk the way of sinners and the wicked in Ps. 1. Opposite these, one finds the divine king depicted in the language of Nathan's oracle as one who, by contrastive implication, walks in the way of the righteous. Consequently, David is represented in Ps. 2 both as the author of the Psalms and also as one who qualifies under the injunction of Ps. 1 to interpret the Torah as a guide to righteousness.

He went on to say (p. 142):

> By his association with Ps. 2, David, who is, in canonical terms, the chief architect of the Psalter, is fully in accord with the ideals of Ps. 1. The entire Psalter, therefore, is made to stand theologically in association with David as a source of guidance for the way of the righteous. In this fashion, the Psalter has gained, among its other functions, the use as a source for Wisdom reflection and a model of prayers based on such a pious interpretation of the Torah.

Joseph Reindl, in an important essay (1981), also argued along these lines (although he ignored the implications of the dominant royal motifs in the Psalter). After reviewing some of the literature devoted to the question of the organization of the canonical Psalter and finding it deficient, either because it was skeptical about any organizing principle or because it saw the principle as being solely liturgical, he cited (p. 336 n. 8) Barth's essay (1976), which argued that there was another principle at work than merely the liturgical, namely, a didactic interest. Reindl saw Psalm 1, as did Brennan, Childs, and Sheppard, as a sort of opening speech ("Prooemium") for the reader and "pray-er" of the psalms, setting out the two ways (pp. 338–39). The "and in his Torah he meditates day and night" of Ps 1:2b is literally meant, and even the Psalter is part of God's Torah. He stated (340; translation mine) that "The original *Sitz im Leben* [of each individual psalm] pales into insignificance (though it does not disappear) in the face of the new *Sitz im Leben* which the Psalter

6. Sheppard has returned to this theme in several later works as well (e.g., 1988, 1991, 1992).

has received.[7] Accordingly, Reindl did not see the final redactor(s) of the Psalter as coming from the ranks of the Temple singers, but belonging to the circles of scribes who adhered to the piety of the Torah and followed the way of the wise in older times, anticipating the ideal picture painted of Jesus Sirach (Sir 39:1–11) (pp. 340–41).

If this were the case, one would expect the editor(s) of the Psalter to leave traces of his/their work. Besides the example of Psalm 1 and its placement, Reindl offered other evidence in support of his thesis. He argued that each of a number of other texts is a gloss, interrupting the poems into which they were inserted, usually toward the ends of the poems. The three individual texts he treated were Pss 50:16a; 146:8b, 9b; and 104:35 (pp. 344–50). Each of these introduces a sudden shift in topic and is concerned with a traditional wisdom motif. He then treated Psalms 90–92 as a group (pp. 350–55), showing that they occur at a strategic location in the Psalter, namely, between the first half of the Psalter, where the organizing principle is fairly clear (Davidic Psalter, Elohistic Psalter, plus appendix), and the second, where the rationale is not so clear. Here, too, he saw a decided wisdom flavor.

Reindl laid out four potential consequences of his study (pp. 355–56).

1. The "wisdom editing" of the Psalter that he attempted to demonstrate should be capable of easy detection throughout the rest of the Psalter, the redactor's hand being seen in glosses or text expansions.
2. The place of the individual psalm in the redactional context should not be neglected in exegesis, as he showed especially in the cases of Psalms 90–92.
3. For the Psalter in its revised, final form, a *Sitz im Leben* different from its earlier, liturgical setting can be seen. Psalms study should not be limited to the study of only one (often hypothetical) early *Sitz.*
4. The psalms, originally the words of men to God, now became the words of God to men, suitable for study and meditation by virtue of the "canonical" outlook, which was sought and found in them by the scribes responsible for the final editing. In the end, the idea of the Psalter as *God*'s word (and not humans') "had as much significance for the reception [as canon] of the already existing book in the developing canon as did its use in the cult" (p. 356; translation mine).

7. Reindl's 1979 essay presumably develops this further, but it has been inaccessible to me, despite repeated efforts to obtain it.

The similarities between Reindl's thesis and the theses of Brennan, Childs, and Sheppard should be clear. All four emphasize (1) that a literary rationale was responsible for the final form of the Psalter; (2) that this rationale reflects a non-liturgical *Sitz im Leben*; (3) that an individualizing tendency can be seen in the use of the psalms; and (4) that wisdom motifs play some part in the scheme.

The most comprehensive treatment to date of the structure of the Psalter is Wilson's (1985a).[8] Wilson is another student of Childs, to whom he is indebted for much of the framework of his ideas. He lays the methodological foundations that the others do not, in tracing examples of collections of hymnic material from the ancient Near East: the Sumerian Temple Hymn Collection and Catalogues of Hymnic Incipits (chaps. 2, 3) and the Qumran Psalms manuscripts (chaps. 4, 5). Each of these exhibits identifiable editorial techniques in the outline of its final form. He then turns to the canonical Hebrew Psalter and looks for evidence of these and other editorial techniques (chaps. 6, 7) and finds two types of evidence: explicit and tacit (nonexplicit). For Wilson, "explicit" indicators are found in the psalm superscriptions or in the postscript to Books I–II at Ps 72:20, while "tacit" indicators are found in editorial arrangements, such as the grouping of psalms with doxologies at the ends of Books I–IV of the Psalter, or the grouping of the *hllwyh* psalms (104–6, 111–17, 135, 146–50) at the ends of certain Psalter segments (Wilson 1985a: 9–10, 182–97).

Like the others, Wilson gives prominence to the placement and contents of Psalms 1 and 2 (but especially Psalm 1). The psalms in their final collection are meant to be read and meditated upon (Psalm 1). The Davidic king and the Davidic covenant are prominent throughout (Psalm 2). This latter concern is seen not only by the predominance of David in the superscriptions, but also in the appearance of royal psalms at the "seams" of the first three books (Psalms 2, 72, 89) (pp. 207–14).[9]

Book IV (Psalms 90–106) stands at the editorial "center" of the final Psalter (1985a: 215):

> As such this grouping stands as the "answer" to the problem posed in Psalm 89 as to the apparent failure of the Davidic covenant with which Books One–Three are primarily concerned. Briefly summarized, the answer given is: (1) YHWH is king; (2) He has been our "refuge" in the past, long before the monarchy existed (i.e., in the

8. Although see now also Millard 1994 (and comments below, pp. 17–18).

9. The end of the first Davidic collection at Psalm 41 accounts for the remaining break, according to Wilson.

Mosaic period); (3) He will continue to be our refuge now that the monarchy is gone; (4) Blessed are they that trust in him!

Book V is rather heterogeneous, but an attitude of dependence and trust on YHWH alone can be seen as the model encouraged there (see especially Ps 107:12–13, 19, 28, at the head of Book V). David is seen as modeling this attitude in Psalms 108–10 and 138–45, an attitude that finds expression in obedience to YHWH's Torah, which is represented in the massive and centrally located Psalm 119. The *maᶜălôt* psalms (120–34) manifest repeated reliance on YHWH alone. The section concludes with the great doxologies of Psalms 146–50, including the theme of YHWH's Kingship in Psalms 146–47, a theme that dominates Book IV and that stands in contrast to the fragile picture of human kingship found in Psalms 2–89. YHWH alone is the eternal King and he alone is worthy of trust in the end (1985a: 220–28).[10]

An oft-overlooked precursor to Wilson's work is the brief essay by Gese (1972), in which he identified nine mini-collections, arranged consecutively within the Psalter:

a. The first Davidic collection (Psalms 3–41)
b. The Korahite collection (42–49), concluded by a psalm of Asaph (50)
c. The second Davidic collection (51–71), concluded by a psalm of Solomon (72)
d. The Asaphic collection (73–83)
e. A concluding appendix to the Elohistic Psalter (85–89)
f. A cohesive grouping in Psalms 90–104, concluded by Psalms 105–7 (which all begin similarly)
g. A short Davidic collection (108–10), followed by *hllw-yh* psalms and the Great Hallel (111–18)

Psalm 119, a monument standing alone

h. The *mᶜlwt* psalms (120–34), followed by four miscellaneous psalms (134–37)
i. The final Davidic collection (138–45), followed by the concluding *hllw-yh* collection (146–50)

In this essay, Gese anticipated many of the questions that scholars are grappling with today.

10. Wilson has written prolifically on the topic since completing his dissertation in 1981, approaching the same thesis from numerous different angles. Of particular note are his 1992 essay, which is a convenient condensation of the major conclusions of his dissertation (1985a), and his 1993b essay, which goes beyond these in attempting to refine the major contours of the Psalter he had outlined earlier.

The work of four additional scholars in the 1970s and 1980s will be reviewed as relevant in one way or another to the present endeavor: Seybold (1978, 1979), Auffret (1982), Collins (1987), and Goulder (1975). The first three do not deal with any psalms in Book IV, but their methods consider collections of psalms within the Psalter.[11]

Seybold's 1978 and 1979 essays represent the most sophisticated work on the *maᶜălôt* psalms in terms of accounting for their origin and development. He analyzed these psalms as originally rural pilgrimage psalms that were redacted by editors with a Zion/Temple perspective to form a collection fit for the pilgrimage to Jerusalem. He noted that the repetitions of Zion/Temple motifs tend to occur at the end or beginning of the poems, or else at spots where they repeat (clumsily, in his view) catch-words or catch-lines from the original "rural" poems. An advantage of this approach is that it sees a coherence among these texts that undoubtedly reflects some of the ancient situation. The obvious weakness is the subjectivity involved in detecting redactional layers. Nevertheless, his sensitivity to the flow of ideas within and especially between poems is instructive, and his emphasis on the Zion/Temple/Jerusalem motifs is certainly well taken.

Auffret's 1982 work is a series of collected structural studies on individual psalms, including three studies on collections in the Psalter (Psalms 15–24, 120–34, and 135–38). His work on Psalms 120–34 differs considerably from Seybold's, since he is not concerned with redactional history but rather with existing surface structure. His method in elucidating the structures of the sections (especially Psalms 15–24) pays close attention to repeated words in both adjacent and non-adjacent psalms. The results generally show close connections of some type or other between adjacent psalms and significant connections between nonadjacent ones as well. Often these latter connections contribute to the understanding of the structure of the entire section.[12]

Collins's work (1987) is from a structuralist perspective. He considers the Psalter as an integrated system, in which the final work "has something to say quite independent of the intentions of the authors of individual psalms, the collectors of groups of psalms or the editors of the psalter" (p. 41). For him, the Psalter's unity is at the implicit, subconscious level. This skepticism concerning the Psalter's ultimate meaning, that it does not reside even in the work of the final editors, sets Collins's

11. The review above (and below) focuses on works dealing primarily on the higher level of the organization of the Psalter itself or of large corpuses within it. Many works are focused more on the lower levels of connections between individual psalms. For an overview of many of these, see Howard 1993a: 66–68.

12. Auffret's interests continue in the same vein in numerous other essays (e.g., 1984, 1986, 1988, 1992, 1993).

work off from the work of most others mentioned above, despite the surface similarities.[13]

Finally, a word about the work of Goulder (1975) is necessary. At first glance, his work is very similar to many of those summarized above, since he stressed that the arrangement of psalms in Book IV was purposeful, that it was an "ordered collection" (pp. 269–70). He cited three features in support of this contention: (1) the presence of marked alternations in Book IV, in the form of repetitions of material, especially among odd-numbered and even-numbered psalms; (2) the likelihood that this alternation was due to a pattern of morning and evening prayer over a period of eight days, likely at the Festival of Tabernacles; and (3) given the second point, time references throughout Book IV suggest that the even-numbered psalms were intended for use in the evening (pp. 270–72).

Goulder went on to propose a detailed liturgical setting for Book IV, one associated with the fall Tabernacles Festival,[14] complete with four motifs that tie the collection and the supposed Tabernacles liturgy together: the king; David and Solomon; Moses; YHWH (pp. 274–75). He then showed how each psalm in Book IV reflects one or more of these motifs.

Two major differences between Goulder's essay and most of the works referred to above can be seen. First, Goulder saw a liturgical rationale for the final form of Book IV, whereas the others (except Seybold) have emphasized a literary basis in the sections they have considered. There is no *necessary* conflict here, though, since most readily admit that the final form of the *Psalter* incorporated fixed sequences of originally liturgical material, the parade example being the *maʿălôt* psalms. Thus, hypothetically at least, a large liturgy such as that postulated by Goulder could have been incorporated undisturbed into the larger canonical corpus.

A second difference is more problematic, however. Goulder paid minimal attention to links *within* the corpus he was analyzing, instead focusing on links between it and two other great blocks of material elsewhere in the canon, namely, "the two great Tabernacles sagas, the J/E version of the Exodus and Desert traditions [Exodus 6–34] on the one side, and the Temple's foundation from 2 Sam. xxiv–I Kgs. ix on the other" (p. 274). As a result, he almost completely neglected investigation of internal links within Book IV. This shows Goulder's approach to be very different. But it is also very doubtful that the many links between psalms in Book IV

13. He does not accept Wilson's arguments about editorial intentionality, for example (p. 58 n. 9).

14. This was the same festival with which Mowinckel associated the "Enthronement of Yahweh" Festival.

are, as Goulder argues, due to these psalms' general use within the same festival and to their specific connections with another, far-removed "liturgy." The solution is more likely to be found in considerations of their similarities with each other.

There are several other problems with Goulder's hypothesis as well.[15] First, his argument for an ordered collection does not rest upon three independent supporting features, as he claimed (pp. 269–70), but rather on one undisputed feature—that of the alternation of subject matter between several odd- and even-numbered psalms—and on two that proceed from it. His second feature is a hypothesis, however plausible, deriving from the first, and does not support in its own right the idea of an ordered collection. The third feature derives from the second and can be similarly judged.

Second, much weight is attached to the hypothesis that these are morning and evening readings. While this is certainly plausible, Goulder's actual support for the theory is rather meager, limited to five references, only two of which are even modestly clear, as he himself admitted (pp. 271–72).

Third, the issue of the theory's hypothetical nature must inevitably arise in this reconstruction. The comment of Childs with reference to the many attempts to reconstruct a lectionary cycle for the entire Psalter is appropriate here as well: "Still the hypothetical nature of the various reconstructions along with sharp disagreement among the experts continues to pose serious problems and prevents anything resembling a consensus from emerging, even on basic issues" (Childs 1976: 381).

Fourth (and in the same vein), as he reconstructed a proposed lectionary out of the two sagas, Goulder was forced to postulate lections of widely varying lengths (cf. the data in his table on p. 286). For example, there are several rather short readings and other rather long readings in the same lection series. In Exodus, compare the following proposed lections: Exodus 6–9 [122 verses] or Exodus 10–13 [112 verses] with Exod 14:1–22 [22 verses] or Exodus 18 [27 verses]; in Kings, compare 1 Kings 3 [28 verses] or 1 Kings 7 [51 verses] with 1 Kgs 6:1–13 [13 verses] or 1 Kgs 8:65–9:9 [11 verses]. Although variety of this degree is found in several of the modern-day reconstructions of supposed lectionary cycles in the Psalter and the Pentateuch, it often appears to be a device forced

15. Further criticism of Goulder's thesis is available in Wilson 1993a: 45–46. Another work oriented in a similar direction to Goulder's (in seeking links within the Psalter to large collections outside of it) is Walton 1991. The latter essay has several strengths, but also numerous weaknesses. For appreciation and evaluation of Walton's work, see below (p. 15) and Wilson 1993a: 43–45.

to fit the scheme, rather than a natural interpretation arising out of the texts (see, e.g., Porter 1963).

### *1990s*

The 1990s have witnessed a rapid expansion of interest in the Psalter's shape and shaping, both in the United States and in Europe (especially Germany). A Book of Psalms Consultation (now "Section") was established in 1989 in the Society of Biblical Literature, and a majority of the papers read since then have dealt with this issue.

Ceresko (1990) has provided a survey of the sage in the Psalms on three levels: (1) the wise man is pictured in the psalms as one who prays and observes Torah; (2) the sages were authors of several psalms, in which they revealed their special concerns for wisdom and order; (3) a sage (or sages) was responsible for the formation and shape of the Psalter itself and, as such, was the "author" of the Psalter. Ceresko develops this last point to emphasize the self-conscious authorial activity behind the collection process, one that displays "a unity intentionally greater than its parts" (1990: 230). The scholar-sage, as one who prays, was a fitting author of the Psalter, the collection par excellence of Israel's prayers.

Seybold's introduction to the Psalms (1990) devotes 14 pages at the outset to matters of the structure and purpose of the collection (1990: 14–28). He sees the existence of five books as arising simply out of analogy to the Pentateuch (1990: 18), but he also argues that the patterns of the Psalter's development were complex and that the final shape betrays a wisdom perspective. Psalm 1's nature and placement show that, in the final analysis, the Psalter was meant to be didactic.

An important work dealing with the overall shape of the Psalter is Brueggemann's 1991 essay. In it he suggests that Psalms 1 and 150 open and close the Psalter by emphasizing simple obedience and praise, respectively. In between, however, the very real struggles of life are indicated by the laments and even the hymns (typified by Psalms 25 and 103, respectively). He argues that a critical turning-point in the Psalter is found at Psalm 73, which encompasses both suffering and hope. Thus, the pure, unmitigated praise that is urged at the end of the Psalter (Psalm 150) is now informed by individuals, and communities, struggles and experiences of God's *ḥesed*.[16]

16. Note that his analysis sees the two major divisions in the Psalter as Psalms 1–72 and 73–150, whereas Wilson's analysis locates the more important break after Psalm 89, the two sections being comprised of Psalms 1–89 and 90–150.

Also writing in 1991, Walton attempts to see in the Psalter a "cantata" (i.e., independent compositions woven together into a secondary framework) organized around the theme of the Davidic Covenant. He argues that Book I addresses "David's Conflict with Saul"; Book II, "David's Reign"; Book III, "Assyrian Crisis"; Book IV, "Introspection about Destruction of Temple and Exile"; and Book V, "Praise/Reflection on Return and New Era." Walton's work is highly original, his focus upon the Davidic Covenant is well taken, and he presents some intriguing possibilities. However, his orientation is somewhat like Goulder's, seeking links to canonical collections outside the Psalter, and as a result, some of the criticisms of Goulder noted above apply to Walton as well. In fact, his work is far more wide-ranging than Goulder's and thus even less susceptible to controls, appearing to be even more arbitrary than Goulder's at several points. At the very least, Walton's hypothesis needs careful and extensive testing.

In 1992, an entire issue of *Interpretation*, honoring J. L. Mays, was devoted to the book of Psalms. Three essays dealt with the question of the shape of the Psalter in one way or another: McCann 1992, Wilson 1992, and Sheppard 1992.[17] McCann's essay deals with the function of the Psalter as a book of instruction, not merely a liturgical manual or a hymnbook.[18] Wilson's essay is a useful reiteration in brief compass of his conclusions about the Psalter in his dissertation (1985a). Sheppard's essay focuses on another aspect of the final form of the Psalter, its function as an instruction manual for prayer.

Kuntz's 1992 work deals with the place of wisdom psalms in the Psalter's final structure, pointing out that, of ten wisdom psalms he identifies,[19] eight are found in Books I (Psalms 1, 32, 34, 37) and V (Psalms 112, 127, 128, 133). Moreover, these tend to cluster near each other in each case. Kuntz's essay serves to reinforce earlier studies emphasizing the importance of wisdom (and especially Psalm 1) in the final shaping of the Psalter.

An important work appeared in 1993 that contains several essays on various aspects of the issues at hand (McCann, editor 1993). Mays's lead essay builds upon his 1986 work on Torah psalms and sets a methodological stage for reading the Psalter in a contextual fashion. He lays out "five kinds of data that can be used to construct a description of the understanding, mentality and piety that led to and used the book of Psalms"

17. M. S. Smith's essay (1992a) does not truly address issues of the Psalter's shape, but another essay in the same year (1992b) is a brief summary and comparison of the work of Childs and Wilson.

18. McCann develops this further in his 1993b work (see below).

19. Psalms 1, 32, 34, 37, 49, 73, 112, 127, 128, 133.

(Mays 1993: 16). These are (1) an interpretive ordering of the psalms; (2) a shift in the conception and use of the genres; (3) a move from ritual to instruction; (4) the combination and consolidation of genres, topics, and motifs; and (5) psalms in reference to books of Scripture. The essays by Murphy and Brueggemann are responses to Mays; Murphy's response (1993) is more skeptical and Brueggemann uses Mays's work as a starting point to suggest his own ways of reading the Psalter (which he develops more fully in his 1991 essay). Wilson's and Howard's first two essays in the volume are overviews and evaluations of work being done on the Psalter from the perspective that it is a unified, coherent collection (Wilson 1993a; Howard 1993a).

Wilson's second essay (1993b) refines and advances his previous work, focusing especially on the framing function of royal and wisdom psalms at different redactional levels in the Psalter. Miller's essay focuses on the function of Psalms 1 and 2 in shaping the Psalter, especially Book I, and he argues that Psalm 2 sets a royalist tone to at least Book I. McCann's essay (1993a), on the other hand, builds on Wilson's argument that Books I–III present a view of the failed Davidic monarchy and that Books IV–V are the eschatological "answer" to this problem; he focuses on indications within Books I–III themselves—especially at the beginning of each book—that the monarchy was inadequate. Howard's second essay (1993b) analyzes the first five psalms of Book IV contextually.

McCann has undertaken the most extensive research dealing with the issue of "the Psalms as Torah" (McCann 1992, 1993b). In his 1993b book, he accepts the conclusion of many preceding him[20] that the psalms were meant not merely to be sung but also to be read as God's instruction. This is a lively and important work that addresses contemporary concerns of worship and relevance, but it does not go beyond the first two Psalms in discussing the canonical shaping of the Psalter per se.

Zenger has devoted two essays (1991, 1994a) to the shape of Book IV of the Psalter, with considerably more productive results than in Goulder's treatment (1975) of Book IV. In both essays, Zenger emphasizes the biblical-theological picture of the kingship of YHWH as it is presented in Book IV. It is a kingship with a world-wide scope yet rooted in covenantal motifs reaching back to the Mosaic covenant. Zenger's method is based on a careful analysis of the chapter-by-chapter (that is, contextual) links in the book. He sees Psalms 93–100 as the heart of the book, with Psalm 100 as the climax of the section (see especially the covenantal language of 100:3).

20. In the tradition of the scholars mentioned above, such as Brennan, Reindl, Childs, Sheppard, Ceresko, Seybold, and extending back as far as John Calvin (McCann 1993b: 20).

Zenger also has addressed the issue of the place and function of Psalms 1 and 2 as an editorial introduction to the Psalter (Zenger 1993), in the tradition of Brennan, Childs, Sheppard, and others (see above). He presents the strongest and most comprehensive case for defining both Psalms 1 and 2 as an introduction to the Psalter. He traces their treatment through early Jewish and Christian interpretations—including the oft-cited reference in the Western Text of Acts 13:33 (Zenger 1993: 40). This version quotes from Ps 2:7 but states, "as it is written in the first psalm," indicating the existence of an early tradition that considered the two psalms to be one (or else that Psalm 1 was by itself a prologue and Psalm 2 was considered to be the first psalm). Zenger also advances an impressive list of reasons for considering the two psalms together as the introduction to the Psalter. One of his most important contributions is his linking of Psalms 2 and 149. Psalm 2 is a royal psalm celebrating YHWH's victory over his enemies and the installation of his king on Zion in language that draws upon 2 Samuel 7, while Psalm 149 is similar, again celebrating YHWH's victory over his enemies, in language reminiscent of Psalm 2. Although YHWH's king is not mentioned in Psalm 149, "Zion" is, keeping alive the memory of Zion as both the historical and the eschatological capital of YHWH's kingdom.

Miller (1994) has recently addressed the problem of the shape and themes of the grouping of Psalms 15–24. He explores the relationship between Torah obedience and (human) kingship in these psalms, both in terms of content and in terms of structure. He shows how they echo Psalms 1 and 2, in combining the way of wisdom with a royal theology: the king himself is to practice prayer and obedience to Torah (cf. Deut 17:18–20), and he highlights the importance of another royal psalm, Psalm 101, in the shape of Book IV.[21] The prayers in this collection are, at least on one level, the king's prayers (Miller 1994: 135).[22]

Gerstenberger (1994: 9, 12) addresses the question of the Psalter's nature as a "book" and/or a "collection," concluding that it is *not* a book in our modern sense but is nevertheless an extraordinarily rich collection that addresses the human condition in profound ways. He attributes its present shape not to literary considerations but to the liturgical needs of the synagogue in contrast to the Second Temple.

Two important works appeared in 1994 dedicated to the overall shape of the Psalter, focusing particularly on the diachronic process of formation (Koch 1994; Millard 1994). Both are similar to Wilson's work in

21. I have also made this point below, in chapter 5 (pp. 181–82).

22. Waltke made the point about David's prayers being, ultimately, the prayers of Christ (Waltke 1981), a point developed further by Shepherd (1995).

attempting to account for the shape of the entire Psalter, and both (especially Koch's) pay attention to clusters of superscriptions.

Millard's work (1994) is especially important as a full-length treatment that parallels Wilson's but devotes more attention than Wilson's to diachronic concerns. Concerning the overall outlook of the Psalter, Millard concludes that the major theme in the Psalter is Torah, with YHWH's kingship as a central motif. In the end, David is an integrating figure as "author" of much of the book but even more importantly as one afflicted: if Israel's greatest king was afflicted like this, then YHWH's kingship is that much greater than his.

A recent essay, whose title "The Division and Order of the Psalms" (Anderson 1994) promises to engage the current discussion, in fact does so very little. This work attempts primarily to account for the stages of the Psalter's formation, assigning the reasons for its compilation to liturgical considerations, from the days of Hezekiah or earlier down to the time of Nehemiah. Anderson (1994: 241) is skeptical about any principle of organization in the Psalter whatsoever: he concludes that "there appears to be no systematic attempt to structure the Psalter internally." This and similar statements are primarily assertions, however, and are not defended in any detail. Furthermore, because Anderson mentions *only* Wilson's dissertation (1985a) among modern-day works in his discussion,[23] one must judge that his work contributes very little to current evaluations of the question at hand.

Beckwith's 1995 essay argues that even before the early (pre-LXX) division of the Psalter into five books, there was a threefold division (Psalms 1–41, 42–89, 90–150). He pays particular attention to liturgical indications in the psalm superscriptions (which he judges to be earlier than commonly supposed) and to data from postexilic books (Chronicles, Ezra, and Nehemiah). He judges that the "eccentric" manuscript traditions from Qumran represent liturgical (and not "canonical") considerations.[24]

Shepherd's work (1995) is a major expansion and full defense of Waltke's idea, presented in brief in 1981, that the entire Psalter should in the final analysis be read Christologically. Shepherd is not convinced that there is an ordering to the Psalter down to the chapter level, but he sees Christ as the overarching "Canon above the Canon." That is, the (perhaps

23. Most of the works cited are pre-1970; aside from Wilson's work (and passing references to the 1987 *Journal of Biblical Literature* review of Wilson and to Beckwith 1985), none of the small handful of post-1970 works that he cites deals with the ordering and arrangement of the Psalter in any case. Anderson's work is especially indebted to Niemeyer's (1950), on which, see above (p. 4).

24. See below, pp. 26–27, for a more complete discussion of this last point.

haphazard) picture of Christ presented in the Psalter is more important than any (well-ordered) *literary* scheme that might be identified.

Davis's 1996 work examines the first twelve psalms in Book V, identifying three major unifying themes: (1) YHWH is deserving of praise, (2) YHWH delivers his people from distress, and (3) YHWH exercises his dominion over the created order. Davis discerns a significant structural break in Book V before Psalm 119, in contradistinction to Westermann, Wilson, and others. He gives five reasons for this, including the inclusio formed by Psalms 107 and 118, the later tradition of a combination involving Psalms 113–18 (the "Egyptian Hallel"), and the unity of subject matter in Psalms 107–18 (Davis 1996: 8–12). Davis's method is to use the lowest levels of analysis, following the word-by-word and motif-by-motif comparisons of my work fairly closely.

Creach's 1996 work forges a third path in the study of the Psalter's organization, between those looking for overarching macrostructures and those concerned with microstructures, that is, connections between individual neighboring psalms. Creach takes a semantic-field (or thematic) approach, studying the associated field of one specific lexeme (in this case, *ḥāsâ* 'to take refuge'). YHWH's 'refuge' is a concept found in a majority of psalms, and it is concentrated in significant sections. Creach then uses his findings to comment on the organization of the entire work. This should prove to be a productive third avenue of approach to the study of the Psalter's shape and shaping.

Four important commentaries that incorporate attention to the shape of the Psalter and to interpsalm links have appeared in the 1990s: Tate (1990), Hossfeld and Zenger (1993), Mays (1994a), and McCann (1996). Hossfeld and Zenger's book is the most self-consciously devoted to studying interpsalm links and the Psalter's shape, and it (along with succeeding volumes) is destined to become a significant landmark in this field. McCann's work also does this in a self-conscious way, but it is limited somewhat by the constraints and demands of the series in which it appears.

## Focus of the Present Study

The present work builds on many of the works reviewed above in that it describes the internal structure of a specific, limited corpus within the Psalter, Psalms 93–100. It is closest in specifics of method to Auffret's approach, in that it pays exhaustive attention to the lowest-level lexical links among the texts dealt with.[25] However, it shares with almost all of

25. See chapter 2 and the introduction to chapter 4 for more on the methods employed here.

the works above the assumption that the observable structure, organization, and coherence of the Psalter are due to intentional editorial activity, rather than being merely the products of a random collecting of psalms. It is especially indebted to Wilson's programmatic dissertation (1985a) for providing an empirical methodological framework, one found not only within the biblical Psalter but also in similar, extrabiblical collections, within which to work.[26]

The objectives here are more modest than those pursued by Brennan, Reindl, Wilson, M. Millard, or others, all of whom have been concerned to describe the higher-level patterns and unifying motif(s) of the Psalter. Most of the work done on the question of the editorial shaping of the Psalter to date has been concerned with its macrostructure. The present work, however, is concerned with its microstructure. As a result, the structure of only one discrete section is described, but in much greater detail than any of the studies mentioned above.

My concern, then, is to describe the structure of Psalms 93–100 as a unified, coherent group of psalms. I attempt to demonstrate that the present order is intentional and significant and that YHWH's kingship is a central focus of *all* the psalms, not just those identified as "kingship" psalms on modern form-critical grounds. I accomplish this by highlighting those lexical, thematic, generic, and structural links that are truly significant. This work is exhaustive in that it considers every lexeme in every psalm and explores all possible combinations of interpsalm links.[27]

The work on Psalms 93–100 begins, after some preliminary methodological considerations (chapter 2), by considering each psalm on its own, with attention given to establishing the text of the psalm and the meanings of particular words and phrases within it. I consider each psalm in depth, from the lowest levels of morphological and lexical analysis to the highest levels of overall poetic structure (chapter 3). I then proceed to consider each psalm in its larger contexts, in its relationships with the other psalms. I accomplish this by laying out, analyzing, and summarizing the raw data of every lexical, thematic, generic, and structural link between each pair of psalms in the group (chapter 4). I conclude by drawing a profile of the entire group of Psalms 93–100, highlighting the most im-

26. Note that Wilson's work appeared when the original version of the present work was already in progress as a dissertation. It thus provided a convenient capstone to my original review of the literature. It also provided the proper methodological framework that had been lacking up to that time, one that demonstrated at the higher levels of analysis what I was attempting to demonstrate at the lower levels.

27. See chapter 4 for the criteria by which links are judged to be significant and for explanation of the rationale for considering every lexeme in these psalms.

portant links in the section, paying brief attention to the links with the remaining psalms in Book IV: Psalms 90–92 and 101–6 (chapter 5). When these psalms are read as a group, consecutively and in relationship to one another, they speak with a voice that is greater than the voices of the individual psalms themselves.

The choice of this particular group of psalms (93–100) is somewhat arbitrary, although not entirely. On strictly form-critical grounds, the psalms that belong together here have often been identified as Psalms 93 and 96–99 (along with Psalm 47), that is, the Kingship (or Enthronement) of YHWH psalms, following Mowinckel's lead (1962: 1.106).[28] Consonant with the interest in form-critical genres and *Sitzen im Leben* mentioned above, there is usually no attempt made to discuss the place of two very different psalms (Psalms 94 and 95) within the otherwise fairly homogeneous corpus or to discuss the function of Psalm 100 in following immediately after several psalms closely related to each other (but less closely to 100). The present order, which includes Psalms 94 and 95 with the others (somewhat intrusively, in most scholars's estimations), is usually attributed by scholars to liturgical considerations. However, they rarely elaborate on this view but merely assert or assume it.[29]

Occasionally (and increasingly), however, Psalms 93–100 *are* referred to in scholarly literature as a coherent group (e.g., Mowinckel 1962: 2.196; Kidner 1973: 6; Mays 1993: 17; Zenger 1991: 240–42; 1994: 157–70). Often, Psalms 93–99 are referred to as a homogeneous group, and Psalm 100 is considered to be a concluding doxology for the group (e.g., Dahood 1966: xxxi–xxxii; Sabourin 1969: 1.7; Kraus 1978: 10–11; Westermann 1981b: 255). There is very little difference in these two formulations, since Psalm 100 is closely linked with the preceding psalms in either case.

There are at least four advantages in the selection of Psalms 93–100 for study. First, it is, for the most part, a relatively homogeneous group of psalms, and this facilitates its study. The exceptions to this homogeneity that I have noted contribute to the conclusion that this group did not exist as a relatively early, independent collection (in the way that Psalms 120–34 undoubtedly did) but rather owes its existence to a relatively late editorial collection process.

A second advantage of the choice of Psalms 93–100 is that they do not stand at a critical juncture in the Psalter; they occupy, rather, a position *in medias res*. This grouping does not have the problems that might

28. See, e.g., Anderson 1972: 33; Drijvers 1964: 164–82; Leslie 1949: 63–83; Oesterley 1937: 67.

29. See, e.g., Briggs 1906: 1.lxxx; 2.299–301; Anderson 1972: 27; Goulder 1975.

be attached to it were it located at a critical juncture, whether at the beginning or end of the Psalter, or at one of the seams between the five books.

A third advantage of the choice of Psalms 93–100 is that their contents are among the most exalted in the Psalter: they proclaim YHWH as King in sustained, joyful outbursts of praise. Largely because of their presence in Book IV, Wilson sees Book IV as the "center" of the Psalter, as I have noted above. Thus, even though they do not stand at a juncture between "books" in the Psalter, Psalms 93–100 are indeed critical to an understanding of the shape of the entire work. As Wilson has noted, these Kingship of YHWH psalms do indeed provide an answer to many of the questions about YHWH's presence and activity raised earlier in the Psalter.

Fourth, from a form-critical perspective, this group coheres as a homogeneous string of psalms of the community. They are bounded by two psalms of the individual (Psalms 92 and 101).[30]

Furthermore, it should be evident to any attentive reader of the Psalter that these eight psalms are by no means divorced from their immediate context in Book IV. There are significant links between Psalms 92 and 93 and between Psalms 100 and 101, as well as many others that also can be traced. Some of these will be noted briefly in chapter 5, especially those among Psalms 90–94. The foundation is thus laid for the obvious next step, a detailed consideration of the entire structure of Book IV, followed by consideration of the rest of the Psalter.[31]

30. While this may not seem to be a very significant point, nor a criterion by which to judge the unity of a section of the Psalter, it does appear to have been a significant factor in the overall organization of the book. See the comments below, in chapter 4, "Structure/Genre Similarities" (pp. 101–2).

31. N. Whybray's critique (1996) of the approaches represented here appeared too late for consideration above. He concludes that "there is no evidence that there was a systematic and purposeful redaction of the whole Psalter in any of the suggested ways." Whybray is an important scholar whose criticisms deserve an extended response; however, here I can make but three points concerning his interaction with my own work. (1) His critique on p. 28 of my expectation that links may eventually be found between every adjacent psalm pair does not take into account my concerns to distinguish between significant key-word links and incidental repetitions (see below in chapter 4, and Howard 1993b: 117). (2) He does not seem to realize (p. 82) that my "forced" claims about Psalm 93 are made in the context of its preceding Psalm 94, not in and of itself. (3) He mistakenly assumes (p. 93) that McCann and I take the same position vis-à-vis Psalm 89 (see appendix 4 below).

## *Chapter 2*
# *Methodological Considerations*

The basic nature and goals of this study have been laid out in chapter 1. Some methodological considerations remain, however, and they are treated here. All of these methodological issues are related to the approach announced in chapter 1, namely, of examining each poem individually, in detail, before proceeding to study the poems in context.

First, the focus of this study is on the Masoretic Text (MT) of the psalms. Thus, it is a synchronic study of Psalms 93–100 within that text tradition. This agrees with many of the approaches common in biblical studies today, including various types of literary criticism and some varieties of "rhetorical" criticism.[1] Part of this chapter deals briefly with synchronic approaches to the Masoretic text tradition, and a second part deals briefly with the question of the Qumran text tradition vis-à-vis the Masoretic text tradition.

A third section of the chapter focuses on a tool that assists structural analysis of poetic texts, syllable counting. Syllable counting is not usually a component of the synchronic or structural analyses practiced by the majority of scholars. However, as will be shown, used judiciously and in conjunction with other tools, such as stress counting and content analysis, the method is productive in elucidating structures and substructures of poems, and these are at least a subsidiary interest here. The syllable-counting method used follows most closely the method developed by D. N. Freedman, and it is interesting to note that J. S. Kselman (1980: 1) included Freedman in his list of rhetorical critics (i.e., scholars with an interest in synchronic, structural analyses).[2] Freedman's studies have used syllable counting, not as an end in itself, but as a means to the larger end of better understanding individual poems (and Hebrew poetry in general).

1. I have reviewed extensively (Howard 1994) the nature of rhetorical criticism in Old Testament studies in a recent essay and it will not be repeated here.

2. Kselman understood rhetorical criticism to be essentially a synchronic, literary, structural endeavor, following J. Muilenburg. I have criticized this understanding (Howard 1994).

## A Synchronic Analysis of the Masoretic Text

At this juncture in the history of biblical studies, there is little need to justify a synchronic approach to biblical texts. The publications by Alter (1981) and Sternberg (1985) are merely the tip of the iceberg of a host of literary studies of narrative texts on the synchronic level, both theoretical and applied to specific corpuses.

Similarly, in studies of biblical poetry, interest in synchronic analysis also is burgeoning. Theoretical studies by Alter (1985) and Berlin (1985) likewise represent but a fraction of the work being done on poetry, and Franke's book (1994) is but one example of synchronic analysis of a specific poetic corpus. The review in chapter 1 of publications by scholars interested in the editorial shaping of the Psalter shows that most are interested in the literary contours of the Psalter's final form.

This is by no means to deny a priori the importance and significance of diachronic and historical analysis, when such analysis can produce results that are more than merely hypothetical. However, diachronic analysis is not the focus here.

A synchronic approach is particularly well suited to a book such as the Psalms in any case, since in the book itself there is a tendency toward a conscious deemphasis of specific historical contexts. This move toward "dehistoricization" often is noted with respect to individual psalms (Childs 1979: 511–23; Wilson 1985a: 142–43). The comments of Miller are typical (1983: 34):

> This situation [that of historical vagueness and stereotypical language used of enemies in the laments] . . . leaves an openness for understanding who these enemies are in a way that pinning them down to one particular category, group, or type of person within the community would not. That is, the enemies are in fact whoever the enemies are for the singers of the psalms.

Again Miller (1983: 36):

> The enemies are an open category, and the content of the category is filled by the predicament and plight not only of the psalmist but also by that of the contemporary singer of the psalm.

This is similar to the situation that obtained for the Mesopotamian canonical collections. Hallo commented on the Sumerian collections (1976: 194):

> [A]lthough the original creative impulse most often arose out of and in response to a specific historical situation, the long process of canonization . . . tended to suppress allusions to these situations. If a

composition resisted such sublimation or ideological updating, it tended to disappear from the canon.

This study, then, is a synchronic study of the Hebrew text, with an eye to its structure and to the strategic markers within the text. In chapter 3, the analysis is applied to the individual poems. In chapter 4, the analysis becomes contextual, extended across the boundaries of the poems.

The Masoretic Text is generally, but not slavishly, followed here. There are four emendations of the consonantal text (at Pss 93:5, 97:11, 98:3, and 98:9). All emendations are based on extant manuscript evidence (not merely hypothetical conjectures), two involving a single letter and two only one or two words. In addition, there are a small number of repointings of the vocalic text.

This synchronic approach by no means indicates a lack of awareness of processes that undoubtedly obtained in finalizing the present text of the Psalter. Indeed, in the individual studies below, attention is given to portions of poems that very likely existed independently at one time or another. However, the primary concern here is not to isolate whatever fragments may have gone into a poem or to reconstruct a history of transmission but rather to analyze the texts in their final form in the Psalter.

The structure of poems is analyzed in chapter 3 at every level relevant to the present task. Morphemes, words, phrases, colons, bicolons (and tricolons), "strophes," and "stanzas" all are analyzed as needed in the individual studies in chapter 3.[3] In chapters 4 and 5, the structure of the entire section (Psalms 93–100) is analyzed, again following a synchronic structural approach.

## Qumran and the Masoretic Text

### *Introduction*

The discovery in the 1940s and since of thousands of fragments of biblical and extrabiblical documents in the caves near Khirbet Qumran, near the Dead Sea, has contributed greatly to many areas of study, biblical and otherwise. One of the most important results has been the contributions to

3. The terms "strophe" and "stanza" as such are not used here, due to the absence of any commonly accepted definition. The terms are often used interchangeably, or they are not defined at all. Watson (1984: 160–200) does distinguish and define them; his "strophes" are subunits of "stanzas," and these correspond fairly closely to the terms "sections" and "units" that are used in the treatments of individual psalms here. See now also Raabe (1990), who follows Watson (see especially pp. 21–28).

textual criticism, since these documents represent a text tradition at least a thousand years earlier than the oldest manuscripts of the Hebrew Bible hitherto known. Among the documents are several copies of the biblical psalms.

The most important of these is the so-called *Psalms Scroll* discovered in Cave 11 (11QPs[a]; published by Sanders [1967]). It contains portions of some 39 psalms from the biblical Psalter, as well as several others. Of Psalms 93–100, it includes vv. 1–3 of Psalm 93, situated between an extrabiblical poem (the "Apostrophe to Zion") and Ps 141:5–10. Its order is radically different from the present canonical order represented by all other manuscript traditions. Another manuscript containing portions of Psalms 93–100 was discovered in Cave 4 (4QPs[b]; published by Skehan [1964]). It contains portions of psalms beginning at Ps 91:5 and ending at Ps 118:26, all in the standard canonical order. It is very fragmentary throughout, but portions of Psalms 93, 94, 99, and 100 are found in this scroll. In addition, fragments of Psalms 95 and 96 are found in a fragment from Cave 1, also in the canonical order.[4]

Two questions arise in a study devoted to the MT of the Psalter as its primary data base, the one "canonical" and the other textual. Both have to do with whether or not the Qumran material represents the same textual tradition as the MT.

## *Qumran and the Canonical Form of the Psalter*

As just noted, the material in 11QPs[a] is not arranged in the same order as that in the canonical Psalter, and there are a few other documents, mostly fragments, that likewise diverge from the canonical arrangement. The majority of the other Psalms material from Qumran, however, does reflect the present canonical order. This has occasioned much discussion as to the exact nature of 11QPs[a], the major document that diverges. It only includes psalms from Books IV and V; its order is radically different from that in the other manuscript traditions; and it includes several psalms not found in any other manuscript tradition.

Sanders and Wilson have argued that this scroll represents a valid edition of the Psalms, from a variant canonical tradition, specifically, that it is the canonical book of Psalms at Qumran. Others, such as Talmon, Goshen-Gottstein, and Skehan have argued (more persuasively, in my

4. See Wilson 1983: 378–80 n. 4 for all of the Psalms manuscripts from Qumran. Flint's new study (1996) is a detailed and comprehensive analysis of all 39 Psalms manuscripts discovered to date; it will be a standard reference work for any future studies in this area.

opinion) that the scroll was not a canonical edition of the Psalter, but rather a liturgical book based upon the canonical Psalter, that is, an anthology of sorts. Thus, it was never understood to be canonical, and the radical divergences in order and the inclusion of the non-canonical psalms are due to liturgical reasons and do not represent a divergent canonical tradition.[5] The debate over the nature of the scroll is not closed, but my view is that the arguments in favor of the scroll being an anthology for liturgical use are the more compelling.[6]

However, even if Sanders and Wilson are correct, the caveat that Leiman advanced must be heeded. He stated (1976: 34) that

> Precisely because of the sectarian nature of the Qumran community, scholars must bear in mind that the content and development of a sectarian canon probably has little or no bearing on the content and development of other sectarian (or normative) canons.

Thus, even if we grant Sanders's and Wilson's point for the sake of argument, study of a text such as the MT remains legitimate, because the MT at the very least represents a legitimate and old canonical tradition, one that certainly reflects the official Pharisaic[7] canon of the turn of the Christian era. Thus, the shape and structure of the canonical text of Psalms 93–100, as found in the MT, are the focus of study here. There is no concern to describe or account for the arrangement in the Qumran *Psalms Scroll* or, for that matter, in any other text tradition (such as the Old Greek).[8]

## *Qumran and Textual Criticism*

The second question arising from the Qumran evidence is textual. The Qumran material can be helpful in illuminating the MT with regard to this question, particularly in cases of variant or defective or plene spellings or in cases of common textual errors (such as haplography or dittography). Thus, for example, in Ps 93:5, 4QPs[b] has *nwh* for MT *n*ᵓ*wh* (Skehan

5. The debate is summarized and bibliography given in Wilson 1983; 1985a: 63–92; 1985b; 1990; see also Leiman 1976: 36 and nn. 177–85 (pp. 154–55); Beckwith 1985: 77–78; Fabry 1987; Flint 1996. See also n. 6 below.

6. See now also Sinclair 1990; Haran 1992, 1993; and Beckwith 1995 for four additional works in support of the "anthology" view. Haran is especially critical of Sanders's position; Beckwith interacts at some length with Sanders's and Wilson's position as well.

7. The term is Leiman's.

8. The Old Greek of the Psalms does not pose problems for consideration of ordering that 11QPs[a] does, however, because it follows the MT ordering in any case (unlike the Old Greek in the case of Jeremiah, for example).

1964: 314, 315), and in the analysis of the psalm below, the Qumran reading is preferred, the *ʾālep* in MT understood as either a later corruption or a vowel letter. On the other hand, the clause *hllwyh* in 11QPs[a] at Ps 93:1 is not dealt with below, because this variant is due to the liturgical nature of the scroll or represents a separate text tradition; it cannot be categorized as a minor textual matter, such as a spelling or scribal error.

## Syllable and Stress Counting and Structural Analysis

An initial step in analyzing the structures of Psalms 93–100 was to perform a complete analysis of the syllabic and stress patterns of the poems (see table 1, p. 32). As will be seen in chapter 3, these processes are helpful in understanding the construction of the individual poems.

### *Syllable Counting*

Methods of poetic analysis vary considerably, and the debate over the nature of Hebrew poetry will not be entered into here. D. N. Freedman has been the champion of the syllable-counting method of descriptive analysis. The great merit of this method is that it is a *description* of observable phenomena. Freedman has shown that ancient poems do break down into fairly consistent lines ("colons")[9] of eight syllables each.[10] The results of this study confirm his observation. The advantage of counting syllables over counting meter or accents is that there is less subjectivity and uncertainty in this endeavor.[11]

It should be noted that Freedman nowhere claims that the ancient poets counted syllables in the detailed fashion he does. Indeed, he has repeatedly insisted that this method is merely descriptive and that the likelihood is that the poets did *not* do an analysis of this sort.[12] Thus criticisms such as Robert Alter's (1981: 14) are misplaced, in that they miss the point of what syllable-counting methods claim. They do not claim to be the "key" to Hebrew poetry, but merely to describe the existing phe-

9. The term "line" is used here in the sense that O'Connor (1980) uses it, to describe what others label a "colon."

10. Freedman's syllable counting is done on a hypothetical, reconstructed text, representing more closely than does the MT the actual spoken language of Hebrew during its classical period. His method will be explained below.

11. Even Freedman, however, has begun counting stresses along with syllables in recent work. Done judiciously, in tandem, the two methods complement each other well (see below).

12. See Freedman 1977: 7; 1971: 304–5; 1972a: xxxii for representative caveats.

nomena. It is a happy result that these phenomena exhibit a high degree of regularity.

The method of counting employed here follows Freedman as he has laid it out in numerous articles.[13] The Masoretic Text is taken as the subject for analysis, with certain variations that attempt to reflect more accurately the pronunciation of Classical Hebrew of the first half of the first millennium B.C.E. In general, the counts are minimal counts and thus are lower than those of the MT.

Counting syllables according to Freedman's reconstructions, rather than counting the MT's data, is primarily for the sake of convenience. For those conversant with syllable counting as a descriptive tool, Freedman's system is the most familiar.

However, since my interest is not on hypothetical reconstruction, but rather to describe synchronically the text as found primarily in the MT (as indicated above), the MT's syllable counts are also included wherever they differ from those of a Freedman-style reconstruction. In general, the Masoretic count is longer. The syllable-counting method does not claim surgical precision, and many individual variations must be allowed for in line lengths; it is most useful in showing general patterns within poems and between poems. Freedman has made this point more clearly in a recent work (1987): poems exhibit both definable, countable "quantities" over the course of large subunits or entire poems and also considerable freedom within smaller units such as the line.[14] The most important factor in syllable counting is consistency in the method of counting, and the method here is consistent.

The salient features of Freedman's method, where it diverges from the MT, are as follows.[15]

1. Segholate nouns are counted as one syllable, since the second syllable, with a secondary vowel, arose later.
2. Likewise, auxiliary vowels (with gutturals) and furtive *pataḥ*s are not counted.[16]
3. Resolved diphthongs in the absolute forms of certain nouns are read as one syllable (e.g., *maym* or *mêm* for MT *mayim*).

13. See Freedman 1972b: 52–53; 1975b: 245; 1972c: 265–67; 1971: 304–6 on his methodology.

14. Freedman has even extended his word-counting techniques to the entire Hebrew Bible, with remarkable results, showing an amazing size balance even among the largest portions of the canon (Freedman 1991).

15. See above, n. 13.

16. However, vocal *shewa is* counted, and thus the *ḥaṭep*-vowels associated with gutturals are counted.

There is one exception to the minimal-count principle that is followed here. The longer forms for the second masculine singular pronominal and verbal suffixes are followed throughout (*-k* and *-kh*, vocalized *-kā*; and *-t* and *-th*, vocalized *-tā*). The problem of the pronunciation of these forms is complex, but it appears that the longer form of the suffix was original in Hebrew and that, even when the shortened form predominated in everyday speech, the longer form survived in elevated speech and literary works. The existing MT represents a mixture of both forms, more commonly preserving the short form in the consonantal orthography. However, it retains the longer pronunciation in the vocalic pointing, and thus is likely very close to the conventions predominating among the writers of the Psalms. Freedman (1972c: 266) noted that the inscriptional evidence shows that, by the early 6th century B.C.E., the short form was standard, but in literary texts and especially in poetry, the expectation is that the long form would have been retained or restored.[17]

We should note that the *qāmeṣ* indicating a long *ā* in the first syllable of forms of the *Qal* Perfect is read as such here (i.e., as a *qāmeṣ gādôl*, following the conventions of the MT tradition). This is so even when BHK and BHS (following the Leningrad Codex itself)[18] do not include the *metheg* that would signal that this *qāmeṣ* is a *qāmeṣ gādôl* (long *ā*) rather than a *qāmeṣ ḥăṭûp* (short *o*).[19] On the other hand, the MT tradition has been strictly followed in those cases where the *dāgēš* is occasionally omitted for euphony (with *s*, *q*, *n*, *m*, *l*, *w*, and *y*), since the presence or absence of the *dāgēš* is consistent in all versions I have consulted.[20] The MT is also followed when *metheg* affects some of these letters.[21] Finally, there are some forms where *dāgeš* is absent in MT, but where it certainly was originally pronounced.[22] In all of these cases the syllable counts would vary slightly. However, it is the overall pattern that is important, and consistency within the limits delineated is adhered to here.

### *Stress Counting*

The advantages of syllable counting as a descriptive method for investigating poetry and as a tool for analysis should not minimized, nor should

17. See Freedman 1972c: 266; Cross and Freedman 1953: 65–68, especially 65–66, on this.

18. See Elliger and Rudolph 1977 [BHS]: xii.

19. See, e.g., *nā-śĕ-ʾû* in Ps 93:3.

20. Thus, for example, in a psalm outside our corpus (but still in Book IV), *way-šal-laḥ* would be read in Ps 106:15; contrast *wat-tĕ-kas* in Ps 106:17.

21. Thus, *wa-yĕ-pat-tĕ-ḥē-hû* in Ps 105:20b, even though there is no *dāgēš* with the *y*.

22. Thus, *yiś-ʾû* in Ps 93:3, which comes from *yiś-śĕ-ʾu* (originally, *yin-śĕ-ʾu*). See Elliger and Rudolph's comments about *rāphê* (1977 [BHS]: xii).

they be overemphasized. Similarly, despite the abuses of metrical analysis as practiced in the past, the analyses here include stress counts for each poem. This method often reinforces judgments reached on the basis of syllable counting, and vice versa.

The major difference in the practice of stress counting as practiced in this study, in contrast with older forms, is that resort is not made to emendation *metri causa*, unless there is some good manuscript evidence to support it (see, e.g., at Ps 98:3). Usually, where the syllable count or meter varies significantly in a poem, other sorts of explanations, such as stylistic variation or intentional emphasis, can be found.[23]

A working method of counting stresses is to assign one stress to every content word, regardless of length. This leads to the extremes of assigning one stress to one-syllable words as well as to five-syllable words. Usually, the lower stress count that results from this approach is balanced by the "normal" syllable count for the line, in the range of 7–8 syllables (see, e.g., Ps 94:5–6).

## *Conclusion*

When used cautiously and in conjunction with each other, the methods of syllable and stress counting are productive in poetic analysis. A general pattern that emerges from these counts is that Hebrew poetry is regularized around a pattern of bicolons of roughly 8:8 syllables[24] and 3:3 stresses. There is much individual variation, of course, and where the variation is significant, reasons for this may be apparent. The poems in Psalms 93–100 conform to the general pattern.

23. See chapter 3, *passim*, and specifically on Pss 94:12a and 97:9.
24. Slightly higher in the MT.

*Table 1.* Psalms 90–106 Syllable and Stress Counts

| *Psalm* | *Lines* | *Syllables* | (MT) | *Syllables/Line* | (MT) | *Stresses* | (MT) | *Syllables/Stress* | (MT) | *Stresses/Line* | (MT) |
|---|---|---|---|---|---|---|---|---|---|---|---|
| 93 | 14 | 101 | (105) | 7.2 | (7.5) | 43 | | 2.4 | (2.4) | 3.1 | |
| 94 | 47 | 379 | (399) | 8.1 | (8.5) | 140 | | 2.7 | (2.9) | 3.0 | |
| 95 | 25 | 204 | (210) | 8.2 | (8.4) | 78 | | 2.6 | (2.7) | 3.1 | |
| 96 | 29 | 251 | (263) | 8.7 | (9.1) | 99 | | 2.5 | (2.7) | 3.4 | |
| 97 | 27 | 222 | (235) | 8.2 | (8.7) | 88 | | 2.5 | (2.7) | 3.3 | |
| 98 | 25 | 181 | (186) | 7.2 | (7.4) | 70 | (68) | 2.6 | (2.7) | 2.8 | (2.7) |
| 99 | 26 | 199 | (206) | 7.7 | (7.9) | 76 | | 2.6 | (2.7) | 2.9 | |
| 100 | 11 | 91 | (92) | 8.3 | (8.4) | 36 | | 2.5 | (2.6) | 3.3 | |
| | 204 | 1628 | (1696) | 8.0 | (8.3) | 630 | (628) | 2.6 | (2.7) | 3.1 | (3.1) |
| 90 | 39 | 335 | (352) | 8.6 | (9.0) | 135 | | 2.5 | (2.6) | 3.5 | |
| 91 | 36 | 328 | (345) | 9.1 | (9.6) | 112 | | 2.9 | (3.1) | 3.1 | |
| 92 | 32 | 258 | (277) | 8.1 | (8.7) | 107 | | 2.4 | (2.6) | 3.3 | |
| 101 | 26 | 173 | (186) | 6.7 | (7.2) | 82 | | 2.1 | (2.3) | 3.2 | |
| 102 | 61 | 467 | (490) | 7.7 | (8.0) | 208 | | 2.3 | (2.4) | 3.4 | |
| 103 | 47 | 386 | (411) | 8.2 | (8.7) | 166 | | 2.3 | (2.5) | 3.5 | |
| 104 | 79 | 640 | (683) | 8.1 | (8.6) | 270 | | 2.4 | (2.5) | 3.4 | |
| 105 | 91 | 677 | (709) | 7.4 | (7.8) | 295 | | 2.3 | (2.4) | 3.2 | |
| 106 | 109 | 857 | (899) | 7.9 | (8.2) | 327 | | 2.6 | (2.7) | 3.0 | |
| | 520 | 4121 | (4352) | 7.9 | (8.4) | 1702 | | 2.4 | (2.6) | 3.3 | |

## *Chapter 3*
# *The Texts*

*Psalm 93*

### Text

| | | *Syllable Count* | *Total* | *Stresses* |
|---|---|---|---|---|
| 1a | *YHWH mlk gʾwt lbš* | 2 + 2 + 2 + 2 | 8 | 4 |
| b | *lbš YHWH ʿz htʾzr* | 2 + 2 + 1 + 3 | 8 | 4 |
| c | *ʾp-tkwn tbl bl-tmwṭ* | 1 + 2 + 2 + 1 + 2 | 8 | 3 |
| 2a | *nkwn ksʾk mʾz* | 2 + 3 + 2 | 7 | 3 |
| b | *mʿwlm ʾth* | 3 + 2 | 5 | 2 |
| 3a | *nśʾw nhrwt YHWH* | 3 + 3 + 2 | 8 | 3 |
| b | *nśʾw nhrwt qwlm* | 3 + 3 + 2 | 8 | 3 |
| c | *yśʾw nhrwt dkym* | 2 + 3 + 2 | 7 | 3 |
| 4a | *mqlwt mym rbym* | 3 + 1(2) + 2 | 6(7) | 3 |
| b | *ʾdyrym mšbry-ym* | 3 + 3 + 1 | 7 | 3 |
| c | *ʾdyr bmrwm YHWH* | 2 + 3 + 2 | 7 | 3 |
| 5a | *ʿdtyk nʾmnw mʾd* | 4 + 3 + 2 | 9 | 3 |
| b | *lbytk [nwh] qdš* | 4 + 2(3) + 1(2) | 7(9) | 3 |
| c | *YHWH lʾrk ymym* | 2 + 2(3) + 2 | 6(7) | 3 |
| | 14 lines | | 101(105) | 43 |

| | |
|---|---|
| 7.2 syllables/line | 2.4 syllables/stress |
| 7.5 syllables/line (MT) | 2.4 syllables/stress (MT) |
| | 3.1 stresses/line |

## Translation

1a YHWH reigns! (With) a proud majesty he is clothed,
b Is clothed YHWH. (With) strength he has girded himself.

c Surely the world is established! It is unmovable.
2a Your throne was established from times past;
b From long ago was you(r throne)!

3a The floods lifted up, O YHWH,
b The floods lifted up their roar!
c The floods lift(ed) up their pounding!

4a More than the thunders of many waters,
b Majestic (waters), breakers of the sea,
c (More) majestic in the heights is YHWH!

5a Your decrees are affirmed, O Mighty One,
b In your house, (your) holy habitation,
c O YHWH, for length of days.

## Translation Notes

**93:1a. *YHWH mlk* "YHWH reigns!"**

This clause occurs only here and in Ps 96:10 // 1 Chr 16:31; Pss 97:1; and 99:1, and it is paradigmatic in classifying these psalms as "Enthronement" or "Kingship" of YHWH psalms. Mowinckel made these psalms the centerpiece of his reconstructed "Enthronement Festival of Yahweh," and he placed heavy emphasis on his translation of the clause as 'Yahweh has become king!'

Both Mowinckel's reconstruction and his translation have attracted vigorous support and attack. The debate over the translation raged through the 1950s, but essentially came to a halt with the appearance of a thorough treatment (Michel 1956) of all the relevant passages where YHWH or *ʾlhym* is described as reigning.[1] In addition, Michel studied all cases of the verb *mlk* used with respect to human accessions to the throne. His conclusion was that Mowinckel's translation was incorrect, and that the correct understanding is something like "YHWH reigns!" or "It is YHWH (and no other) who reigns/exercises kingship!"[2]

Michel's conclusion has prevailed, and no major English Bible version translates the clause following Mowinckel.

**93:1a. *gʾwt lbš* "(With) a proud majesty he is clothed"**

The basic meaning (5 times) of *gʾwt* is 'majesty' (BDB, KB³). However, a connotation of arrogance or pride is found in its use in Ps 17:10. Its references to nature in Ps 89:10 and Isa 9:17 carry the sense of natural forces opposed (arrogantly) to God. In Isa 28:1, 3, it refers to the proud crown of those in Ephraim. Furthermore, other related words (*gʾh, gʾwh, gwh*) carry a prideful connotation (cf. *gʾym* 'proud ones' in Ps 94:2). In each of its references to God (Ps 93:1; Isa 12:5, 26:10), there is a contrast (implicit or explicit) between God's majesty and the wickedness of nations or forces of nature. Thus, the idea of a proud (even arrogant) majesty, a pride in God's person and glory, is not foreign to the texts, but emphasizes

1. The clause is slightly different in each of the following: Exod 15:18; Isa 24:23, 52:7; Ezek 20:33; Mic 4:7; Pss 47:9, 146:10.

2. Other treatments that have come to a similar conclusion, using a variety of approaches, include Koehler 1953; J. Ridderbos 1954; Combs 1963: 34–38, 81–82, 107–8, 219–21; Gelston 1966; Kitchen 1966: 102–6; Kraus 1966: 203–8; 1978: 94–108, especially 99–108, also 817; Lipiński 1968: 336–91. Brettler's recent treatment (1989: 125–58, especially 139–54) concludes that one cannot make a judgment either way, grammatically, but he criticizes Mowinckel's hypothesis of a cultic ritual enthronement for being "based upon a faulty set of interpretations of this phrase [i.e., *YHWH mlk*]" (1989: 157).

the legitimate continuities with other uses of the word, and thus the word is translated here as 'proud majesty'.

**93:2b. *mᶜwlm ᵓth* "From long ago was you(r throne)!"**

The translation suggested here departs from the commentaries and the versions but does justice to the parallelism in the verse.[3] It reflects the reinforcement of the verbal suffix by the independent personal pronoun, a phenomenon seen in both Hebrew and Ugaritic with both nouns and verbs. Dahood (1970: 101, on Ps 109:4) mentioned the phenomenon, and cited Ugaritic *šmk at* 'your own name' (also seen in Ps 83:19), Ps 86:2 (*ᶜbdk ᵓth* 'your own servant'), and Gen 27:34 (*brkny gm ᵓny* 'bless me, even me') in support.

In Psalm 93, v. 1c is scanned as one line but naturally falls into two parallel halves, with *tbl* serving as subject of both verbs. The second part of Section II, consisting of vv. 2a and b, can be seen in the same manner, that is, it consists of two parallel halves, with *ksᵓ* serving as subject of both halves. There is one verb here (*nkwn*), doing double duty for the two lines. The subject itself is not repeated but is recalled in v. 2b by the echoing and reinforcing of its suffix through the use of the independent personal pronoun. This analysis is confirmed by the chiastic pattern now apparent in v. 2, whereby *ksᵓk* and *ᵓth* (both referring to YHWH's throne) bracket *mᵓz* and *mᶜwlm* (both laying out the time frame of the throne's existence), with the verb doing double duty for both lines of the verse. The parallelism between vv. 1c and 2a–b, particularly in the repetition of *kwn*, suggests by means of merismus[4] that YHWH's sovereignty is over all things, both the world and the heavens. The establishment of his throne likely refers to the heavens,[5] which complements the establishment of the world.

Another support for this analysis comes in noting the parallels between vv. 2 and 5 (see also below, on "Form-Critical Genre and Structure," p. 43). In v. 5, the second-person possessive suffix (*-k*) occurs twice, referring to YHWH. In v. 2, it occurs once, but it is balanced by the occurrence of the independent personal pronoun (understood here possessively).

Note that the picture advanced is apparent even if the verse is read in the traditional way ('Your throne was established from times past, / From long ago art Thou!'). That is, the direct reference to YHWH via the personal pronoun also carries with it a reference to YHWH's throne, by means of metonymy (or perhaps synechdoche). Thus, reference to God also echoes

3. The suggestion comes from Freedman (private communication).

4. Merismus is a figure of speech in which a subject is broken into two or more essential (usually complementary) parts, which nevertheless signify the whole.

5. See, e.g., Ps 11:4, where his throne is in the heavens, or Isa 66:1, where the heavens are his throne and the earth is his footstool.

things associated with him; in this context, the throne mentioned in v. 2a is naturally recalled in v. 2b when reference to YHWH himself is made.[6]

Finally, it should also be noted that this verse is the only one in the psalm that does not have an occurrence of *YHWH*. Furthermore, v. 2b, where one would naturally expect an occurrence, is two syllables shorter than the norm for the psalm, suggesting that it may have occurred there. The psalm may have suffered in transmission.[7] However, the phenomenon may be nothing more than a stylistic variation, a deliberate variation from the norm, for added emphasis, as is common in Hebrew poetry. The most dramatic example of this occurs in Amos 1–2, where in six of the seven oracles the verb used for the promised destruction is *šlḥ* 'to send' and in the seventh (the oracle against the Ammonites) the verb is *yṣt* 'to kindle', reflecting either a special outrage at the sins of Ammon (or a special hatred for the nation in general) or simply a variation for stylistic reasons.[8]

**93:3. Verb sequence**

We find a *qṭl–qṭl–yqṭl* sequence in this verse, and it is a prime datum used to make the case for a "preterite" aspect for some cases of prefixing verbs. These are usually found in the early Hebrew poems, reflecting the apparent pattern in Ugaritic. This conclusion is accepted as a given by many[9] and has been defended in more detail by Held (1962) and Robertson (1972: 7–55).[10]

As a general pattern across Hebrew grammar, this phenomenon certainly cannot be sustained. Furthermore, the presence of *yqṭl* "preterite" cannot be given undue weight as a criterion for dating, since a circular argument may result. Its effectiveness is mainly when used in conjunction with other, independent criteria. However, careful, contextual study of individual passages (see Held and Robertson) does suggest that preterites of this sort exist. The present verse is a case in point. The entire psalm is concerned with YHWH's sovereignty over the world (v. 2) and over the waters (vv. 3–4). Furthermore, his sovereignty is seen as having been established in ages past, and the rebellious waters are no longer any

6. On figures of speech such as metonymy (substituting one related noun for another) and synechdoche (substituting one related idea for another) in general, see Bullinger 1898, an old, but still useful compendium (although he does not specifically discuss Ps 93:2); see also Watson 1984: 273–348.

7. Note that the Targum has *ʾlhʾ* here, that BHS suggests addition of *ʾēl* (on metrical grounds), and that Gunkel, Weiser, Kraus, and others added it in their translations.

8. See also on Ps 97:9a, below (pp. 71–72).

9. See, e.g., Gordon 1967: 68–69; Cross and Freedman 1953: 20; Cross 1973: 125 and n. 44.

10. See appendix 1, "Dates of Psalms 93–100," for fuller discussion.

threat (if indeed they ever were). YHWH's established throne prevents them from any longer lifting up their voices in opposition to him (which would be the case if *yśʾw* were translated with present habitual or durative connotations).

An alternative would be to read *yśʾw* as a past habitual. The verbs would then read 'lifted up . . . lifted up . . . used to lift up'. This sense is little different from reading the verb as a preterite. Another alternative would be to explain the form as indicating that even if the waters that have been rebellious in the past (v. 3a–b) should be so in the future (v. 3c), YHWH still remains stronger. This reading must be admitted as a possibility, especially if v. 4 may be read as stating that the waters continue to be rebellious but that YHWH, nevertheless, is greater than they are.

**93:4. YHWH and the waters**

The translation here reads the *mîn* of v. 4a in its common, comparative sense. The picture in both vv. 3 and 4 is of rebellious or contentious waters and the absolute sovereignty of YHWH over them. He is more terrible or majestic (*ʾdyr*) than the most terrible of the waters (the use of *ʾdyr* to describe both YHWH and the waters is doubtless deliberate). The *mîn* in v. 4a is linked with *ʾdyr* in v. 4c. A smooth English translation of the verse would be: 'More majestic in the heights is YHWH than the thunders of many waters, majestic waters, breakers of the sea'.

*Mym rbym* and (*mym*) *ʾdyrym* are read as stock phrases here. The former is common in the Bible, occurring 28 times, 7 times in Psalms (but nowhere else in Book IV). In Ezekiel, the *mym rbym* are usually seen as abundant, favorable waters (9 of 11 times). Elsewhere, they are seen as overwhelming individual humans. Only in Pss 29:3, 93:4, and Isa 17:13 are the waters seen as deliberately rebellious against YHWH after the fashion of Yamm's struggle with Baʿal in Ugaritic mythology.[11]

The phrase *mym ʾdyrym* is found only in Exod 15:10, where the Egyptians are seen as sinking like lead in the mighty waters, but it is undoubtedly meant here as well. It is interesting to note the parallels between Psalm 93 and Exodus 15 and Psalm 29. The latter two, along with Judges 5, are the three poems that Freedman groups in his Phase I of early Hebrew poetry (1976: 118; and see appendix 1, "Dates of Psalms 93–100").

The Ugaritic parallels with vv. 3–4 in the psalm are clear and are mentioned in almost every treatment of the psalm.[12] The personification of

11. The Ugaritic texts are in Gordon 1967: nos. 129, 137, 68; English translations are in Gordon 1977: 67–74; see also Gray 1956: 269–73.

12. However, in the Bible itself, as well, there is at least one other place where the waters are clearly in opposition to YHWH: Hab 3:15 (another poetic text).

the forces of nature present in the Ugaritic texts might be seen here as well, and the titles for the waters may legitimately be rendered as names, not descriptions: "Floods" (or even "Neharot"), "Many Waters," "Terrible Waters," and "Breakers of the Sea" (or "Yamm's Breakers").

Freedman notes (private communication) that *mqlwt . . . mšbry-ym* 'than . . . Breakers of Yamm' can be read as a broken construct chain.[13] The terms *mym rbym ᵓdrym* 'Many Waters, Majestic (Waters)' are synonymous with (or modifiers of) the *mšbry-ym.* They are stock phrases in their own right, as noted, and they are retained intact, inserted into the chain.

**93:5a. *ᶜdtyk* "Your decrees"**

The idea of YHWH's decrees (or precepts, testimonies, or Law) is usually seen as chronologically late, and thus attempts are made to reinterpret *ᶜdtyk.* Dahood (1968: 342) read it as 'your enthronement'; Shenkel (1965: 404–9) read it as 'your throne'; Bentzen (cited by Shenkel: 404) read it as 'sacred assemblies'. These interpretations have the advantage of paralleling *bytk* 'your house'.

The related terms *ᶜēdōt*/*ᶜēdôt* and *ᶜēdut*/*ᶜēdût* occur some 83 times in Biblical Hebrew (BH), the majority of the time in texts considered late. They occur 23 times in Psalm 119 and often in the so-called "P" material of the Pentateuch, and they are associated with Torah in Pss 19:8 and 78:5. They occur twice in Psalm 78 (vv. 5 [*ᶜēdût*], 56 [*ᶜēdôt*]), a psalm that is certainly earlier than "P," however.[14]

While the terms often refer to the code of law in general, they are used several times in Exodus and Numbers to refer specifically to the ark of the testimony, and they have strong covenantal overtones. The term here, *ᶜēdōt,* especially has covenantal connections, referring to YHWH's covenant stipulations or expectations.[15] The Aramaic cognate occurs in several forms in the Sefire inscriptions (*ᶜdy, ᶜdyᵓ,* or *ᶜdn*), and Fitzmyer rendered it as 'treaty stipulations' or simply 'treaty, pact'. Given what is known about the Israelite covenant as a treaty[16] and the early dates (relative to many scholars's "P") of the Sefire material (8th century B.C.E.) and the Akkadian cognates,[17] there is no need to reinterpret the Hebrew term on the basis of supposed lateness.

13. On the phenomenon, see GKC §130; Freedman 1972d; Dahood 1970: 381–83.

14. Freedman (1976: 118) placed it in his Phase III (10th–9th centuries B.C.E.).

15. Van Leeuwen 1979: cols. 218–19; for another discussion of the term and its cognates, see Fitzmyer 1967: 23–24.

16. The foundational studies are those of Mendenhall (1954a, 1954b); see the updated discussion by Mendenhall and Herion (1992) for more recent studies.

17. The term *adē* occurs in Middle and Neo-Assyrian and Middle and Neo-Babylonian (ca. 15th–7th centuries B.C.E.), according to von Soden (quoted by Fitzmyer [1967: 23]).

**93:5a. *n*ʾ*mnw* "are affirmed"**

The common meaning of ʾ*mn* is 'confirmed, sure, established'. It is a short semantic leap to 'affirmed', understanding it to refer to an action by the people, that is, that they are involved in a liturgy or ceremony affirming or testifying to the surety of YHWH's decrees.

**93:5a. *m*ʾ*d* "O Mighty One"**

The word is read tentatively as an epithet of YHWH, 'the Mighty One', or 'the Almighty', as a parallel with *YHWH*. Dahood documented numerous such occurrences in his discussions at Pss 109:30 and 142:7 (1970: 109, 318–19). To these, Freedman (1973) added the example of Ps 78:59. In almost all the cases cited by Dahood and Freedman, *m*ʾ*d* (vocalized *mā*ʾ*ēd*) is parallel to *YHWH* or ʾ*ĕlōhîm*.

Reading *mā*ʾ*ēd* in this way yields a better parallelism here and elsewhere, but it must be acknowledged that the traditional renderings make perfectly good sense.[18]

**93:5b. [*nwh*] *qdš* "(your) holy habitation"**

The MT has *n*ʾ*wh qdš*, and most commentators understand the root to be *n*ʾ*h*, meaning 'to be fitting, suited' (see BDB, $KB^3$, s.v.). However, there is support from Qumran ($4QPs^b$) for reading *nwh* instead of *n*ʾ*wh* here. The term *nwh* refers to the abode of shepherds or flocks, or, in poetic texts, to habitation in general (BDB). The phrase *nwh qdšk* 'your (YHWH's) holy habitation' in Exod 15:13 provides a parallel. The preposition is read 'in'[19] and the verb in v. 5a is carried over into v. 5b. The result is a balanced pair of lines: 'Your decrees are affirmed, O Mighty One, / In your house, (your) holy habitation, O YHWH'.[20] In earlier stages of the poem, YHWH's "house" would have meant something similar to a house of shepherds, that is, the wilderness tent, or even the wilderness itself. In later periods, the association in the poem would have been with the Temple.

## Form-Critical Genre and Structure

There is no disagreement among modern scholars on the form-critical genre of the poem. It is a hymn, one of the Kingship (or Enthronement) of YHWH psalms, along with Psalms 47, 96–99. It is one of only three (along with Psalms 97, 99) that begin with the formula *YHWH mlk*.

18. This interpretation is disputed by some, most specifically by Loretz (1974c) and Marcus (1974).

19. For this reading of *l*-, see Dahood 1968: 342; 1970: 395.

20. It is not strictly a balanced bicolon here, since *YHWH* occurs in the third (and not the second) line of the verse. The metrical analysis, however, is 3:3:3; the syllabic structure is not quite as symmetrical but is roughly balanced.

The structure of the poem breaks easily and logically into five sections. Section I is introductory to the poem. It has a different metrical pattern (4:4) from the rest of the poem (which follows a 3:3:3 pattern in each of the next four sections, with one exception). The syllable count of Section I totals 16, and it does not fit into the alternating pattern of the other four sections.[21] There are three verbs associated with clothing/girding here, but they are not repeated in the remainder of the poem. YHWH is referred to in the third person here, and he is the subject of all four verbs in the section, but he is referred to in the second person in Sections II, III, V, and possibly even in IV. He is not the subject of any verbs in II–V.

The syllable and word counts for the psalm are as follows:

| | | |
|---|---|---|
| I | (v. 1a–b) | 16 (MT 16) syllables and 8 words |
| II | (vv. 1c–2) | 20 (MT 20) syllables and 10 words |
| III | (v. 3) | 23 (MT 23) syllables and 9 words |
| IV | (v. 4) | 20 (MT 21) syllables and 9 words |
| V | (v. 5) | 22 (MT 25) syllables and 9 words |

The placement of divine names and epithets, especially *YHWH*, is often instructive in discerning poetic structure, and the position of *YHWH* in

21. The word count is less conclusive, but the metrical and syllabic patterns carry more weight in this case.

---

*Psalm 94*

## Text

| | | *Syllable Count* | *Total* | *Stresses* |
|---|---|---|---|---|
| 1a | *ʾl-nqmwt YHWH* | 1 + 3 + 2 | 6 | 3 |
| b | *ʾl nqmwt hwpyʿ* | 1 + 3 + 2(3) | 6(7) | 3 |
| 2a | *hnśʾ špṭ hʾrṣ* | 3 + 2 + 2(3) | 7(8) | 3 |
| b | *hšb gmwl ʿl-gʾym* | 2 + 2 + 1 + 2 | 7 | 3 |
| 3a | *ʿd-mty ršʿym YHWH* | 1 + 2 + 3 + 2 | 8 | 3 |
| b | *ʿd-mty ršʿym yʿlzw* | 1 + 2 + 3 + 3(4) | 9(10) | 3 |
| 4a | *ybyʿw ydbrw ʿtq* | 3 + 4 + 2 | 9 | 3 |
| b | *ytʾmrw kl-pʿly ʾwn* | 4 + 1 + 3 + 1(2) | 9(10) | 3 |
| 5a | *ʿmk YHWH ydkʾw* | 3 + 2 + 4 | 9 | 3 |
| b | *wnḥltk yʿnw* | 5(6) + 3 | 8(9) | 2 |
| 6a | *ʾlmnh wgr yhrgw* | 3 + 2 + 3(4) | 8(9) | 3 |
| b | *wytwmym yrṣḥw* | 3 + 4 | 7 | 2 |

this poem confirms this principle. In Section I, it occurs twice as the outer components of an inclusio. It occurs again, delimiting an inclusio in Sections III–IV. These two sections can be seen to fit naturally together on other grounds as well, namely, in the imagery of powerful waters in both. The divine name *YHWH* occurs for the last time in v. 5. It is not matched by another occurrence of *YHWH*, a pairing that might be expected, because of the preceding pairs. However, *ʾth* in v. 2 is a substitute for *YHWH*, perhaps as a poetic variation, and forms the inclusio between Sections II and V.

The link between these two sections is further confirmed by at least three factors: (1) by the second masculine singular suffix, which occurs only in these two sections (once in II and twice in V); (2) by the references to places of YHWH's dwelling—his throne (II, established from times long past) and his house (V, continuing in times to come); and (3) by the only two occurrences of *Niphal* verbs (once each in II and V). This is a very neatly constructed poem, with an introduction followed by four sections, alternating in length and linked with each other in a chiastic (II–V, III–IV) pattern. I conclude that the poem is complete as it stands, although some might find the absence of a concluding unit that corresponds to Section I to be somewhat puzzling.

---

## Translation

1a God of vengeances, O YHWH,
 b God of vengeances, shine forth!
2a Rise up, O Judge of the earth!
 b Return due recompense upon the proud ones!
3a How long will the wicked ones, O YHWH,
 b How long will the wicked ones exult?
4a (How long) will they bubble forth, will they speak arrogantly?
 b (How long) will they boast, all the evil-doers?
5a Your people, O YHWH, they crush,
 b And your inheritance they afflict.
6a Widow and sojourner they kill,
 b And orphans they murder,

| | | | | |
|---|---|---|---|---|
| 7a | *wyʾmrw lʾ yrʾh-*YH | 4 + 1 + 2 + 1 | 8 | 3 |
| b | *wlʾ-ybyn ʾlhy yʿqb* | 2 + 2 + 3 + 2(3) | 9(10) | 3 |
| 8a | *bynw bʿrym bʿm* | 2 + 3 + 2 | 7 | 3 |
| b | *wksylym mty tśkylw* | 4 + 2 + 3 | 9 | 3 |
| 9a | *hnṭʿ ʾzn hlʾ yšmʿ* | 3 + 1(2) + 2 + 2 | 8(9) | 3 |
| b | *ʾm-yṣr ʿyn hlʾ ybyṭ* | 1 + 2 + 1(2) + 2 + 2 | 8(9) | 3 |
| 10a | *hysr gwym hlʾ ywkyḥ* | 3 + 2 + 2 + 2(3) | 9(10) | 3 |
| b | *hmlmd ʾdm dʿt* | 4 + 2 + 1(2) | 7(8) | 3 |
| 11a | YHWH *ydʿ mḥšbwt ʾdm* | 2 + 2(3) + 3 + 2 | 9(10) | 4 |
| b | *ky-hmh hbl* | 1 + 2 + 1(2) | 4(5) | 2 |
| 12a | *ʾšry hgbr ʾšr-tysrnw* YH | 2 + 2(3) + 2 + 5 + 1 | 12(13) | 5 |
| b | *wmtwrtk tlmdnw* | 6 + 5 | 11 | 2 |
| 13a | *lhšqyṭ lw mymy rʿ* | 3 + 1 + 2 + 1 | 7 | 3 |
| b | *ʿd ykrh lršʿ šḥt* | 1 + 3 + 3 + 1(2) | 8(9) | 3 |
| 14a | *ky lʾ-yṭš* YHWH *ʿmw* | 1 + 1 + 2 + 2 + 2 | 8 | 3 |
| b | *wnḥltw 1ʾ yʿzb* | 4(5) + 1 + 2(3) | 7(9) | 2 |
| 15a | *ky-ʿd-ṣdq yšwb mšpṭ* | 1 + 1 + 1(2) + 2 + 2 | 7(8) | 3 |
| b | *wʾḥryw kl-yšry-lb* | 3(4) + 1 + 2 + 1 | 7(8) | 3 |
| 16a | *my-yqwm ly ʿm-mrʿym* | 1 + 2 + 1 + 1 + 3 | 8 | 3 |
| b | *my-ytyṣb ly ʿm-pʿly ʾwn* | 1 + 3 + 1 + 1 + 3 + 1(2) | 10(11) | 4 |
| 17a | *lwly* YHWH *ʿzrth ly* | 2 + 2 + 3 + 1 | 8 | 3 |
| b | *kmʿṭ šknh dwmh npšy* | 2 + 3 + 2 + 2 | 9 | 4 |
| 18a | *ʾm-ʾmrty mṭh rgly* | 1 + 3 + 2 + 2 | 8 | 3 |
| b | *ḥsdk* YHWH *ysʿdny* | 3 + 2 + 4 | 9 | 3 |
| 19a | *brb śrʿpy bqrby* | 2 + 3 + 3 | 8 | 3 |
| b | *tnḥwmyk yšʿšʿw npšy* | 4 + 4 + 2 | 10 | 3 |
| 20a | *hyḥbrk ksʾ hwwt* | 5 + 2 + 2 | 9 | 3 |
| b | *yṣr ʿml ʿly-ḥq* | 2 + 2 + 2 + 1 | 7 | 3 |
| 21a | *ygwdw ʿl-npš ṣdyq* | 3 + 1 + 1(2) + 2 | 7(8) | 3 |
| b | *wdm nqy yršyʿw* | 2 + 2 + 3 | 7 | 3 |
| 22a | *wyhy* YHWH *ly lmśgb* | 3(2) + 2 + 1 + 3 | 9(8) | 3 |
| b | *wʾlhy lṣwr mḥsy* | 3 + 2 + 2 | 7 | 3 |
| 23a | *wyšb ʿlyhm ʾt-ʾwnm* | 3 + 3 + 1 + 2 | 9 | 3 |
| b | *wbrʿtm yṣmytm* | 5 + 3 | 8 | 2 |
| c | *yṣmytm* YHWH *ʾlhynw* | 3 + 2 + 4 | 9 | 3 |
| 47 lines | | | 380(399) | 140 |

| | |
|---|---|
| 8.1 syllables/line | 2.7 syllables/stress |
| 8.5 syllables/line (MT) | 2.9 syllables/stress (MT) |
| | 3.0 stresses/line |

7a And they have said, "YH does not see!
b Nor does the God of Jacob understand!"

---

8a Understand, O dull ones among the people!
b And, you stupid ones, when will you become wise?
9a Does he who plants the ear not hear?
b Or he who forms the eye not see?
10a Does he who instructs nations not reprove?
b Is he who teaches man (without) knowledge?
11a YHWH knows the thoughts of man,
b That they are but a breath.

---

12a Happy is the man whom you instruct, O YH,
b And whom you teach from your Torah,
13a In order to give him rest from evil days,
b Until a pit is dug for the wicked.
14a For YHWH will not forsake his people,
b And his inheritance he will not abandon.
15a For justice will return to the righteous one,
b And after it, (to) all the upright in heart.

---

16a Who stands up for me against the evil ones?
b Who takes a stand for me against evil-doers?
17a If YHWH were not a help to me,
b I soon would have dwelt in (the land of) silence.
18a If I said, "My foot has slipped,"
b Your steadfast love, O YHWH, supported me.
19a When many were the cares within me,
b Your consolations cheered my soul.
20a Can a seat of destruction be allied with you,
b One which creates trouble in accordance with a statute?
21a They band together against the life of a righteous man,
b And innocent blood they condemn.
22a So YHWH has become to me a secure high retreat,
b And my God the mountain of my refuge,
23a And he has returned their iniquity upon them,
b And for their wickedness he will exterminate them;
c YHWH our God will exterminate them.

## Translation Notes

**94:1. *nqmwt* "vengeances"**

The word *nqmwt* often occurs denoting the plural of totality, and here it signifies the totality of YHWH's legitimate exercise of executive power (see Mendenhall 1973: 85 and below, on Ps 99:8).

**94:3–4. *ʿd-mty* "How long?"**

The translation "How long?" borrows from Dahood, who has pointed out that the force of particles is often carried over at least into the next verse.[22] The JB, NJPSV, and NAB translations all reflect the carry-over of the question from v. 3 to v. 4. The signal for the termination of the question is the introduction of the verbs describing the loathsome activities of the wicked; they occur in rapid succession, each time without a subject or object attached. In vv. 5ff., not only are the clauses lengthened and transitive verbs introduced, but the objects are placed in clause-initial position, probably to emphasize disjunction. Another indication of a break is the bracketing of verbs in referring to the exulting ones in vv. 3–4: the *ršʿym* and the *pʿly ʾwn* (vv. 3b, 4b).

**94:5–7. On verb forms**

If the psalm could clearly be shown to have been early, then Dahood's rendering of the prefixing verbs in vv. 5–7 (as well as in vv. 12, 16, 18, 19, 21, 23) as preterites would be supportable.[23] However, there is no such evidence, and, in any case, the psalm is perfectly intelligible when these forms are read as present or past habituals and the *wāw*-consecutive form in v. 7a is understood as a stylistic variant or as a form for closing off the section (v. 8 begins a new section).[24]

**94:8a. *bʿm* "among the people"**

Dahood's reading of *ʿm* as 'sagacity' is unconvincing and unnecessary here. See also his discussion at Ps 18:28, where the same judgment applies.[25]

**94:10b. *hmlmd ʾdm dʿt* "Is he who teaches man (without) knowledge?"**

The last line of the verse does not fit the parallelism of the previous three lines. BHS and Anderson suggest that the reading might have been *hlʾ ydʿ* 'does he not know?' However, there is no manuscript evidence for this. BHS alternatively suggests *hlʾ mdʿt* 'does he lack knowledge?' but this also is conjecture.

22. See his comments on *lmh* in Ps 2:1–2 and *mh* in Ps 3:2–3.

23. See discussion of the phenomenon in appendix 1, under dating of Psalm 93.

24. See also below on v. 18, p. 48.

25. See Loretz (1974a: 183–84), who also disagrees with Dahood on this point.

A less drastic suggestion is the mere loss of one *mêm* (BHS, Anderson, Kraus), reading 'Is the one who teaches man without knowledge?' My reading is the same, but with Dahood, I understand the *mêm* in *ʾdm* as doing double duty.[26]

Thus, v. 10b concludes the short series of questions begun in v. 9a. Verse 10b is similar to the others, because it is a rhetorical question that demands an emphatic answer affirming YHWH's wisdom and power. However, the answer to the first three questions is "Yes!" while here it is "No!" The slight difference in structure serves to tie off this subsection (vv. 8–11). The omission of a negated verb form here is compensated by the use of a longer word (*mlmd*) and by the addition of a final word (*dʿt*). Understanding the *mêm* in *ʾdm* as doing double duty results in an additional syllable (*ʾādām* [*mid*]*daʿat*), and the syllable count comes closer to the count of the other three lines.[27] Verse 11 picks up where v. 10 leaves off, by repeating the root *ydʿ*.

### 94:12a. *ʾšr* "whom"

There is some meager manuscript evidence for omitting the word *ʾšr*.[28] This is the only occurrence of the relative pronoun in the psalm, and its inclusion causes the line to be the longest in the poem. Without *ʾšr*, the line is 10 (11) syllables long, and four stresses, and it fits the context better structurally. Verse 12 then has a stress pattern of 4:2, which matches that of v. 11, immediately preceding (although the number of syllables still varies somewhat).

However, the meaning of the line clearly demands the presence of *ʾšr*, and the majority of manuscripts do have it. Furthermore, it fits the pattern of the use of *ʾšry* in the Psalter. That is, in 23 of the 26 occurrences of the word, *ʾšry* is followed by a relative pronoun such as *ʾšr* or *š-*, or (more commonly) a participle.[29] If *ʾšr* is dropped here, the line would not fit the pattern. There are exceptions to the pattern, in Pss 34:9 and 65:5, where *ʾšry* is followed by a prefixing verb form, and Ps 84:6, where neither a verb nor a relative pronoun follows, so the pattern is not inviolable. However, majority use and the occurrence of this exact clause (and clause structure) in several psalms argue for retaining *ʾšr* here. The metrical asymmetry introduced by the presence of *ʾšr* does not upset the balance

26. On this phenomenon of *scriptio continua*, see Dahood at Pss 94:10 and 60:11; also see Watson 1969. Even a skeptic such as Millard (1970) has conceded that the phenomenon probably did exist (p. 14).

27. If a *mêm* dropped out here, the result is the same.

28. Two manuscripts manifest this omission, according to BHS, but note that 4QPs[b] includes *ʾšr* (Skehan 1964: 317). Freedman (1985b: 426) omits the word.

29. In two cases (Pss 40:5, 127:5), the clause is exactly the same (*ʾšry hgbr ʾšr*), and in Ps 1:1 and 33:2 the clause structure is identical (*ʾšry* NOUN *ʾšr*).

excessively, since v. 12a is among the longest lines in the poem in any case. Clearly the "heaviness" of this verse signals a major structural break, whether *ʾšr* is dropped or not.

**94:13a. *mymy rʿ* "from evil days"**

The reading *mymy rʿ* follows the major commentaries and versions. Dahood's citing of Ps 30:4 to support his reading 'after the evil days' is unconvincing. The example he cited from Hos 6:2 is a better one, but the usage seems to be restricted to references to a specific time (particular days or a past time) rather than to general periods of time or to descriptions of these general periods, as in v. 13b (see Andersen and Freedman 1980: 422).

**94:14a, 15a. *ky* "For"**

The causal sense of *ky* is understood here. The happy state in v. 12a is due to the conditions described in vv. 14–15. Muilenburg (1961) has shown that *ky* often has an asseverative force; however, the difference between causative and asseverative would be slight in this case.

**94:15a. *ṣdq* "the righteous one"**

Two late versions (Symmachus and the Syriac) read *ṣdyq* 'the righteous one' in line 15a, a reading that renders the verse more intelligible because it parallels *yšry-lb* 'the upright in heart'. Kissane, Weiser, and the RSV also translate 'the righteous one'. Freedman points out (private communication) that even without emendation, the abstract noun ('righteousness') can be interpreted to represent the concrete referent ('righteous one') by metonymy.[30]

The second line of the verse is thus parallel to the first, and *ʿd* 'to' in v. 15a also serves v. 15b. Some (e.g., Kissane, Leslie, and Kraus) emended *ʾḥryw* 'after it' to *ʾḥryt* 'a reward'. This makes good sense, and it would parallel *mšpṭ* 'justice'. However, the MT is intelligible as it stands, and there is no manuscript support for such a change. The implication in v. 15a is that *mšpṭ* is carried forward into v. 15b as well.

**94:18. Verb forms**

The best example in the psalm of the "conditioned variation" (Robertson 1972: 28) between prefixing and suffixing forms is arguably in this verse (*ʾmr* [and also the verb *mṭh* in 18a] and *ysʿdny*). It is difficult to see any true variation in aspect between these forms.[31] However, the syntax here is likely affected by the first word in the verse, *ʾim*, which is commonly followed by a suffixing form (BDB 49–50; GKC §159 1), and thus no definitive conclusion can be based on this example.

**94:21a. *ygwdw* "they band together"**

Reading *gdd* II (KB$^3$) here.

30. On this phenomenon, see Bullinger 1898: 587–89.

31. Thus a pre–eighth-century date might be assigned to the psalm (see appendix 1).

## Form-Critical Genre and Structure

Generic and structural analyses of the psalm have varied greatly. Briggs glossed away approximately half of the psalm and obtained a unified psalm of vengeance. Leslie divided it into two independent psalms, one a community lament and one an individual lament (vv. 1–15, 16–23). Gunkel also interpreted it as composed of independent fragments but dominated by lament (the community lament in vv. 1–7 and the individual lament in vv. 16–23). Anderson followed Leslie's division but saw no need to regard the psalm as a composite, suggesting rather that it might have been used by a representative of the community. In this he agreed with Mowinckel (1962: 1.227), who interpreted this representative as most likely being the king. Weiser likewise saw a unity in the psalm, but he divided it into a prayer for vengeance (vv. 1–11) and a thanksgiving for help rendered (vv. 12–23). Schmidt's division was identical to Weiser's, but he proposed two independent psalms. Kraus described it as a unified psalm of mixed style, divided into a description of need (community lament, vv. 1–7), a didactic and hortatory address against the wicked (vv. 8–15), and a prayer of an individual (vv. 16–23).

Kraus's division is the most appropriate. The presence of an individual lament form at the close cannot be disputed, and the integrity of vv. 1–7 is also clear, whereas vv. 8–15 have conspicuous wisdom motifs. However, he and all the others observed the break at v. 12, as well, where the subject matter and the poetic structure change. This break is incorporated into my analysis. Thus, the syllable and word counts for the sections are as follows:

| | | |
|---|---|---|
| I | (vv. 1–7) | 110 (MT 117) syllables and 46 words |
| II | (vv. 8–11) | 61 (MT 67) syllables and 29 words |
| III | (vv. 12–15) | 67 (MT 73) syllables and 32 words |
| IV | (vv. 16–23) | 140 (MT 143) syllables and 62 words |

The psalm is well known for the wisdom interlude in vv. 8–15. This is marked not only by the reference to the Torah in v. 12, but also by the *ʾašrê* formula, by the picture of YHWH as Teacher in vv. 10 and 12, and by the occurrence of other wisdom vocabulary (*byn, bʿr, ksyl* [v. 8]; *lmd, dʿt* [v. 10]; *ysr* [vv. 10, 12]; etc.).[32] While most scholars have not considered this evidence sufficient to warrant classifying the psalm as belonging to the wisdom genre,[33] they have identified it with the next level, psalms with major wisdom emphases.

32. See the list in Scott 1971: 121–22.

33. See Murphy 1963: 165–67; Crenshaw 1974: 249–51; Kuntz 1974: 202, 208, 210; 1977: 232.

Within the wisdom interlude, there is a natural break at v. 12. The psalmist turns from rebuking the wicked (vv. 8–11) to describing the advantages of life under YHWH's tutelage and protection (vv. 12–15). YHWH as Teacher links the two sections here (vv. 10, 12). The two subsections are almost equal in length: vv. 8–11 consist of 61 (MT 67) syllables and 29 words, whereas vv. 12–15 have 67 (MT 73) syllables and 32 words.

On a strictly formal level, Freedman notes (private communication) that this break at v. 12 comes near the midpoint of the psalm. If vv. 12–13 are taken as the midpoint, there are 22 lines preceding and 23 lines following them. The syllable counts also match closely: 171 (184) in vv. 1–11 and 169 (174) in vv. 14–22.[34] The affirmations in v. 12 about YHWH's instruction and his Torah appropriately sum up the message of the wisdom interlude.

There are clear connections between the various sections, as well, especially between I and II/III, and so there is no justification for the radical surgery that Briggs, Leslie, and Schmidt performed. The link between the initial community lament form in vv. 1–7 and the hortatory/didactic address in vv. 8–16 is immediately obvious in v. 8, which is the psalmist's derisive answer to the foolishness expressed in v. 7b (note the repetition of *byn*). The scoffing by the wicked in v. 7a is more than answered by the psalmist in vv. 9–10 (also v. 11). YHWH's care for his inheritance (v. 14b) is the answer to the abuse of his inheritance in v. 5b. There is an ironic twist in the use of *mty* in Sections I and II. In v. 4, it expresses longing in two requests to God (*ᶜd-mty*); in v. 8b it constitutes part of the psalmist's derisive rhetorical question in response to the stupidity of v. 7.

The divine names are evenly distributed across the psalm. *YHWH* occurs three times in Section I, once in II, once in III, and four times in IV. *YH* occurs twice, once in I (v. 7) and once in III (v. 12). The word *ᵓl* only occurs in v. 1, but *ᵓĕlōhê* occurs in vv. 7 and 23, and *ᵓĕlōhay* is found in v. 22.

Aside from the divine name distribution, the links between the first three sections and the last one are not quite as strong as those among the first three. Both Sections I and IV are laments, however, and the despairing question typical of laments is found in both ("How long . . . ?" [v. 3] and "Who will rise . . . ?" [v. 16]). More substantially, the evildoers are seen in both sections (vv. 4 and 16), and the poem's three *wāw*-consecutives appear at the end of each section (vv. 7, 22, 23). The stress patterns of I and IV are more consistently 3:3 than in Sections II and III, which exhibit greater variety. Finally, links between the wisdom inter-

34. Freedman's counts are slightly lower (private communication, and 1986: 426), because he counts the shorter form of the 2 m.s. suffix, although he admits the longer form may have obtained (see above, p. 30, on syllable counting).

lude and the concluding individual lament form can also be seen in the use of *yṣr* in vv. 9, 20. The word *yṣr* in v. 9 refers to YHWH and is echoed ironically in v. 20 in the reference to the seat of destruction.

One very significant link, however, has not been noted by most writers: the very presence of v. 23c, *yṣmytm YHWH ʾlhynw* 'YHWH our God will exterminate them'. This clause is intrusive, in two ways. First, it creates the only tricolon in the psalm; the regular pattern is bicolons. Second, the pronominal reference is plural (*-nw* 'our'), rather than singular, as in the rest of Section IV (the individual lament). The function of v. 23c is at least twofold. First, the verb in the clause stands in a chiastic relationship with the verb in v. 23b. The repetition of the verb in this way functions to close off the present thought (and, indeed, the entire psalm). A second function—and a far more important one—is that v. 23c connects the individual lament form in vv. 16–23b with the community lament form in vv. 1–7 and the address to the people in vv. 8–15 by means of the plural possessive pronominal suffix. If the various sections of the psalm originated from different hands, this phrase can only have been a gloss by the final author to tie the poem together. If the entire composition came from one hand, the phrase nevertheless performs the same function.

A final note concerns the structural similarity of this psalm to the typical structure of the acrostic poem. By definition, an acrostic poem's structure is very regular: it tends to have 22 bicolons (or a multiple of 22). In Freedman's study of 13 acrostic poems (1972b), he found a major group of 9 poems that tend to have bicolons averaging approximately 16.5 syllables and a minor group (4 poems) with slightly shorter line lengths, averaging 13–14 syllables per bicolon.[35]

The total syllable count in Psalm 94 is 379 (disregarding the higher MT count for the moment), and the stress count is 140. There are 47 lines (colons) in the psalm, and thus the average number of syllables per line is 8 (16 for the bicolon), and the average stresses per line is 3 (6 for the bicolon). The optimum counts, assuming a regular poem with 8:8 and 3:3 syllabic and stress patterns, would be 376 syllables and 141 stresses. The differences between the hypothetical and the actual totals here (376/379 and 141/140, respectively) are negligible, and thus the psalm fits the classic acrostic structure quite well. The extra verse (23) fits the pattern of the undisputed acrostics in Psalms 25 and 34 (v. 23 in Psalm 25 and v. 22 in Psalm 34 are outside the acrostic patterns there as well).[36]

35. The larger group consisted of Lamentations 5; Prov 31:10–31; and Psalms 25, 34, 37, 111, 112, 119, 145. The smaller group consisted of Lamentations 1–4.

36. Freedman's numbers here are slightly lower, due to the above-mentioned lower counts for the second masculine singular suffix and Freedman's omission of *ʾăšer* in v. 12, but the differences are negligible.

The obvious difference between Psalm 94 and the acrostic poems is that it does not follow an alphabetic pattern at all (after v. 1, at any rate). However, the structural cohesiveness of the acrostic poems is so distinctive, and Psalm 94 fits the pattern so well, that it may legitimately be included among the acrostics. Freedman notes (private communication) that he would now include it in the study he did in 1972.[37] Note also that Skehan (1971: 9–10; 1979: 373) similarly analyzed Proverbs 2, a 22-verse poem that fits the acrostic structure. The first word of the poem begins with *ᵓālep*, the first letter of the alphabet, and the first word at the midpoint of the poem (v. 12) begins with *lāmed*, the middle letter of the alphabet.

There is undoubtedly more to the relationship between Psalm 94 and the acrostics than merely the coincidence of structural similarity, however. Alphabetic structure is one of the stylistic features typical of wisdom literature (see Murphy 1963: 159–60 and n. 1; Skehan 1971). Of the seven acrostic psalms treated by Freedman (Psalms 25, 34, 37, 111, 112, 119, and 145), three are listed by Murphy as belonging to the wisdom genre he identified in the Psalms (Psalms 34, 37, 112).[38] Furthermore, Murphy

37. See Freedman's study on "non-alphabetic" acrostics, in which he discusses Psalm 94, among others (1985b).

38. Murphy's list has become something of a standard reference, it should be noted. His list of seven includes Psalms 1, 32, 34, 37, 49, 112, and 128 as "wisdom"

---

*Psalm 95*

## Text

| | | *Syllable Count* | *Total* | *Stresses* |
|---|---|---|---|---|
| 1a | *lkw nrnnh lYHWH* | 2 + 4 + 3 | 9 | 3 |
| b | *nryᶜh lṣwr yšᶜnw* | 3 + 2 + 3 | 8 | 3 |
| 2a | *nqdmh pnyw btwdh* | 4 + 2 + 3 | 9 | 3 |
| b | *bzmrwt nryᶜ lw* | 3 + 2(3) + 1 | 6(7) | 2 |
| 3a | *ky ᵓl gdwl YHWH* | 1 + 1 + 2 + 2 | 6 | 3 |
| b | *wmlk gdwl ᶜl-kl-ᵓlhym* | 2(3) + 2 + 1 + 1 + 3 | 9(10) | 4 |
| 4a | *ᵓšr bydw mḥqry-ᵓrṣ* | 2+ 3 + 3 + 1(2) | 9(10) | 4 |
| b | *wtwᶜpwt hrym lw* | 4 + 2 + 1 | 7 | 2 |
| 5a | *ᵓšr-lw hym whwᵓ ᶜśhw* | 2 + 1 + 2 + 2 + 3 | 10 | 4 |
| b | *wybšt ydyw yṣrw* | 3(4) + 2 + 3 | 8(9) | 3 |

included Psalm 25, another acrostic, in his second level, psalms with major wisdom motifs. If the later identification of the Torah motif with wisdom literature is allowed, then certainly Psalm 119 must also be seen as a wisdom psalm at some level.[39] Thus, of the seven acrostics treated by Freedman, five have significant links with wisdom. Even the other two have traces of wisdom motifs: Ps 111:10 is clearly a wisdom passage, echoing as it does Prov 1:1–7, and Ps 145:19–20 also speaks in sapiential terms.

The confluence of a structural pattern typical of wisdom literature and content typical of wisdom literature in Ps 94:8–15 can hardly be coincidental. Indeed, it could even be argued that this is sufficient reason to classify the entire psalm as belonging to the wisdom genre identified by Murphy, especially when the links between the wisdom section and the lament sections noted above are taken into account. The structure argues for a unity of authorship of the psalm (or, at the very least, for a careful, conscious arrangement by the author/editor of the final form of the psalm). The confluence of content and structure suggests that the author's primary concerns were sapiential, despite the prominence of the lament forms.

---

psalms per se. Kuntz, in a more recent listing of wisdom psalms, detects ten in the Psalter: Psalms 1, 32, 34, 37, 49, 73, 112, 127, 128, and 133 (Kuntz 1992, building on Kuntz 1974, where he did not include Psalm 73).

39. So also Kuntz 1992: 22.

---

## Translation

1a Come, let us sing for joy to YHWH,
b Let us raise a glad cry to the Mountain of our salvation!
2a Let us come into his presence with thanksgiving,
b With songs of praise we will raise a glad cry to him!
3a For a great God is YHWH,
b And a great King above all gods!
4a In whose hand are the depths of the earth;
b And, the mountain peaks belong to him.
5a To whom the sea belongs—and it was he who made it—
b And dry land his hands formed.

| | | | | |
|---|---|---|---|---|
| 6a | *bʾw nštḥwh wnkrʿh* | 2 + 3(4) + 4 | 9(10) | 3 |
| b | *nbrkh lpny-YHWH ʿśnw* | 3 + 2 + 2 + 3 | 10 | 4 |
| 7a | *ky hwʾ ʾlhynw* | 1 + 1 + 4 | 6 | 2 |
| b | *wʾnḥnw ʿm mrʿytw* | 4 + 1 + 3 | 8 | 3 |
| c | *wṣʾn ydw* | 2 + 2 | 4 | 2 |
| d | *hywm ʾm-bqlw tšmʿw* | 2 + 1 + 2 + 3 | 8 | 3 |
| 8a | *ʾl-tqšw lbbkm kmrybh* | 1 + 2 + 3 + 3 | 9 | 3 |
| b | *kywm msh bmdbr* | 2 + 2 + 3 | 7 | 3 |
| 9a | *ʾšr nswny ʾbwtykm* | 2 + 3 + 4 | 9 | 4 |
| b | *bḥnwny gm-rʾw pʿly* | 4 + 1 + 2 + 2(3) | 9(10) | 3 |
| 10a | *ʾrbʿym šnh ʾqwṭ bdwr* | 3 + 2 + 2 + 2 | 9 | 4 |
| b | *wʾmr ʿm tʿy lbb hm* | 3 + 1 + 2 + 2 + 1 | 9 | 4 |
| c | *whm lʾ-ydʿw drky* | 2 + 1 + 3 + 3 | 9 | 3 |
| 11a | *ʾšr-nšbʿty bʾpy* | 2 + 3 + 3 | 8 | 3 |
| b | *ʾm-ybʾwn ʾl-mnwḥty* | 1 + 3 + 1 + 4 | 9 | 3 |
| | 25 lines | | 204(210) | 78 |

| | |
|---|---|
| 8.2 syllables/line | 2.6 syllables/stress |
| 8.4 syllables/line (MT) | 2.7 syllables/stress (MT) |
| | 3.1 stresses/line |

## Translation Notes

### 95:1b. *ṣwr* "Mountain"

The term *ṣwr*, used as a title of YHWH, usually means 'Mountain' (cf. Ps 94:22 and Freedman 1976: 114). However, in the present context, vv. 8–11 recall the wilderness experiences of Exod 17:1–7 and Num 20:2–13, where water flowed from a rock. The meaning of *ṣwr* 'Mountain' undoubtedly plays on the more common meaning of *ṣwr* 'rock' from the wilderness story.

### 95:2b. *nryʿ* "we will raise a glad cry"

This translation reflects the difference between the three preceding cohortatives (including this same verb in v. 1b) and the apparent indicative here. Some manuscripts have *nryʿh* instead of *nryʿ*, and therefore all the major Bible versions and most commentators accordingly translate *nryʿ* as cohortative. These are the only two occurrences of *rwʿ* in the first-person plural form of the cohortative. However, the MT clearly uses the indica-

6a Come, let us worship and bow down,
b Let us kneel before YHWH our Maker!
7a For he is our God,
b And we are the people of his pasture,
c And the sheep of his hand.

---

d O that today you would listen to his voice:
8a "Do not harden your heart, as (at) Meribah,
b As (on) the day (at) Massah, in the wilderness,
9a Where your fathers tested me,
b (Where) they tried me, even though they had seen my work.
10a Forty years I loathed a generation,
b And I said, 'An errant-hearted people are they:
c They have not known my ways!'
11a So that I swore in my anger,
b 'They will surely not come into my rest!' "

---

tive, and it is certainly acceptable here, neatly closing the opening section of the call to praise immediately before introducing the reasons for praise in v. 3. Thus, I prefer the indicative.

**95:3a.** ***ʾl gdwl*** **"a great God"**

The alternative to 'a great God' is the translation 'the great El' or 'El, the Great One', alluding to the Canaanite pantheon: in other words, YHWH occupies the high position that the Canaanites assigned to El. This may very well have been intended as a secondary meaning, but the meaning 'a great God' is likely the primary one because of the parallelism with 'a great King' in v. 3b; both refer to a position or an office occupied by YHWH.

**95:5a.** ***whwʾ ʿśhw*** **"and it was he who made it"**

YHWH is seen in vv. 4–5 as the powerful and sovereign Creator whose dominion extends over all parts of the natural world, even the sea (v. 5a). There may be a veiled polemical thrust at Yamm of the Ugaritic texts here, but it is not as obvious as elsewhere.

**95:6b. *YHWH ʿśnw* "YHWH our Maker"**

In addition to his position as Creator of the sea and the land (v. 5), YHWH is the Creator (lit. 'Maker') of his covenant people in vv. 6bff. The idea that YHWH created (*ʿśh*) his people (*ʿm* or *gwy* 'nation') is fairly common.[40] God's people as his 'work' (*mʿśh*) is seen in Isa 29:23, 60:21, 64:7. Isaiah also uses the term 'form' (*yṣr*) ten times to refer to YHWH's forming his people.[41] Interestingly enough, the only other reference in the Psalms to the idea that YHWH created his people (using one of these verbs) is Ps 100:3. YHWH created his covenant people through the exodus, Sinai, desert, and land possession experiences.

**95:7. *ky hwʾ ʾlhynw . . .* "For he is our God . . . "**

The text of v. 7 is variously translated. In v. 7b–c, Gunkel, Kraus, and Weiser, for example, all follow the Syriac, reading 'we are his people, the sheep of his pasture', adding a suffix to *ʿm* and transposing *wṣʾn* and *mrʿytw*. BHS, Gunkel, and Kraus then add *dʿw* 'know' and read *ydw* with *hywm*: 'Know today (of) his rule/works (lit. "hand")' in v. 7d. It appears that the Syriac rendering is due to the common phrase *ṣʾn mrʿytw/k/y* 'sheep of his/your/my pasture', which appears in Pss 74:1, 100:3; Jer 23:1; and Ezek 34:31. Ps 79:13 provides an even closer parallel, because it contains the preceding clause as well: *wʾnḥnw ʿmk* 'and we are your people'.

However, the MT makes perfectly good sense as it stands, and all the major Bible versions follow it, as do many commentators (e.g., Dahood, Anderson, Delitzsch, and Leslie). There is no reason why the poet could not have broken up standard phrases, transposing parts of them, and stating, "the people of his pasture and the sheep of his hand" in place of the more stereotypical "the sheep of his pasture (and the people of his hand)." Looked at syntactically, the parallels between Ps 79:13 and 95:7 are exact and the semantic differences are slight, as the following shows:

| | | | |
|---|---|---|---|
| Ps 79:13 | (1) *wʾnḥnw* | (2) *ʿmk* | (3) *wṣʾn mrʿytk* |
| Ps 95:7 | (1) *wʾnḥnw* | (2) *ʿm mrʿytw* | (3) *wṣʾn ydw* |

In each of the passages, element (1) is identical, and elements (2) and (3) both consist of a noun or compound noun that carries a suffix referring to YHWH and that depicts YHWH's tender care for his people.[42]

40. See Gen 12:2; Exod 32:10; Num 14:12; Deut 9:14; 32:6, 15; Isa 43:7, 44:2, 46:4; Ezek 37:19, 22.

41. For these, see the list in the discussion of Ps 100:3b, below p. 93.

42. On the parallels between Ps 95:6b–7 and Ps 100:3, see the discussion at Ps 100:3b on p. 94 (see also pp. 138–40).On the place of the phrase *ky hwʾ ʾlhynw* and of vv. 6–7c in the scheme of the psalm, see below on "Form-Critical Genre and Structure," pp. 58–59.

**95:7d.** ***hywm ᵓm . . .*** **"O that today . . . !"**

I follow the major Bible versions and the majority of commentators, reading *ᵓm* with an optative sense. Dahood's objection that this reading results in a case of aposiopesis (a sudden, sharp break in the sentence), especially with a negative clause following, is weak. The parallel usually given here is Ps 81:9, where a negative clause also follows. (It should be noted that Dahood read an optative sense there.)

**95:9b.** ***pᶜly*** **"my work"**

YHWH's work referred to in line 9b may be that of causing water to come from the rock (at Massah and Meribah). However, it more likely refers to all of YHWH's saving work (so also Davies 1973: 194; Anderson; Weiser). This is especially likely in light of the earlier emphasis on YHWH's work in creating his people (vv. 6b–7c; see above on v. 6b, p. 56).

**95:11a.** ***ᵓăšer*** **"so that"**

Refer to Gen 11:7, 13:16; Deut 28:27, 51; and others for this use of *ᵓăšer.*[43]

**95:11b.** ***ᵓm-ybᵓwn*** **" 'They will surely not come' "**

"After an oath (expressed, or merely implied) אִם (the formula of imprecation being omitted) becomes an emph. negative and אִם־לֹא an emph. affirmative" (BDB 50, §1.b.[2]). The paragogic *nûn* (GKC §47m) makes the clause even more emphatic.

**95:11b.** ***ᵓl-mnwḥty*** **"into my rest"**

Braulik makes the perceptive observation (1987: 41) that only in Ps 95:11 and Deut 12:9 do we find the expression *bwᵓ ᵓl* (*h*) *mnwḥh* 'to come into (the) [place of] rest'. Deuteronomy 12 speaks clearly of centralization of worship in the place of YHWH's choice (which came to be Jerusalem, and, more specifically, its Temple). Braulik notes that later, Solomon's prayer echoed this idea of YHWH's giving rest to his people Israel, after the Temple had been completed (1 Kgs 8:56). Thus, 'my rest' in Ps 95:11 points beyond the land of the inheritance to the Temple, where YHWH's presence and true rest are to be found. The psalm, then, despite its clear references to the Exodus and wilderness periods, brings the readers into the present, the period of the monarchy.

## Form-Critical Genre and Structure

There are two main units in the poem, a two-part hymn (A) in vv. 1–7c and a prophetic oracle (B) in vv. 7d–11. The juxtaposition of such

43. See also BDB 83/§8b; Delitzsch.

diverse genres has caused considerable discussion. Gunkel called the psalm a "prophetic liturgy," but he also termed it a "composite liturgy" (1933: 329 and n. 6). Mowinckel referred to it as a complex liturgical composition (1962: 1.106; 2.76), but he classified it as one of the Enthronement psalms on the basis of the first part (1962: 1.122, 156). Kraus follows Gunkel in seeing it as a composite prophetic liturgy. The majority of scholars follows Gunkel and Mowinckel, both regarding the division into two parts and the classifications of these as hymn and prophetic oracle. Most have seen it as an entrance liturgy, possibly at the Feast of Tabernacles.[44]

The hymn is divided into two parallel sections, unequal in length: I (vv. 1–5), consisting of a call to praise (vv. 1–2) and reasons for praise (vv. 3–5); and II (vv. 6–7c), likewise consisting of a call to praise (v. 6) and reasons for praise (v. 7a–c). The syllable and word counts for the psalm are as follows:

| | | |
|---|---|---|
| A | I (vv. 1–5): | 81 (MT 85) syllables and 36 words |
| | II (vv. 6–7c): | 37 (MT 38) syllables and 15 words |
| B | III (vv. 7d–11): | 86 (MT 87) syllables and 38 words |

The verbs in the first call to praise (vv. 1–2) are verbs of audible praise (interpreting *qdm* in v. 2a in this way by its context), whereas the verbs in the second call to praise (v. 6) are verbs of physical acts of worship. The reasons for praise in the first part are expanded by two clauses describing attributes of YHWH, both introduced by *ʾăšer* (vv. 4a, 5a). A double call to praise/worship such as we find in vv. 1a and 6a[45] is relatively rare. Usually only one verb of motion is present, followed by a series of imperative or cohortative verbs of actual praise activity ("Sing!" "Worship!" "Bow down!" etc.). However, the double call does occur, in the double ending of Psalm 24 with the verb *nśʾ* 'Lift up!' (vv. 7–8 // 9–10), and in Psalm 100, again with the verb *bwʾ* (v. 2b // 4a). There may have been a liturgical reason for the double invitation (Davies 1973: 190–91).

The second section of the hymn (vv. 6–7c) forms the center of the psalm, both in structure and in content. The sections on each side of the structural center are almost identical in length. Within the section, the affirmation of Israel's relationship with YHWH (v. 7a–c) forms the central message of the psalm. Indeed, Freedman notes (private communication) that the statement 'For He is our God' (*ky hwʾ ʾlhynw*) in v. 7a

44. For a nearly complete survey of the views on the psalm, see Davies 1973: 183–87.

45. Both begin with verbs of motion (*lkw*, *bʾw* 'Come!'), denoting the activity enjoined.

stands almost at the exact midpoint of the poem: the preceding material is 100 (105) syllables and 43 words long, and the following material is 98 (99) syllables, also 43 words long.

In terms of content, vv. 6–7c form a bridge between vv. 1–5 and vv. 7d–11. This section belongs to the hymnic genre and naturally echoes vv. 1–5; both sections include the call to praise and reasons for praise, as noted above. The bridge also introduces the last section by narrowing the psalm's focus from the great, universal God who is above all of nature and other gods to the personal God of Israel who made and cares for his people (v. 7a–c) and who exhorts and warns them (vv. 7d–11).

The third section of the psalm is a prophetic oracle from the mouth of YHWH (v. 7d). It presents a sharp contrast to the first two sections, consisting as it does of a harsh warning to the people against behaving as their forebears did. The actual lexical links between it and the other two sections are few, the principal one being *ᶜm* 'people'. The people appear once in a tender relation to YHWH (v. 7b) and once in a rebellious relation (v. 10b).

A few other links are present, as well. First, Dahood points out that the flock metaphor of v. 7 is repeated in v. 10, as both *tᶜy* and *ydᶜw drky* are elsewhere predicated of sheep (see Jer 1:6 and Prov 3:5–6, respectively). This adds force to any argument for unity in both parts of the psalm. Second, we may note the correspondence between *mrᶜytw* 'his (YHWH's) (place of) pasture' (v. 7b) and *mnwḥty* 'my (YHWH's) (place of) rest' (v. 11b) that Girard (1981: 188) points out. Third, Girard is also correct in discerning (p. 187) a large inclusio marked by the verbs of entering: *ybᵓwn* in v. 11b and *lkw* and *bᵓw* in vv. 1a and 6a.[46] This reinforces the already-noted role of the middle section as a bridge between the others. Verse 6a obviously echoes v. 1a, as a call to worship, but is itself echoed by the root *bwᵓ* in v. 11b. The contrast is between the call to a faithful generation to enter YHWH's place of worship (in the hymn) and the warning that YHWH's rest will not be entered by a rebellious generation (in the oracle).

Despite the contrast in genre and content between the first two and the third sections of the psalm and the paucity of lexical connections, the *logical* progression from the hymnic section to the oracle is clear, and it is facilitated by the psalm's middle section, as noted. The fact that Israel was YHWH's covenant people, both in the wilderness days and presently, unites the psalm. The emphasis in the middle section on YHWH as the one who gave birth to and cares for his people (vv. 6b–7c) provides the justification for the stern warning in the last part. The covenant people

46. This is despite the fact that his overall analysis is forced at a number of points.

are reminded now of their covenant responsibilities. The reminder that YHWH made them appears in both parts (vv. 6b, 9b).[47]

Psalm 95 has several connections with the Song of Moses. These connections have some significance for the dating (see appendix 1), and they also aid in understanding the prophetic oracle. First, Freedman notes (private communication) that the general situation underlying the psalm easily corresponds to that of the Song. That is, the psalm speaks of the rebellious wilderness generation but in the context of addressing a later generation (vv. 7d–11). The first generation addressed in this way was the generation in Deuteronomy 32, namely, the children of the rebellious generation. In the Song, Moses is seen exhorting them at some length not to repeat the mistakes of their fathers. In the psalm the message of the prophetic oracle is much the same. The psalmist assumes the same role that Moses did in the Song, the role of one who addresses the people and exhorts them on behalf of YHWH. The psalmist speaks directly, quoting YHWH (vv. 8–11), while Moses in the Song usually refers to YHWH in the third person, but at times quotes him directly (vv. 20–27, 34–35, 37–42). Like the Song, the psalm does not mention any of Israel's history

47. Using the verbs *ʿśh* and *pʿl*; see the comments above, pp. 56 and 57.

---

*Psalm 96*

**Text**

| | | *Syllable Count* | *Total* | *Stresses* |
|---|---|---|---|---|
| 1a | *šyrw lYHWH šyr ḥdš* | 2 + 3 + 1 + 2 | 8 | 4 |
| b | *šyrw lYHWH kl-hʾrṣ* | 2 + 3 + 1 + 2(3) | 8(9) | 3 |
| 2a | *šyrw lYHWH brkw šmw* | 2 + 3 + 3 + 2 | 10 | 4 |
| b | *bśrw mywm-lywm yšwʿtw* | 3 + 2 + 2 + 4 | 11 | 4 |
| 3a | *sprw bgwym kbwdw* | 3 + 3 + 3 | 9 | 3 |
| b | *bkl-hʿmym nplʾwtyw* | 2 + 3 + 4 | 9 | 3 |
| 4a | *ky gdwl YHWH wmhll mʾd* | 1 + 2 + 2 + 4 + 2 | 11 | 4 |
| b | *nwrʾ hwʾ ʿl-kl-ʾlhym* | 2 + 1 + 1 + 1 + 3 | 8 | 3 |
| 5a | *ky kl-ʾlhy hʿmym ʾlylym* | 1 + 1 + 3 + 3 + 3 | 11 | 4 |
| b | *wYHWH šmym ʿśh* | 3 + 2(3) + 2 | 7(8) | 3 |
| 6a | *hwd-whdr lpnyw* | 1 + 2 + 3 | 6 | 3 |
| b | *ʿz wtpʾrt bmqdšw* | 1 + 4 + 4 | 9 | 3 |

after Moses, such as the Conquest and Settlement or any part of the monarchy.[48]

Second, in addition to the general situational outlook, the two poems share several divine names and titles. *YHWH* of course occurs in both. The word *ṣwr* 'Mountain' occurs in Ps 95:1a and six times, referring to YHWH, in the Song.[49] The word *ʾl* 'God' occurs in Ps 95:3a and at least twice in the Song; *ʾlhynw* 'our God' occurs in Ps 95:7a and once in the Song; *hwʾ* 'he', referring to YHWH, occurs in Ps 95:5a and 7a and occurs three times in the Song.

The prophetic oracle could, therefore, easily fit the situation seen in the Song of Moses. However, as noted above, the hymnic portion of the psalm is sufficiently general and common that it could be dated at any time. Certainly the psalm in its final form lent itself to any generation that considered itself to be in the same position as the generation addressed in the oracle and thus wished to appropriate the psalm for itself.

48. Except in the indirect reference to the Temple in v. 11b (see second note on v. 11b, above).

49. See Freedman 1976: 99–102 for the data in the Song.

---

## Translation

1a Sing to YHWH a new song,
b Sing to YHWH, all the earth!
2a Sing to YHWH, bless his name!
b Proclaim from day to day his salvation!
3a Declare among the nations his glory,
b Among all the peoples his wonderful works!

---

4a For great is YHWH, and worthy of praise is the Mighty One;
b To be feared is he above all gods.
5a For all the gods of the peoples are worthless idols,
b But it was YHWH who made the heavens.
6a Splendor and majesty are before him,
b Strength and beauty are in his sanctuary.

| | | | | |
|---|---|---|---|---|
| 7a | *hbw lYHWH mšpḥwt ʿmym* | 2 + 3 + 3 + 2 | 10 | 4 |
| b | *hbw lYHWH kbwd wʿz* | 2 + 3 + 2 + 2 | 9 | 4 |
| 8a | *hbw lYHWH kbwd šmw* | 2 + 3 + 2 + 3 | 10 | 4 |
| b | *śʾw-mnḥh wbʾw lḥṣrwtyw* | 2 + 2 + 3 + 4 | 11 | 4 |
| 9a | *hštḥww lYHWH bhdrt-qdš* | 3(4) + 3 + 3 + 1(2) | 10(12) | 4 |
| b | *ḥylw mpnyw kl-hʾrṣ* | 2 + 3 + 1 + 2(3) | 8(9) | 3 |
| 10a | *ʾmrw bgwym YHWH mlk* | 2 + 3 + 2 + 2 | 9 | 4 |
| b | *ʾp-tkwn tbl bl-tmwṭ* | 1 + 2 + 2 + 1 + 2 | 8 | 3 |
| c | *ydyn ʿmym bmyšrym* | 2 + 2 + 4 | 8 | 3 |
| 11a | *yśmḥw hšmym wtgl hʾrṣ* | 3 + 3(4) + 3 + 2(3) | 11(13) | 4 |
| b | *yrʿm hym wmlʾw* | 2 + 2 + 4 | 8 | 3 |
| 12a | *yʿlz śdy wkl-ʾšr-bw* | 2(3) + 2 + 2 + 2 + 1 | 9(10) | 4 |
| b | *ʾz yrnnw kl-ʿṣy-yʿr* | 1 + 4 + 1 + 2 + 1(2) | 9(10) | 4 |
| 13a | *lpny YHWH ky bʾ* | 2 + 2 + 1 + 1 | 6 | 3 |
| b | *ky bʾ lšpṭ hʾrṣ* | 1 + 1 + 2 + 2(3) | 6(7) | 3 |
| c | *yšpṭ-tbl bṣdq* | 2 + 2 + 2(3) | 6(7) | 2 |
| d | *wʿmym bʾmwntw* | 3 + 4(5) | 7(8) | 2 |
| | 29 lines | | 252(264) | 99 |

| | |
|---|---|
| 8.7 syllables/line | 2.5 syllables/stress |
| 9.1 syllables/line (MT) | 2.7 syllables/stress (MT) |
| | 3.4 stresses/line |

## Translation Notes

### 96:2b. *mywm-lywm* "from day to day"

Dahood's rendering of this phrase, 'from sea to sea', assuming a defective original spelling or else a Phoenician pronunciation, is attractive because of the parallelism with v. 3 and the universal picture seen there. However, the MT clearly reads 'from day to day'. Furthermore, for all of its attractiveness (due to its consistency), Dahood's rendering does not allow for the refreshing variety that is also a part of Hebrew poetry. YHWH's virtues are being proclaimed not only in all places (v. 3), but also at all times (v. 2b). The phrase encompasses all of time, via merismus: from the first day of time until the last (Freedman, private communication).[50]

50. The picture is not unlike the one in Ps 113:2–3. There Dahood understands it (correctly, in my view) both temporally and spatially, even though some commentators understand *mmzrḥ-šmš ʿd-mbwʾw* in v. 3a temporally, because it corresponds to the same idea in v. 2.

7a Give to YHWH, O families of the peoples,
b Give to YHWH glory and strength!
8a Give to YHWH the glory due his name!
b Bring an offering and enter into his courts.
9a Worship YHWH in (his) holy splendor,
b Tremble before him, all the earth!

---

10a Say among the nations, "YHWH reigns!
b Surely the world is established! It is unmovable.
c He will judge peoples with equity."

---

11a Let the heavens rejoice, and the earth be glad!
b Let the sea roar, and all that fills it!
12a Let the field exult, and all that is in it!
b Then all the trees of the woods will sing for joy
13a Before YHWH, for he comes,
b For he comes to judge the earth;
c He will judge the world with (his) righteousness,
d And the peoples with his faithfulness!

---

**96:4a. *mʾd* "the Mighty One"**

See the discussion at Ps 93:5a.

**96:9a. *bhdrt-qdš* "in (his) holy splendor"**

The word *hdrt* has been the basis for a great deal of discussion. It has traditionally been rendered 'adornment, array' (BDB, $KB^3$, NAB, NASB, RSV), based on parallels between the verbal *hdr* and *lbš* 'to be clothed' in Job 40:10, Ps 104:1, Prov 31:25, and Isa 53:1. However, the clothing in these passages is metaphorical, and the likelihood is that *hdrt* means 'splendor, honor, dignity' in all of the cases, as BDB renders it in Prov 14:28 (and compare *hdr* 'majesty' in v. 6a in this psalm). Furthermore, *hdrt* occurs in Ugaritic, parallel with *ḥlm* 'dream'. The context makes it clear that there is an appearance of El associated with the dream. Thus the idea of a theophany is implicit in 96:9a, a fact that is supported by 9b. The meaning intended, therefore, is that the reader should worship YHWH in *YHWH's* holy splendor, displayed as it were, in a theophany. Thus, it is not the worshipers who put on garments to worship him, as understood in most Bible versions. The Old Greek and the Syriac both include the suffix, but it is not needed if the holy splendor is understood correctly as YHWH's, not the worshipers'.[51]

**96:12a. *śdy* "field"**

This is a rarer, original form of *śdh*, used only 13 times (compared to 318 times for *śdh*). *Śdy* occurs only in poetry. The parallel in 1 Chr 16:32b has *śdh*.

**96:13a–b. *ky bʾ* "for he comes"**

I read *bʾ* as a participle here.

**96:13c. *bṣdq* "with (his) righteousness"**

The suffix pronoun on the parallel term *ʾmwnh* in v. 13d is understood to serve the word *ṣdq* as well.[52]

## Form-Critical Genre and Structure

This psalm is a hymn, one of the Kingship of YHWH psalms. There is no disagreement about this classification, just as there is none about Psalm 93; the debate revolves around the *Sitz im Leben* and the significance of the clause *YHWH mlk*.[53] However, in contrast to the other psalms that contain *YHWH mlk* (93, 97, 99), in Psalm 96 it appears as part of an injunction (line 10a): the people are told to say, "YHWH reigns!" In this psalm, the phrase also appears *within* the psalm, rather than at the outset. The hymn is dominated by praise motifs. Eighteen of the 28 verb forms[54] in the psalm (14 imperatives and 4 jussives) urge the people or the elements of creation to praise or to have an attitude of praise.

Almost all commentators agree that the clause *YHWH mlk* introduces a major break and that the climax of the psalm is in vv. 10–13. Structural analyses typically divide the psalm into the following sections:

I Call to worship/praise (vv. 1–3)
II Reasons for praise (vv. 4–6)
III Second call to worship (vv. 7–9)
IV Exaltation of YHWH as king (vv. 10–13)[55]

51. See Kraus, Dahood, and especially Ackroyd (1966).

52. The phenomenon is well known in Hebrew poetry; see Dahood 1970: 429–31, especially 429–30.

53. See first translation note on Ps 93:1.

54. Or 30, if *mhll* and *nwrʾ* in v. 4 are counted.

55. So Gunkel, Anderson, Kraus, and Leslie (who omitted v. 4!).

Dahood saw two strophes: vv. 1–9 and vv. 10–13. Syllable and word counts in the divisions of most scholars are as follows:

| | | |
|---|---|---|
| I | (vv. 1–3) | 55 (MT 56) syllables and 22 words |
| II | (vv. 4–6) | 52 (MT 53) syllables and 24 words |
| III | (vv. 7–9) | 58 (MT 61) syllables and 24 words |
| IV | (vv. 10–13) | 86 (MT 93) syllables and 42 words |

The clause *YHWH mlk* in v. 10 sounds the keynote for vv. 11–13, which tell of the implications of YHWH's kingship.[56] It is also true, however, and less often noted, that an imperatival clause precedes *YHWH mlk*. It is of a piece with the series of imperatives in vv. 7–9. Furthermore, the formulas in vv. 3a and 10a are identical in meaning and almost identical in expression: *sprw bgwym* 'declare among the nations' and *ʾmrw bgwym* 'say among the nations'. Each occurs at the end of a series of imperatives, and there is no compelling syntactical reason to postulate a major break at v. 10.

Accordingly, it is attractive to see v. 10 as a bridge between sections, with ties to both the preceding and the succeeding material. Syntactically, it fits closely with vv. 7–9 and echoes v. 3. Thematically, it continues sounding the note of praise that permeates the earlier sections. It also introduces a new theme, YHWH's kingship, and serves as a natural opening to the section that follows, which develops the theme.

Thus, in order to emphasize the unique function of v. 10 in the psalm, I consider it an independent section, with ties both to vv. 1–9 and vv. 11–13. Accordingly, the syllable and word counts of the psalm may be diagramed this way:

| | | | |
|---|---|---|---|
| A | I | (vv. 1–3) | 55 (MT 56) syllables and 22 words |
| | II | (vv. 4–6) | 52 (MT 53) syllables and 24 words |
| B | III | (vv. 7–9) | 58 (MT 61) syllables and 24 words |
| | IV | (v. 10) | 25 (MT 25) syllables and 12 words |
| | V | (vv. 11–13) | 61 (MT 68) syllables and 30 words |

The result is that the poem divides into four roughly equal sections (I, II, III, V), and the keynote of the composition is sounded in a separate, shorter section (IV), which has structural links to the rest of the psalm.[57]

56. On the emphasis in the Kingship psalms on the *consequences* or implications of YHWH's sovereignty rather than the establishment of it, see Gelston 1966: 511–12.

57. Westermann's analysis (1981a: 148) is comparable, partly on the basis of similar reasoning.

The structural analysis can be refined further. Sections I and II form a natural unit (A): call to praise (vv. 1–3), reasons for praise (vv. 4–6); this is paralleled by Sections III–V (unit B): second call to praise (vv. 7–12), reasons for praise (v. 13); though the two units are somewhat different in length.

The connections within these units are clear. In unit A, Sections I and II are almost identical in length, and the use of *YHWH* is significant: it occurs three times in parallel in Section I (vv. 1a, b, 2a) and then forms an inclusio around the core reasons for praise in Section II (vv. 4a and 5b). A similar structural pattern obtains in the use of *YHWH* in unit B: it again occurs in the opening tricolon (vv. 7a, b, 8a) and forms an inclusio around a succeeding section (vv. 10a, 13a).[58] *YHWH* in v. 9a has no correspondent, but it is introduced by the preposition *l-*, as it is in vv. 7–8a (and vv. 1–2a). Thus it is consistent with the rest of Section III.

As noted above, v. 10 has ties with both vv. 7–9 (by virtue of the imperatives) and with vv. 11–13 (by virtue of the new subject matter introduced). The links with vv. 11–13 are somewhat stronger, something that the majority of scholars also have discerned. For this reason, I include v. 10 with the last section. Verses 10 and 13 form an inclusio around vv. 11–12, since v. 13 picks up the judgment motif left off in v. 10, while vv. 11–12 are a unified praise section characterized by jussives.[59]

58. The succeeding section in this case, however, is not a "reasons for praise" section, as is the section bounded by *YHWH* in vv. 4a and 5b.

59. Note that the lengths of the paired verses are similar: v. 10 has 25 (25) syllables and v. 13 likewise has 25 (28) syllables; v. 11 has 19 (21) syllables and v. 12 has 17 (19) syllables.

---

*Psalm 97*

## Text

| | | Syllable Count | Total | Stresses |
|---|---|---|---|---|
| 1a | *YHWH mlk tgl hʾrṣ* | 2 + 2 + 2 + 2(3) | 8(9) | 4 |
| b | *yśmḥw ʾyym rbym* | 3 + 2 + 2 | 7 | 3 |
| 2a | *ʿnn wʿrpl sbybyw* | 2 + 3(4) + 3 | 8(9) | 3 |
| b | *ṣdq wmšpṭ mkwn ksʾw* | 1(2) + 3 + 2 + 2 | 8(9) | 4 |
| 3a | *ʾš lpnyw tlk* | 1 + 3 + 2 | 6 | 3 |
| b | *wtlhṭ sbyb ṣryw* | 4 + 2 + 2 | 8 | 3 |

The universal emphasis in the psalm is clear. All the earth, the nations, and the peoples figure prominently. YHWH's sovereignty over the nations (v. 3a), the peoples (v. 3b), the gods of the peoples (vv. 4b, 5a), and the heavens (v. 5b) is asserted in Sections I and II, and the various elements of creation are urged to praise him in Section V. The psalm ends with the assertion that the earth (*ʾrṣ* and *tbl*) and its peoples are subject to his judgment (v. 13).

Psalm 96 is one of the most unified of Psalms 93–100. It is the most purely praise-oriented of the group, sustaining the laudatory note throughout the 13 verses. Lexically, numerous words are repeated throughout the poem. The word *ʾrṣ* occurs in Sections I, III, and V; in fact, it brackets Sections I and III (vv. 1b and 9b) and Section V (vv. 11a and 13b). Its synonym *tbl* brackets Sections IV and V (vv. 10b and 13c), as does *špṭ* (vv. 10c and 13b, c). The word *ʿmym* is found in all five sections (vv. 3b, 5a, 7a, 10c, 13d), while *gwym* links Sections I and IV (vv. 3a and 10a). *Šmym* links Sections II and V (vv. 5b and 11a), and *kbwd* (vv. 3a and 7b) and *šm* (vv. 2a and 8a) link Sections I and III. *YHWH* occurs 11 times, at least once in each section, with structural significance, as noted above.

Structurally, the two main units of the psalm (A: vv. 1–6; B: vv. 7–13) are roughly parallel. Section III (vv. 7–9) parallels Section I (vv. 1–3) as a call to praise, consisting of 6 lines, all introduced by imperatives. Furthermore, both sections begin with a tricolon whose component colons begin with the same verb (*šyrw* in vv. 1–2a and *ḥbw* in vv. 7–8a). Sections I, II, and III are all approximately the same length. The end of the psalm (vv. 10 and 11–13) is different structurally from the other sections. However, we should note that vv. 11–12a do parallel vv. 1–2a and 7–8a in consisting of a tricolon, one which repeats (jussive) verbs of praise.

---

## Translation

1a YHWH reigns! Let the earth be glad!
b Let the many coastlands rejoice!
2a Cloud and thick darkness surround him;
b Righteousness and judgment are the foundation of his throne.
3a A fire goes before him,
b And it consumes his adversaries all around (him).

| | | | | |
|---|---|---|---|---|
| 4a | *hʾyrw brqyw tbl* | 3 + 3 + 2 | 8 | 3 |
| b | *rʾth wtḥl hʾrṣ* | 3 + 3 + 2(3) | 8(9) | 3 |
| 5a | *hrym kdwng nmsw* | 2 + 3 + 3 + 3 + 2 | 13 | 5 |
| | *mlpny* YHWH | | | |
| b | *mlpny ʾdwn kl-hʾrṣ* | 3 + 2 + 1 + 2(3) | 8(9) | 3 |
| 6a | *hgydw hšmym ṣdqw* | 3 + 3(4) + 2 | 8(9) | 3 |
| b | *wrʾw kl-hʿmym kbwdw* | 3 + 1 + 3 + 3 | 10 | 3 |
| 7a | *ybšw kl-ʿbdy psl* | 3 + 1 + 3 + 1(2) | 8(9) | 3 |
| b | *hmthllym bʾlylym* | 5 + 4 | 9 | 3 |
| c | *hštḥww-lw kl-ʾlhym* | 3(4) + 1 + 1 + 3 | 8(9) | 3 |
| 8a | *šmʿh wtśmḥ ṣywn* | 3 + 3 + 2 | 8 | 3 |
| b | *wtglnh bnwt yhwdh* | 4 + 2 + 3 | 9 | 3 |
| c | *lmʿn mšpṭyk* YHWH | 2(3) + 4 + 2 | 8(9) | 3 |
| 9a | *ky-ʾth* YHWH *ʿlywn* | 1 + 2 + 2 + 2 + 1 + 1 + 2(3) | 11(12) | 5 |
| | *ʿl-kl-hʾrṣ* | | | |
| b | *mʾd nʿlyt ʿl-kl-ʾlhym* | 2 + 3(4) + 1 + 1 + 3 | 10(11) | 4 |
| 10a | *ʾhby* YHWH *śnʾw rʿ* | 3 + 2 + 2 + 1 | 8 | 3 |
| b | *šmr npšwt ḥsydyw* | 2 + 2 + 3 | 7 | 3 |
| c | *myd ršʿym yṣylm* | 2 + 3 + 3 | 8 | 3 |
| 11a | *ʾwr zr[ḥ] lṣdyq* | 1 + 2(3) + 3 | 6(7) | 3 |
| b | *wlyšry-lb śmḥh* | 4 + 1 + 2 | 7 | 3 |
| 12a | *śmḥw ṣdyqym b*YHWH | 2 + 3 + 3 | 8 | 3 |
| b | *whwdw lzkr qdšw* | 3 + 2(3) + 2 | 7(8) | 3 |
| | 27 lines | | 222(235) | 88 |
| | 8.2 syllables/line | 2.5 syllables/stress | | |
| | 8.7 syllables/line (MT) | 2.7 syllables/stress (MT) | | |
| | | 3.3 stresses/line | | |

## Translation Notes

**97:1b. *ʾyym rbym* "the many coastlands"**

The NEB's rendering, 'let coasts and islands all rejoice', best captures the meaning of the term here.

**97:3b. *sbyb ṣryw* "his adversaries all around (him)"**

Dahood read v. 3b 'and blazes round his back', understanding *ṣryw* as cognate to Ugaritic *ẓr* 'back'. It is an attractive suggestion, because of the parallelism created—of fire burning before and behind YHWH. It might be

4a His lightning flashes lit up the world;
b The earth saw and trembled.
5a Mountains melted like wax
from before YHWH,
b From before the Lord of all the earth.
6a The heavens declared his righteousness,
b And all the peoples saw his glory.

---

7a All who serve an image are put to shame:
b Those who boast in worthless idols;
c All gods have worshiped him!
8a Zion has heard and rejoiced,
b And the villages of Judah have been glad,
c Because of your judgments, O YHWH!
9a For you, O YHWH, are the Most High,
above all the earth,
b (You,) O Mighty One, are exalted, above all gods!

---

10a O lovers of YHWH, hate evil!
b He preserves the lives of his devoted ones;
c From the hand of the wicked ones he will deliver them.
11a Light [dawns] for the righteous one,
b And for those upright in heart, joy.
12a Rejoice, O righteous ones, in YHWH,
b And give thanks to his holy name!

---

rendered 'and blazes around behind him', understanding *zr* as a preposition, and thus maintaining an even closer parallelism with *lpnyw* 'before him' in v. 3a.[60]

However, there is nothing here that compels this reading other than the aesthetic satisfaction of creating a synonymously parallel line pair: 'before him' (v. 3a) // 'behind him' (v. 3b). The traditional reading of the MT

60. See Gordon 1967: 407, #1047, where *zr* is seen primarily as a preposition, 'top, above', with an earlier meaning of 'the back'.

(adopted here) makes perfectly good sense, and it is consistent with standard Hebrew poetry (despite the fact that there is no synonymous parallelism). The only departure in my translation from the majority MT is in allowing for the possibility of a pronominal suffix on *sbyb*: *sbybyw* 'around him', as found in some manuscripts (BHS). However, the presence of the pronoun is implicit even if only *sbyb* is read.

**97:5a and 5b. *mlpny* "from before"**

There is a slight difference in nuance between *mlpny* and *lpny*, in that *lpny* indicates position in front of, and *mlpny* (as in 5a and 5b) indicates movement away from (BDB 817–18; $KB^3$ 889). *Mlpny* is closer in meaning to *mpny*; this is illustrated by the occurrence of *mpny* in Ps 96:9b and the occurrence of *mlpny* in the parallel passage of 1 Chr 16:30. It is conceivable that the first occurrence of the phrase *mlpny YHWH*, in Ps 97:5a, is an addition (as suggested by BHS and Kraus, for example), since without it, the line length would be 8 syllables (3 stresses), which fits the pattern of its surrounding lines.[61]

**97:7c. *hštḥww-lw kl-ʾlhym* "All gods have worshiped him!"**

I read the verb as an indicative here. Many versions (JB, NASB, NEB, NIV; also Dahood) read it as an imperative; the forms are identical. The understanding here is that the statements in 7a–b are dependent on 7c: precisely because all the gods have worshiped (or do worship) YHWH (v. 7c), anyone who puts his trust in worthless idols or images is put to shame, doomed (vv. 7a and 7b). The NJPSV, NAB, RSV, Anderson, Kraus, Gunkel, and Delitzsch all see an indicative here. Either form is possible, and the difference is slight, but it does seem a bit anomalous for the imperative to be inserted in the midst of a string of indicative verbs.[62]

An alternative understanding of the suffixing form (*hštḥww*) is raised by Freedman (private communication), who points out that it might be a precative "perfect": 'May all the heavenly beings bow down to him'.

It is debated whether a precative sense can attach to a suffixing conjugation. In GKC (§109b), for example, a precative sense is given only for prefixing conjugations, and most other grammars do not mention the precative in connection with suffixing forms. On the other hand, Dahood found it many times in the Psalms (1970: 414–17) and defended its ex-

61. However, see below, on v. 9, for a discussion of the name *YHWH* and the "extra-metrical" phenomenon.

62. The word *ybšw* in v. 7a is read by some (NASB, NEB, and Dahood) as a jussive, but, even if it is a jussive, it is the first nonindicative verb form since v. 1 and does not seriously weaken the point just made, since it is a prefixing form.

istence in many of the passages listed (see especially his comments on Pss 3:8 and 4:2), as did Buttenwieser in a long excursus (1938: 18–25) and throughout his commentary. Even a scholar such as Craigie, who more often than not disagrees with Dahood's nontraditional readings, allows for the existence of the phenomenon in this case (see his comments at Ps 4:2).

Thus, we may agree that a precative "perfect" does occur in Biblical Hebrew. If *hštḥww* is read this way, then presumably *ybšw* in v. 7a would be read as a jussive. However, while there is nothing in the present context that specifically militates against seeing a jussive or precative mood for both verbs, neither is there anything in the context that compels such a reading or that militates against interpreting both verbs as simple indicatives. Indeed, if anything, the common understanding of the "precative" as a request or entreaty and the "jussive" as a wish or desire, which is actually the sense of Freedman's suggestion, is an argument against reading a precative here. There is no request per se in v. 7, but there is either an expressed wish ('May all gods worship . . . ') or a declarative statement ('All gods have worshiped . . . '). For these reasons, I still prefer the indicative in 7c.

**97:9a.** ***ky-ʾth* Yhwh *ʿlywn*** **"For you, O Yhwh, are the Most High"**

I read *Yhwh* (v. 9a) and *mʾd* (v. 9b) as appositional to *ʾth* (v. 9a), thus rendering the two clauses following *ky ʾth* parallel to each other. The words *ʿlywn* and *nʿlyt* are not precisely parallel, since one is a divine title and the other is a finite verb, but the wordplay between the verb *ʿlh* and the divine title *ʿlywn* explains the parallelism.[63] Dahood saw *ʿlywn nʿlyt* as a composite divine title, broken up here to serve the wordplay and structural considerations.

The metrical pattern in the verse is longer than that in most of the rest of the psalm. Some scholars delete the word *Yhwh* in v. 9a for metrical reasons (e.g., BHS and Kraus). Omission of *Yhwh* does yield four stresses for each line in the verse, rendering the verse symmetrical. However, if *mʾd* is indeed a divine title here, its presence argues against deleting *Yhwh*, since the two are parallel. Furthermore, deleting *Yhwh* still would not solve the "problem" that the entire verse is metrically anomalous in any case. Each line can be subdivided before the prepositional phrase introduced by *ʿl-*, yielding a 7:4(5) // 5(6):5 pattern. If the word *Yhwh* were deleted, the pattern would be almost exactly symmetrical: 5:4(5) // 5(6):5. However, the presence of the name fits well with the common practice of deviation from the norm, either for stylistic reasons (deviation for the sake

63. Noted by A. R. Johnson at Ps 47:6 (1967: 75 n. 2).

of deviation) or for reasons of emphasis (especially when the divine name is involved), and there is no compelling reason to delete it here. Freedman has developed this argument on several occasions, notably in his essay on "Acrostics and Metrics" (1972b; cf. also 1972a: xv).[64] Freedman has also noted (private communication) that the extrametrical occurrence of the name *YHWH* is not unique to this psalm. The metrical irregularity is found, for example, all three times the name occurs in Lamentations 5 (vv. 1a, 19a, and 21a).

**97:10a.** ***ʾhby YHWH śnʾw rʿ*** **"O lovers of YHWH, hate evil!"**

The text in v. 10 is not easy to understand. A common reading emends *ʾhby* to *ʾhb* (citing dittography with following *YHWH*) and *śnʾw* to *śnʾ*, and repoints *šmr* from a participle to a "perfect," thus yielding a balanced verse: 'YHWH loves those who hate evil; he preserves the lives of his devoted ones' (so, e.g., JB, NAB, NEB, RSV; Gunkel, Kraus, Anderson).

My reading of v. 10a follows the MT, however, both consonantally and vocalically (as do, e.g., NJPSV, NASB, NIV; Delitzsch, Weiser). Aside from the general preference for following the MT, support for this reading can be seen in the parallels between vv. 10a and 12a. The two lines are closely related structurally, since both contain imperatives, and in both, YHWH's supporters are addressed by these imperatives. YHWH's name also occurs in both lines, although with different syntactical functions in each. Since vv. 10–12 constitute the final section of the psalm, this bracketing of it at beginning and end with similar constructions makes the MT reading perfectly acceptable. The disjunction in v. 10a, which addresses the hearers, emphasizes the change at the beginning of a new section and the fact that YHWH is no longer being addressed.

**97:11a.** ***ʾwr zr[ḥ] lṣdyq*** **"Light [dawns] for the righteous one"**

The MT here reads 'Light is sown [*zrʿ*] for the righteous one'. Delitzsch explained the sowing of light as "strewn along [the righteous one's] life's way, so that he . . . advances step by step in the light." However, the imagery is rather strange, unparalleled elsewhere, and the picture drawn by Delitzsch is somewhat strained.

Accordingly, many Bible versions and scholars (JB, NAB, RSV; Kraus, Gunkel, and others) read *zrḥ* 'to dawn' for MT *zrʿ*, based on the versions (a Hebrew manuscript, Old Greek, Syriac, Targum, and Jerome). This yields the more comprehensible 'light dawns for the righteous one'. This is

64. See also above, on Ps 94:12a.

similar to the picture in Ps 112:4: "Light dawns in the darkness for the upright ones," and it is the reading adopted here.

Dahood offered an equally comprehensible reading (although very different and much less plausible): "a sown field awaits the just." He retained the MT analysis of *zrʿ* but interpreted *ʾwr* as *ʾūr* 'field'. However, there is no other Semitic evidence for this reading of *ʾwr*. Although some of the passages Dahood cited (1966: 222–23) in support are plausible enough with this reading (especially Isa 26:19 and Ps 56:14), they can also be understood reading *ʾwr* as 'light'. Furthermore, Dahood's suggestion concerning Ps 56:14, which (according to him) speaks of walking in the "field" of life, is weakened somewhat by Ps 89:16, which speaks of walking in the light of YHWH's countenance. In this passage, Dahood followed the MT pointing and translated *ʾwr* as 'light'.[65]

## Form-Critical Genre and Structure

The psalm is a hymn, one of the Kingship of YHWH psalms.[66] The syllable and word counts for the sections as divided here are:

| | | | |
|---|---|---|---|
| A | I | (vv. 1–6) | 100 (MT 106) syllables and 42 words |
| | II | (vv. 7–9) | 71 (MT 76) syllables and 31 words |
| B | III | (vv. 10–12) | 51 (MT 53) syllables and 22 words |

The major break in the psalm, at v. 10, divides it into two main units. Verses 1–9 (unit A) describe YHWH's sovereignty; vv. 10–12 (unit B) are an admonition to the faithful, employing various wisdom motifs. The syntactical and semantic coherence of unit B is clear.[67] The main lexical links between the two units are the recurrence of the roots *śmḥ* in vv. 1a, 8a, 11b, and 12a; *ṣd(y)q* in vv. 2b, 6a, 11a, and 12a; and the divine name, *YHWH* (see below). The coherence of unit A is also clear, since it is a

65. While it is true that *ʾwr pnyk* 'the light of your countenance' in Ps 89:16 is a more easily understood image than *ʾwr hḥyym* 'the light of life' in Ps 56:14 (thus perhaps justifying Dahood's search in 56:14 for a more understandable word picture), it is also true that walking in the light of life, namely, in 'earthly existence as God intended it to be' (Anderson 1972: 424), is far from obscure. Certainly it is no more obscure than the walking in 'the field of life' that Dahood postulated in Ps 56:14. The expression 'light of life' also occurs at Qumran (1QS III 7 [Anderson 1972: 424]), a fact that further weakens Dahood's case.

66. See the comments above on Ps 93:1 and on the form-critical genre of Psalms 93 and 96.

67. See the discussion on v. 10a, above.

hymn praising YHWH's kingship. However, its internal structure is not easily determined. I propose four divisions within unit A, based on the pattern of prefixing and suffixing verb forms.[68]

The most significant break occurs at v. 7. Verses 1–6 present the majesty of YHWH, revealed in the theophany of vv. 2–6, and vv. 7–9 describe the effects of YHWH's majesty. The break is marked grammatically by the prefixing verb form in v. 7a, following a series of suffixing forms in vv. 4–6.

A second, more minor break exists at v. 4, where the series of suffixing verb forms begins, following the prefixing forms in v. 3. Delitzsch's analysis reflected a break here, but his translation of the verbs did not distinguish between the prefixing and suffixing forms. Indeed, the flow of thought in vv. 2–6 continues uninterrupted, and any real temporal distinction between the events in vv. 2–3 and those in vv. 4–6 appears to be nonexistent.

The third break based on verb forms occurs in v. 8, where a suffixing form is followed by two *wāw*-consecutive prefixing forms. Verses 8–9 are in second-person form, addressing YHWH directly (the only such verses in the psalm), and they do not appear to be directly related to v. 7. Zion and the Judahite villages in v. 8 are rejoicing because of YHWH's judgments and exaltation in v. 9 rather than because of the information about other gods in v. 7.

The following figure reveals all of these breaks in a more detailed analysis:

| | | | |
|---|---|---|---|
| A | I | (vv. 1–3) | 45 (MT 48) syllables and 20 words |
| | II | (vv. 4–6) | 55 (MT 58) syllables and 22 words |
| | III | (v. 7) | 25 (MT 27) syllables and 10 words |
| | IV | (vv. 8–9) | 46 (MT 49) syllables and 21 words |
| B | V | (vv. 10–12) | 51 (MT 53) syllables and 22 words |

A more symmetrical structure appears than before, with four sections similar in length (I, II, IV, V) surrounding a short middle section. In this analysis, v. 7 functions as a bridge of sorts, since it links with the reference to 'all gods' (*kl-ʾlhym*) in v. 9 and also is a concluding statement on the theophany described in vv. 2–6. This is a somewhat artificial analysis, however, if it gives the impression that the five sections are equally independent, particularly when content (and not merely verb forms) is taken into account, as noted above in regard to vv. 1–3 and 4–6. Further-

68. I am omitting consideration of *hštḥww* in v. 7c, given the uncertainty attached to the form and the fact that v. 7c obviously belongs with vv. 7a–b.

more, while vv. 8–9 clearly belong together, v. 9c also echoes v. 7c, since the reference to "all gods" is found in both. The links between v. 7 and vv. 8–9 are stronger than the links between v. 7 and vv. 1–6 (or vv. 2–6). Thus, the five sections should not be seen as equally independent. They fit into the pattern seen in the first figure above, in which four subsections (vv. 1–3, 4–6, 7, and 8–9) combine to form two main units (unit A) that comprise the hymnic portion of the psalm, all of which is appropriately combined with the final hortatory address (unit B; see also below).

Verse 9 serves to conclude the second main section of the poem (vv. 7–9), in testifying to YHWH's exalted place, especially in v. 9b, and in the reference to all the gods, who were introduced in v. 7. It also aptly closes its immediate section (vv. 8–9), in affirming that YHWH, whose judgments cause rejoicing in the land (v. 8), is high and exalted (v. 9). This high position legitimates his judgments. However, with its reference to all the earth, v. 9 also echoes the earlier sections, where *ʾrṣ* occurs three times in vv. 1–5. Indeed, v. 9 is a fitting summary to all of vv. 1–8, since both speak of YHWH's exalted position above all the earth and all gods.

The third section (vv. 10–12) is only slightly linked with the others. Connections can be seen in the references to joy in YHWH in vv. 1b, 11b, and 12a. Otherwise, its subject matter is different, since it is a hortatory address to YHWH's followers to remain faithful to him.[69] It is couched in terms of traditional piety, often characteristic of wisdom circles (*rʿ*, *ḥsydyw*, *ršʿym*, *ṣdyq*[*ym*], *yšry*, *lb*).[70] Kraus (1978: 843) notes that Psalm 24 shows the connections between *YHWH mlk* and the *ṣdyqym* 'righteous ones'. Here the "King of glory" is prominent, and YHWH's *ṣdqh* 'righteousness' (as well as access to his holy hill; compare Psalm 15) is given to the one who is blameless. This shows that the section certainly is not misplaced and that the final form of the psalm indeed has coherence, although Delitzsch (see n. 69) may be correct about the later date of the third section.

The universal outlook of the psalm (like that of Psalm 96) is clear, particularly in vv. 1–9. For instance, the frequency of *kl* 'all'—referring to the earth (vv. 5b, 9a), the peoples (v. 6b), and the gods (vv. 7c, 9b)—is striking. All of creation marvels at YHWH's awesome power in vv. 1–9. References to the earth figure prominently throughout and even bracket the entire section (vv. 1a, 4a [*tbl*], 4b, 5b, 9a).

69. And, it may be later chronologically than the first two sections (Delitzsch).
70. See Scott 1971: 121–22 for some of this vocabulary.

*Psalm 98*

## Text

| | | Syllable Count | Total | Stresses |
|---|---|---|---|---|
| Title: *mzmwr* | | | | |
| 1a | *šyrw lYHWH šyr ḥdš* | 2 + 3 + 1 + 2 | 8 | 4 |
| b | *ky-nplʾwt ʿśh* | 1 + 3 + 2 | 6 | 2 |
| c | *hwšyʿh-lw ymynw* | 3 + 1 + 3 | 7 | 3 |
| d | *wzrwʿ qdšw* | 3(4) + 2 | 5(6) | 2 |
| 2a | *hwdyʿ YHWH yšwʿtw* | 2(3) + 2 + 4 | 8(9) | 3 |
| b | *lʿyny hgwym* | 3 + 3 | 6 | 2 |
| c | *glh ṣdqtw* | 2 + 3 | 5 | 2 |
| 3a | *zkr ḥsdw [lyʿqb]* | 2 + 2 [+ 3] | 7(4) | 3(2) |
| b | *wʾmwntw lbyt yśrʾl* | 4(5) + 2 + 3 | 9(10) | 3 |
| c | *rʾw kl-ʾpsy-ʾrṣ* | 2 + 1 + 2 + 1(2) | 6(7) | 3 |
| d | *ʾt yšwʿt ʾlhynw* | 1 + 3 + 4 | 8 | 2 |
| | | | | |
| 4a | *hryʿw lYHWH kl-hʾrṣ* | 3 + 3 + 1 + 2(3) | 9(10) | 3 |
| b | *pṣḥw wrnnw wzmrw* | 2 + 4 + 4 | 10 | 3 |
| 5a | *zmrw lYHWH bknwr* | 3 + 3 + 3 | 9 | 3 |
| b | *bknwr wqwl zmrh* | 3 + 2 + 2 | 7 | 3 |
| 6a | *bḥṣṣrwt wqwl šwpr* | 4(5) + 2 + 2 | 8(9) | 3 |
| b | *hryʿw lpny hmlk YHWH* | 3 + 2 + 2(3) + 2 | 9(10) | 4 |
| | | | | |
| 7a | *yrʿm hym wmlʾw* | 2 + 2 + 4 | 8 | 3 |
| b | *tbl wyšby bh* | 2 + 4 + 1 | 7 | 2 |
| 8a | *nhrwt ymḥʾw-kp* | 3 + 3 + 1 | 7 | 3 |
| b | *yḥd hrym yrnnw* | 1(2) + 2 + 4 | 7(8) | 3 |
| 9a | *lpny-YHWH ky bʾ* | 2 + 2 + 1 + 1 | 6 | 3 |
| b | *[ky bʾ] lšpṭ hʾrṣ* | [1 + 1 +] 2 + 2(3) | 6(5) | 3(2) |
| c | *yšpṭ-tbl bṣdq* | 2 + 2 + 2(3) | 6(7) | 3 |
| d | *wʿmym bmyšrym* | 3 + 4 | 7 | 2 |
| | 25 lines | | 181(186) | 70(68) |

7.2 syllables/line
7.4 syllables/line (MT)

2.6 syllables/stress
2.7 syllables/stress (MT)
2.8 stresses/line
2.7 stresses/line (MT)

## Translation

Title: *A Psalm*

1a Sing to YHWH a new song,
b For he has worked wonders!
c His right hand has worked salvation for him—
d Indeed, his holy arm.
2a YHWH has made known his salvation—
b In the eyes of the nations—
c He has revealed his righteousness.
3a He has remembered his steadfast love [to Jacob]
b And his faithfulness to the house of Israel.
c All the ends of the earth have seen
d The salvation of our God!

---

4a Raise a glad cry to YHWH, all the earth!
b Break forth, and sing for joy, and sing praises!
5a Sing praises to YHWH with a lyre,
b With a lyre and the sound of a song of praise!
6a With trumpets and the sound of a horn,
b Raise a glad cry before the King, YHWH!

---

7a Let the sea roar, and all that fills it!
b The world, and those who dwell in it!
8a Floods, let them clap their hands!
b Let the mountains sing for joy together,
9a Before YHWH, for he comes,
b [For he comes] to judge the earth;
c He will judge the world with righteousness,
d And the peoples with equity.

## Translation Notes

**98:1b. *ky-npl*ʾ*wt* ʿ*śh* "For he has worked wonders!"**

The Old Greek adds *kyrios* (= *YHWH*) at the end of this line, yielding 'for YHWH has worked wonders!' The line then has 8 syllables and 3 accents, a pattern that better balances v. 1a. The loss of the word could easily be explained by homoioteleuton,[71] which is an attractive reading, but there is no compelling need to adopt it. The poetic structure of vv. 1a–b without *YHWH* (8 and 6 syllables) is not seriously out of balance, and the verb does not require it. Thus, I retain the MT's reading.

**98:1c. *hwšy*ʿ*h* "has worked salvation"**

The verb is singular, with *ymynw* as subject. The *wāw* attached to *zrw*ʿ is thus understood as an emphatic *wāw*, which places *zrw*ʿ *qdšw* in apposition to *ymynw*, not in conjunction with it. The sense of lines 1c and 1d is thus: 'His right hand—indeed, his holy arm—has worked salvation for him'.[72] The verb may also be read as 'has won victory', both here and in v. 2a (see also the noun in v. 3d), reflecting a divine warrior motif (so most Bible versions and many commentators). The idea is essentially the same in either case.

**98:2b. *l*ʿ*yny hgwym* "in the eyes of the nations"**

The phrase modifies both the preceding and following clauses, and the line division above reflects this fact. The actual poetic division may have been only two lines, as follows:

2a *hwdy*ʿ *YHWH yšw*ʿ*tw*
2b *l*ʿ*yny hgwym glh ṣdqtw*

The syllable counts would have been 8(9):11 and the meter 3:4. I prefer the three-line division, however, since it is slightly better balanced syllabically and since it better reflects the dual function of the phrase in v. 2b.[73]

Note that the calculations above would be altered if there were only two lines here. The figures would then be as follows: 24 total lines; 7.5 (MT 7.8) syllables per line; and 2.9 (MT 2.8) stresses per line.

**98:3a. *zkr* "He has remembered"**

Dahood reads *zkr* (along with *r*ʾ*w* in v. 3c) as an imperative, seeing it as the first in the series of imperatives extending through v. 6. There is

71. Homoioteleuton is the loss of a word when an adjoining word ends similarly. In this case, the letter is *-h*, at the end of both ʿ*śh* and *YHWH*.

72. The JB, NJPSV, and NAB translations all have captured this nuance. See Dahood 1970: 401–2 on emphatic *wāw* of this type.

73. See Longman 1984: 268 n. 7 for studies developing this well-known phenomenon at the lower levels of structure, and Parunak 1983: 540–42 for exposition of it on a larger scale.

nothing in theory that would militate against his analysis here (including the idea of a vocative *lāmed*), but the context does not in any way demand it. The (traditional) reading that I have adopted makes good sense. In fact, the ideas in v. 3 are more closely linked with those of vv. 1–2 than vv. 4ff. The imperatives and jussives in vv. 4–8 all speak of praise activities, which is not at all true in v. 3. This verse speaks of the attributes of YHWH, which have been already introduced in vv. 1–2. Furthermore, there are six (indicative) suffixing forms in vv. 1–3—if *zkr* is read 'he has remembered'—that balance the six imperative plural forms in the next section (vv. 4–6); this is another argument against Dahood's reading.

**98:3a. [*lyᶜqb*] "[to Jacob]"**

I insert *lyᶜqb* 'to Jacob', provisionally, following the Old Greek rendering. The words 'Jacob' and 'Israel' are parallel in this reading (as is common elsewhere), as are YHWH's attributes *ḥsd* and *ᵓmwnh*. The actual phrases, 'Jacob' // 'house of Israel' are parallel elsewhere only in Mic 1:5 and 3:1. However, the more expanded phrases, 'house of Jacob' // 'house of Israel' do occur in Isa 46:3; Jer 2:4; 5:15, and 20 (also see Ezek 28:25).

**98:4b. *pṣḥw* . . . "Break forth . . . !"**

The cumulative effect of three imperatives following one after the other is not adequately captured by my translation. The verb *pṣḥ* always occurs with the roots *rnn* or *rnh* and means 'to break out into a glad song' ($KB^3$, s.v.). The NIV captures the sense of the line: 'Burst into jubilant song with music'.

**98:9b. [*ky bᵓ*] "[For he comes]"**

I favor the Old Greek's Codex Alexandrinus in my translation: 'for he comes' (so also, for example, Gunkel, Kraus). This is the reading found in Ps 96:13, which is almost identical to 98:9, and the reading is justifiable not only on the basis of the similarities between the two verses, but especially because of the extremely close relationship between the two psalms as a whole. (The loss of the clause is easily explainable by haplography.) This reading has the further advantage of balancing the poetic structure of the verse. The syllabic and metrical patterns are then 6:6(5):6(7):7 and 3:3:3:2, the last line's variation signaling the end of the section (and the poem). Finally, it should be noted that restoration of this phrase creates a "stairstep" pattern in vv. 9a–c, with the repeated words being *ky bᵓ* (vv. 9a and 9b) and *špṭ* (vv. 9b and 9c). This pattern is not foreign to the poem; it is also found in vv. 4b–5b (see below, under "Form-Critical Genre and Structure").

## Form-Critical Genre and Structure

Psalm 98 is a hymn in praise of YHWH. It is classified as a Kingship of YHWH psalm (1) on the strength of its position between two other kingship psalms, both of which begin with *YHWH mlk*, (2) its similarities with Psalm 96, and (3) the reference to 'the King, YHWH' in v. 6b (Gunkel; Mowinckel 1962: 1.106ff.; Kraus). Gunkel (1926: 427; 1933: 82–83), however, saw it as an eschatological hymn.

Psalm 98 divides easily into three sections: (1) vv. 1–3, call to worship and celebration of YHWH's victory; (2) vv. 4–6, exaltation of YHWH as King; (3) vv. 7–9, exaltation of YHWH as Judge. The first section especially emphasizes his victory (or 'salvation'; see above, on v. 1c) by using the term *yšʿ* as a bracket around the reasons-for-praise section (vv. 1c and 3d) and using it in v. 2a as well. There is also an unmistakable inclusio in vv. 2–3 involving *yšʿ* and the divine names. This is formed by the fact that both vv. 2a and 3d speak of divine victory and that the common expression *YHWH ʾlhynw* 'YHWH our God' is broken up and forms the outer limits of the inclusio.

The second section (vv. 4–6) is more purely praise-oriented. It also is bracketed by an inclusio at its outer limits, both extremes of which contain very similar clauses: imperatives of the verb *rwʿ* 'to raise a glad cry' and the divine name *YHWH* (vv. 4a, 6b). Within the section many words are repeated, some in intentional poetic patterns. We see a stairstep parallelism of sorts in vv. 4b–5b: the repeated terms are *zmrw* 'sing praises' (vv. 4b and 5a) and *bknwr* 'with a lyre' (vv. 5a and 5b). The term *wqwl* 'and the sound [of X]' is also found in vv. 5b and 6a. Lines 5b and 6a do not exactly fit the stairlike progression of the preceding lines, but they are syntactically identical to each other. The metrical pattern of vv. 4–6 is three stresses per line, with the final line breaking the pattern (4 stresses [or else 2:2]).

The third section (vv. 7–9) praises YHWH as Judge. It also is bracketed by an inclusio of sorts, formed by the repetition in vv. 7b and 9c of the relatively rare word *tbl* 'world' and the parallels between the world's inhabitants (7b) and the peoples (9d).

---

*Psalm 99*

## Text

| | | *Syllable Count* | *Total* | *Stresses* |
|---|---|---|---|---|
| 1a | *YHWH mlk yrgzw ʿmym* | 2 + 2 + 3 + 2 | 9 | 4 |
| b | *yšb krwbym tnwṭ hʾrṣ* | 2 + 3 + 2 + 2(3) | 9(10) | 4 |
| 2a | *YHWH bṣywn gdwl* | 2 + 3 + 2 | 7 | 3 |
| b | *wrm hwʾ ʿl-kl-hʿmym* | 2 + 1 + 1 + 1 + 3 | 8 | 3 |

Seven divine names are found in this poem: *YHWH* appears six times and *ʾlhynw* once. The number *seven* may have been intentional, with *ʾlhynw* used in v. 3d as the variant from an established pattern. *Seven* also figures in other ways. There are seven imperative plural verbs of praise (six in vv. 4–6 and one in v. 1a) and seven different verbs of which YHWH is the subject (*ʿśh*, v. 1b; *hwšyʿh*, v. 1c; *hwdyʿ*, v. 2a; *glh*, v. 2c; *zkr*, v. 3a; *bʾ*, v. 9a [and 9b]; and *špṭ*, vv. 9b and 9c).

As noted above (first note on v. 3a), the connections between vv. 1–3 and 4–6 are less marked than the connections between vv. 4–6 and 7–9, because the latter two groups have in common the exhortation to praise (by means of imperatives in vv. 4–6 and jussives in vv. 7–8). The links between the latter can be seen in the syllable and word counts for the sections as well:

| | | |
|---|---|---|
| I | (vv. 1–3) | 75 (MT 76) syllables and 32 (31) words |
| II | (vv. 4–6) | 52 (MT 55) syllables and 20 words |
| III | (vv. 7–9) | 54 (MT 55) syllables and 25 (23) words |

We should note that the words added by emendation (*lyʿqb* and *ky bʾ*) in Sections I and III decrease the expected differences between the minimal and the MT syllable counts. The metrical patterns throughout the poem are reasonably consistent, averaging just under three stresses per line; where there is variation, there is usually a balancing compensation.

The terms for praise in the last two sections are prevalent, repeated with an insistence that is impossible to ignore. The psalm reflects much of the outlook of Psalm 96, and the connections with Isaiah 40–66 are clear, although the direction of the influence is debated.[74]

74. See the discussion in appendix 1 of the dating of Psalm 96. On the connections with Isaiah 40–66, see, for example, the list in Kraus 1978: 846.

## Translation

1a YHWH reigns! Let the peoples tremble!
b The One enthroned (upon) cherubim (reigns). Let the earth quake!
2a YHWH is great in Zion,
b And exalted is he over all the peoples!

| | | | | |
|---|---|---|---|---|
| 3a | *ywdw šmk gdwl wnwrʾ* | 2 + 2 + 2 + 3 | 9 | 4 |
| b | *qdwš hwʾ* | 2 + 1 | 3 | 1 |
| 4a | *wʿz mlk mšpṭ ʾhb* | 2 + 1(2) + 2 + 2 | 7(8) | 4 |
| b | *ʾth kwnnt myšrym* | 2 + 3 + 3 | 8 | 3 |
| c | *mšpṭ wṣdqh byʿqb* | 2 + 4 + 3(4) | 9(10) | 3 |
| d | *ʾth ʿśyt* | 2 + 3 | 5 | 2 |
| 5a | *rwmmw YHWH ʾlhynw* | 3 + 2 + 4 | 9 | 3 |
| b | *whšthww lhdm rglyw* | 4(5) + 2(3) + 2 | 8(10) | 3 |
| c | *qdwš hwʾ* | 2 + 1 | 3 | 1 |
| 6a | *mšh wʾhrn bkhnyw* | 2 + 3(4) + 4 | 9(10) | 3 |
| b | *wšmwʾl bqrʾy šmw* | 4 + 4 + 2 | 10 | 3 |
| c | *qrʾym ʾl-YHWH* | 3(2) + 1 + 2 | 6(5) | 2 |
| d | *whwʾ yʿnm* | 2 + 2(3) | 4(5) | 2 |
| 7a | *bʿmwd ʿnn ydbr ʾlyhm* | 3 + 2 + 3 + 3 | 11 | 4 |
| b | *šmrw ʿdtyw* | 3 + 3 | 6 | 2 |
| c | *whq ntn-lmw* | 2 + 2 + 2 | 6 | 3 |
| 8a | *YHWH ʾlhynw ʾth ʿnytm* | 2 + 4 + 2 + 3 | 11 | 4 |
| b | *ʾl nśʾ hyyt lhm* | 1 + 2 + 3 + 2 | 8 | 3 |
| c | *wnqm ʿl-ʿlylwtm* | 3 + 1 + 4 | 8 | 3 |
| 9a | *rwmmw YHWH ʾlhynw* | 3 + 2 + 4 | 9 | 3 |
| b | *whšthww lhr qdšw* | 4(5) + 2 + 2 | 8(9) | 3 |
| c | *ky qdwš YHWH ʾlhynw* | 1 + 2 + 2 + 4 | 9 | 3 |
| | 26 lines | | 199(206) | 76 |

7.7 syllables/line — 2.6 syllables/stress
7.9 syllables/line (MT) — 2.7 syllables/stress (MT)
2.9 stresses/line

## Translation Notes

**99:1b. *yšb krwbym* "The One enthroned (upon) cherubim (reigns)"**

I understand the phrase as parallel to *YHWH mlk*, with the verb *mlk* gapped and *krwbym* providing the compensating balance in the verse. The verb, although it is gapped, is understood to serve this phrase as well. Note that the syllable count for both lines is exactly the same. My translation differs from most translations, which render the phrase 'he sits enthroned on/above cherubim', understanding the phrase as making a new, declarative

3a Let them praise your name, O Great and Awesome One!
b Holy is it!

---

4a Indeed, the Victorious One is King! He loves justice!
b You have established equity;
c Justice and righteousness in Jacob—
d You have wrought (them).
5a Exalt YHWH our God!
b And worship at his footstool!
c Holy is he!

---

6a Moses and Aaron were among his priests,
b And Samuel among those who would call on his name,
c Who would call on YHWH,
d And he would answer them;
7a From the pillar of cloud he would speak to them.
b They obeyed his decrees,
c And the law he gave to them.

---

8a O YHWH our God, you answered them;
b A forgiving God you were to them
c And One who vindicates (them) despite their evil deeds.
9a Exalt YHWH our God!
b And worship at his holy mountain,
c For holy is YHWH our God!

---

statement.[75] A slightly different explanation of the deep structure would be to translate the phrase as appositional to *YHWH*, after the fashion of *y(w)šb hkr(w)bym* in 1 Sam 4:4, 2 Sam 6:2, 2 Kgs 19:15, Isa 37:16, Ps 80:2, and 1 Chr 13:6. In each of these cases the phrase is appositional to the divine name or a divine title. The complete divine name and title here (*YHWH yšb krbym*) are split for poetic reasons.

75. The NJPSV translation is similar to my understanding: 'The LORD, enthroned on cherubim, is king'.

**99:2a. *YHWH bṣywn gdwl* "YHWH is great in Zion"**

It is tempting to translate *YHWH bṣywn* as a title, 'YHWH of Zion'. The exact phrase (*YHWH bṣywn*) occurs only one other time, in Lam 2:6, but the parallelism of the last two lines in that verse argues against its being a divine title. At Kuntillet Ajrud, the phrases *YHWH šmrn* ('YHWH of Samaria') and *YHWH tmn* ('YHWH of Teman') have both appeared in the inscriptions, and *YHWH bṣywn* could conceivably be analogous to them. This translation, of course, would accord well with the predominant biblical picture of YHWH in close association and identification with Zion, especially in the Psalms. However, the two syntactical constructions are somewhat different and cannot be strictly compared. In Psalm 99, the syntax is:

divine name / preposition (*b*-) / place-name,

whereas in the other cases, there is no preposition:

divine name[76] / place-name.

Furthermore, the preposition *b*- does not appear to be used to indicate a construct relationship in this type of construction; it does occasionally intrude in a construct chain (GKC §130a) but not in a divine title or in a personal or place-name. Consequently, I translate *bṣywn* adverbially, describing where it is that YHWH is great, 'in Zion'. This understanding still accords with the predominant biblical picture mentioned above.[77]

**99:2b. *ʿl-kl-hʿmym* "over all peoples"**

Dahood's rendering of *ʿmym* as 'Strong Ones' is not verified by Ugaritic or any other Semitic parallels. Dahood cited many passages as examples in his explication of Ps 18:28, but they are all fairly weak support. Indeed, in 1966 (p. 112) he rendered *ʿmym* in Ps 99:1a as 'gods', but in his actual translation of the verse (1968: 377), he rendered it 'peoples'.[78]

**99:3a. *ywdw šmk gdwl wnwrʾ* "Let them praise your name, O Great and Awesome One!"**

Addressing YHWH in the second person in 99:3a, following the third-person address in vv. 1–2 and elsewhere in the psalm, may be an example of court style, as noted by Dahood here and at Ps 61:8.

Most versions (JB, NAB, NASB, NIV, RSV) treat the adjectival phrase *gdwl wnwrʾ* as attributive: 'your great and awesome name'. However, strictly speaking, one would expect to find the definite article attached to any adjectives modifying a definite noun (in this case, the noun is *šmk*); since

76. Possibly in construct (see Emerton 1982: 3–9).

77. See Dever 1984 and especially Emerton 1982 for the literature and a discussion of the Kuntillet Ajrud materials in general and the above phrases in particular.

78. For further criticism, see Loretz 1974a: 183–85.

it is lacking, the paired words should be read as predicate adjectives: 'Your name is great and awesome'.

This rendering, however, ignores the first word in the line. The NJPSV and NEB are sensitive to the problem, and their renderings are similar: 'They praise your name as great and awesome' (NJPSV). Weiser, with a slightly different nuance, translated: 'Let them praise thy name; great and terrible'. These translations do justice to the grammar of this difficult line.

The reading I prefer slightly above others interprets *gdwl wnwrʾ* as titles of YHWH himself: 'O Great and Awesome One'.[79] YHWH is the Great and Awesome One par excellence. This reading is consistent with the canons of the grammar, and it strengthens the second-person addresses in v. 3 (see next note). It is identical to Dahood's reading, although based on different reasons.[80]

**99:3b.** ***qdwš hwʾ*** **"Holy is it!"**

In my view, the words of this line are still addressing YHWH, in the second person, and the pronoun refers to YHWH's name (so also Weiser; Freedman [private communication]). The clause recurs in the refrain in v. 5c, where it refers to YHWH himself (based on the parallel with v. 9), and most Bible versions read it the same way: 'Holy is he!' There is no doubt a wordplay involved here, as Delitzsch long ago noted: "[YHWH] and His Name are notions that easily glide into one another" (1881: 3.101). In this way, vv. 3b and 5c consciously echo each other while nonetheless denoting different referents.

**99:4a.** ***wʿz mlk mšpṭ ʾhb*** **"Indeed, the Victorious One is King! He loves justice!"**

This line is most difficult to translate. Literally, the MT reads 'And strength of a king loves justice', and this enigmatic construction has occasioned many readings and proposed solutions.[81]

My interpretation is similar to Kraus's, who reads (repointing *wĕʿōz* to *wĕʿāz*) 'A strong one is king! He loves justice!' However, I read *ʿōz* as a divine title: 'Strong One' or 'Victorious One'.[82] The metaphor of YHWH

79. For *nwrʾ* as a divine title, see Exod 15:11 and Ps 68:36 (Freedman 1976: 80, 82, 106). It may also occur as a title in conjunction with *rbh* in Ps 89:8. On the occurrence of double divine names such as this, see Freedman and Franke Hyland 1973: 242 n. 8.

80. His principal reason seems to be the parallelism created with 'O Enthroned upon the Cherubim' in v. 1b; however, the phrase in v. 1b is not a vocative in my view.

81. See Eaton 1968: 555 for a review of the various readings.

82. See Freedman 1976: 80, 82 on *ʿōz* as a divine title; and Freedman and Franke Hyland 1973: 238, 242; Dahood 1966: 180 on the reading of *ʿōz* as 'Victorious One'.

as a victorious king is repeated obliquely in vv. 4b and 4c, where the establishment of equity, justice, and righteousness in Jacob can be interpreted as the result of YHWH's victory. Whether the victory was over the primordial forces or over the Egyptians is difficult to say, but perhaps it was the latter, given the reference in v. 4c to the entity "Jacob" and to Moses and Aaron in v. 6a. I consider the *wāw* before *ʿz* to be emphatic.[83]

The emphatic *wāw* thus emphasizes the break between vv. 3 and 4, a break with which many scholars agree, based on the repeated line *qdwš hwʾ* that occurs in vv. 3b, 5c and, with modification, in 9c. In fact, the first clause in v. 4 can then be seen as paralleling v. 1a: "YHWH reigns! . . . Indeed, the Victorious One is king!' *Mlk* can either be read as a noun (*melek*; so MT) and the clause thus seen as a standard verbless clause, or it can be repointed to *mālak* (so Kraus), in which case the parallel with v. 1a becomes even more striking.

**99:6b–7a. Verb forms**

I read the participle in vv. 6b and 6c (*qrʾy*[*m*]) in a durative/habitual sense, consonant with the reading of the prefixing verb forms in vv. 6d and 7a (*yʿnm* and *ydbr*).

**99:7a. *bʿmwd ʿnn* "From the pillar of cloud"**

The preposition *b-* is translated 'from' here. This sense is defended by Dahood, with references and bibliography at Pss 15:2 and 60:8. Craigie, at Ps 15:2, also recognizes this sense. The phrase modifies both v. 6d and the end of v. 7a.[84]

**99:8c. *wnqm ʿl-ʿlylwtm* "And One who vindicates (them) despite their evil deeds"**

This phrase has caused a great deal of difficulty.[85] The reason for the difficulty is that the root *nqm*, commonly translated 'to avenge', occurs in the midst of a discussion about God's grace and forgiveness. The point made in vv. 6–8 is that YHWH forgives in response to obedience and intercession of the type demonstrated by Israel's leaders Moses, Aaron, and Samuel. The presence of *nqm* (as commonly translated, 'avenge') introduces a discordant note into a psalm otherwise concerned with God's merciful and just dealings with his people. While YHWH certainly is seen as an avenger in Scripture, and this use of the word would merely serve as

83. On this use of *wāw*, see above on Ps 98:1c.

84. On this "pivot" or "hinge" phenomenon, see Dahood's commentary here, and also my comments above on Ps 98:2.

85. See Whybray 1969; Whitley 1973 for the best reviews of the proposed solutions.

a reminder of this fact (Delitzsch, Weiser), more plausible solutions have been advanced.

One such solution is offered by Whitley (1973), who proposes that *nqm* comes from the root *nqh* 'to cleanse', with a pronominal suffix (*-m*), and points it as a *Qal* participle, *nōqām*. *Nqh* occurs primarily in *Niphal* and *Piel* stems, but it does occur once in *Qal* (an infinitive absolute in Jer 49:12). Furthermore, it does not occur at all as a participle in *Niphal* or *Piel*.[86] Whitley understood the suffix on *ᶜlylwtm* as possessive, referring to Israel's sins, from which YHWH cleansed her, and he read *ᶜl* as 'from', justified on the basis of several texts from the Bible as well as from Northwest Semitic inscriptions.[87] Another, less plausible solution, is Whybray's (1969). He concluded that the suffix of *ᶜlylwtm* is an objective suffix.

The best solution is far more simple than these, however. One must remember that *nqm* connotes more than merely 'vengeance'; it is perhaps best rendered as 'vindication'. In this context, it denotes the legitimate exercise of YHWH's executive power against those who do not call on his name.[88] The translation of *ᶜl* as 'despite' is rare but not unknown in Biblical Hebrew (BDB 754), and it clarifies the nature of YHWH's activity as a *nōqēm*: YHWH's vindication is directed against his enemies.[89] The entire verse thus portrays YHWH as acting on behalf of the faithful in Israel: he answered them (v. 8a), he forgives them (v. 8b), and he vindicates them (v. 8c)—all of this in spite of their sins. Indeed, this is the essence of forgiveness: God forgives and acts on behalf of sinners, who do not intrinsically merit his favor.

## Form-Critical Genre and Structure

Psalm 99 opens with *YHWH mlk*, as do Psalms 93 and 97, and it is thus classified as a Kingship/Enthronement of YHWH psalm. Formally, it is a hymn, which can be divided into two major units (A and B) on the basis of the refrain in vv. 5 and 9. The two verses are identical, except for the following substitutions: in v. 9b, *hr qdšw* 'his holy mountain' replaces *hdm rglyw* 'his footstool', and in v. 9c, *YHWH ᵓlhynw* 'YHWH our God' replaces

86. Its occurrence as a *Piel* participle would weaken the case for seeing a *Qal* participle here.

87. Whitley 1973: 228–29 and n. 13; see also Dahood 1966: 26 (on Ps 4:7); 1968: 264 (on Ps 81:6) and references there.

88. The relevant work is Mendenhall's (1973), especially pp. 70–77 and 82–88.

89. Whether these enemies of YHWH are internal (to Israel) or external is not relevant in the discussion of *nqm*; both types of enemies are objects of YHWH's exercise of this power (Mendenhall 1973: 82–83).

*hwʾ* 'he, it'. The two units are almost identical in length: unit A consists of 94 (MT 99) syllables and 42 words; unit B consists of 105 (107) syllables and 41 words (see below).

Within these units, we also find significant breaks. In unit A, there is a natural break between vv. 3 and 4, and vv. 1–3 are parallel to vv. 4–5. The parallels between vv. 1a and 4a were noted in the comments on v. 4a. Besides these, the parallels between vv. 3 and 5 are also instructive. That is, both verses end with the clause *qdwš hwʾ*, and both consist of exhortations to praise or exalt YHWH (via a jussive in v. 3 and two imperatives in v. 5). Both sets of exhortations follow verses describing YHWH's attributes and actions (vv. 2, 4bc).[90] In unit B, there is also a break, at v. 8, which is signaled by the change in address: YHWH is referred to in the third person in vv. 6–7, in the second person in v. 8, and in the third person again in the refrain. The subject matter in vv. 6–8 is closely related, however, so the break is more purely a structural one than the break at v. 4.

My analysis reflects these two secondary breaks, as well, and thus I see the psalm as being composed of four main sections combined into two larger units, displaying a remarkable symmetry. The syllable and word counts of these sections are:

| | | |
|---|---|---|
| A | I (vv. 1–3) | 45 (MT 46) syllables and 22 words |
| | II (vv. 4–5) | 49 (MT 53) syllables and 20 words |
| B | III (vv. 6–7) | 52 (MT 53) syllables and 20 words |
| | IV (vv. 8–9) | 53 (MT 54) syllables and 21 words |

The psalm is full of references to YHWH, in uses of his name proper, in divine titles, and in pronouns and suffixes referring to him that are distributed evenly across the psalm. The name *YHWH*, for example, occurs precisely seven times, three times in unit A (once in the refrain) and four times in unit B (twice in the refrain, due to the expanded v. 9c). Sections I and II both begin and end with a divine name, title, or pronoun. (See appendix 3 on "Divine Names and Titles.")

The repeated clause (*qdwš hwʾ*), referring to YHWH's (or his name's) holiness, which is identical in vv. 3b and 5c and is expanded in v. 9c, also links the sections. Indeed, it has formed the basis for some divisions of the psalm into only three major sections (e.g., Delitzsch and Dahood). It is less of a refrain, however, than a repeated structural device, and thus my analysis is based on the two major refrains in vv. 5 and 9. This clause does

90. There is even a purely formal link, in the occurrence of *b-ṣywn* (v. 2a) and *b-yʿqb* (v. 4c) in the verses immediately preceding the exhortations of vv. 3 and 5.

contribute to the complex unity of the poem, however. It strongly links the end of section II with the end of section I, and it also recurs as an echo at the end of section IV. Although section I does not, strictly speaking, have a refrain, it does echo the refrain in vv. 5 and 9 in another way: in v. 2b, YHWH is referred to as exalted (*rwm*); this root is precisely the root found in vv. 5a and 9a, also referring to YHWH. Weak links between sections II and III can also be seen in the references to what YHWH has established or proclaimed: justice, righteousness, and equity in v. 4, and his decrees and statutes in v. 7.

However, most of the examples of unity between sections occurs between the sections within each major unit. That is, sections I and II are both short paeans to YHWH's kingship, dominated by praise vocabulary. Sections III and IV are likewise related to each other, concerned with the relationship of YHWH to those who have called on his name. They deal with praise of YHWH only indirectly (v. 8), except for the refrain in v. 9. Units A and B display this internal unity, but the connections between them are much less pronounced. However, the poem as a whole displays a remarkable balance and symmetry, as seen in the balanced lengths of each section.

I should also note that vv. 6–8 appear on the surface to refer to the Exodus and Sinai experiences. However, the inclusion of Samuel along with Moses and Aaron indicates that there is another central theme: relationship with YHWH, in *all* periods and *all* locations. If vv. 6–8 were an independent psalm, the holy mountain of v. 9b could conceivably be Sinai. However, the presence of Samuel argues against this. Furthermore, in the context of the entire psalm, the holy mountain can only be Zion. YHWH is enthroned above the cherubim (v. 1b), which are in the Temple at Zion. Zion itself is mentioned in v. 2. The reference in v. 5b to YHWH's footstool echoes v. 1b: YHWH's footstool is either the ark or Mt. Zion itself. The reference to YHWH's holy mountain in v. 9b occurs in exactly the same syntactical locus as the reference to "footstool" in v. 5b and can thus only refer to Mt. Zion.

The emphasis on Moses and Aaron as priests confirms this interpretation. They are important in this context, not as leaders or recipients of the covenant, but as YHWH's priests and worshipers of his name (thus the inclusion of Samuel). There were also priests and worshipers of YHWH's name at Zion in later periods. Thus the psalm exhibits a unity of outlook and structure, despite the major disjunction at v. 6. It is a unity centered around worship of YHWH at Zion and around his various attributes.

*Psalm 100*

## Text

| | | Syllable Count | Total | Stresses |
|---|---|---|---|---|
| Title: | *mzmwr ltwdh* | | | |
| 1a | *hryʿw lYHWH kl-hʾrṣ* | 3 + 3 + 1 + 2(3) | 9(10) | 3 |
| 2a | *ʿbdw ʾt-YHWH bśmḥh* | 2 + 1 + 2 + 3 | 8 | 3 |
| b | *bʾw lpnyw brnnh* | 2 + 3 + 3 | 8 | 3 |
| 3a | *dʿw ky-YHWH hwʾ ʾlhym* | 2 + 1 + 2 + 1 + 3 | 9 | 4 |
| b | *hwʾ-ʿśnw wlʾ ʾnḥnw* | 1 + 3 + 2 + 3 | 9 | 4 |
| c | *ʿmw wṣʾn mrʿytw* | 2 + 2 + 3 | 7 | 3 |
| 4a | *bʾw šʿryw btwdh* | 2 + 3 + 3 | 8 | 3 |
| b | *ḥṣrtyw bthlh* | 4 + 3 | 7 | 3 |
| c | *hwdw-lw brkw šmw* | 2 + 1 + 3 + 2 | 8 | 3 |
| 5a | *ky-ṭwb YHWH lʿwlm ḥsdw* | 1 + 1 + 2 + 3 + 2 | 9 | 4 |
| c | *wʿd-dr wdr ʾmwntw* | 2 + 1 + 2 + 4 | 9 | 3 |
| | 11 lines | | 91(92) | 36 |

8.3 syllables/line | 2.5 syllables/stress
8.4 syllables/line (MT) | 2.6 syllables/stress (MT)
3.3 stresses/line

## Translation Notes

**Title: *mzmwr ltwdh* "A Psalm of Thanksgiving"**

The term *twdh* can mean 'thank offering' as well as 'thanksgiving', and it is translated that way by some versions and scholars (e.g., RSV; Gunkel, Leslie, Weiser). The translation 'thank offering' would accord well with an original cultic setting for the psalm. However, I translate it with the more general 'thanksgiving', on the basis of its occurrence in v. 4. There it is parallel to *thlh* 'praise' and followed by the imperatives *ydh* and *brk*, verbs of thanking and blessing. It is more likely that *twdh* in v. 4 means 'thanksgiving' in general. It is of course possible that the title was added later, intended to appropriate a general psalm of thanksgiving for use in the cultic

## Translation

Title: *A Psalm of Thanksgiving*

1a Raise a glad cry to YHWH, all the earth!
2a Serve YHWH with joy!
b Come before him with joyful song!

---

3a Know that YHWH, it is he who is God.
b It is he who has made us, and we are his!
c (We are) his people, and the sheep of his pasture!

---

4a Enter his gates with thanksgiving,
b His courts with praise!
c Give thanks to him! Bless his name!

---

5a For YHWH is good! Forever is his steadfast love,
b And to all generations is his faithfulness.

---

ceremony, but it is equally possible that the psalm was used in the cult for more than just the thank offering, regardless of when the title arose. The JB, NJPSV, NAB, NASB, NEB, NIV, Dahood, Anderson, and Kraus all follow this reading.

**100:1a. *kl-hʾrṣ* "all the earth"**

*Kl-hʾrṣ* is a stock phrase, and it is used throughout the Psalter, especially in the Kingship of YHWH psalms. It usually denotes YHWH's sovereignty over the earth and the nations and peoples inhabiting the earth. In the context of this psalm, however, one should allow for the possibility of a more narrow meaning of 'all the land', referring to Israel as YHWH's chosen people. The justification for this lies in v. 3, where the people in view are the covenant people of Israel and not all the peoples of the earth (see next note, under the discussion of *ʿśh*). Furthermore, YHWH's *ḥsd*, referred to in v. 5b, has strong connections to his covenant with his people (Glueck 1967; Sakenfeld 1978).

If *kl-hʾrṣ* does indeed refer here to the broader meaning 'earth' (as most versions and commentators render it, and as I prefer), then the psalm progresses from a generalized call to all the earth at its outset, in stylized language, to a specific focus on Israel in vv. 3–5.

**100:3b. *wlʾ ʾnḥnw* "and we are his"**

The MT *Kethiv* reads 'and not we ourselves' here, which makes good sense grammatically, and this is the traditional reading, found in the KJV and the NASB. However, this rendering does violence to common sense and to the biblical world view. Human beings in general, and Israel specifically, are created by God; there is no suggestion anywhere of self-creation. The traditional reading answers a question that few people, if any, were asking or even thought to ask. The contrast in the verse is not between YHWH's creative activity and humanity's (or Israel's) potential for self-creation. Rather, it is between YHWH and other gods. The verse states that it is YHWH who has created. The double occurrence of the independent personal pronoun *hwʾ* in the first two lines underscores this. The phrase in v. 3b (*hwʾ ʿśnw*) is similar to the clause *YHWH mlk* in its emphasis on the distinctiveness of the grammatical subject.[91]

On the other hand, the MT *Qere* reads 'and we are his', understanding *lʾ* not as a negative particle, but as a preposition followed by a 3d masculine-singular suffix. It is one of fifteen passages in which the Masora indicates that *lô* is to be read for *lōʾ*.[92] This reading has several advantages. First, it does not answer a question scarcely or never asked. Second, it reinforces the references to YHWH in the rest of the verse. That is, the term *YHWH* occurs in the first half of v. 3a, and YHWH is then referred to by an independent personal pronoun or a possessive suffix in each half of each line in the rest of the verse, a total of five times. It is more reasonable to see *lʾ* in v. 3b (as well as in the rest of the verse) as a reference to YHWH than as a disruptive intrusion. A third advantage of this reading is that it reinforces the theme of the close relationship between YHWH and humanity or Israel that is being developed in the verse. Since he made them, they belong to him.

We should note that the creation of Israel in particular is in view here, and not YHWH's general creating activity. The word *ʿśh* is used here to

91. See the discussion of *YHWH mlk* above, at Ps 93:1a.

92. See the list in Delitzsch's note, p. 105, and his full discussion at Job 13:15.

denote YHWH's creation of his own people Israel—in the events of the Exodus and later—and not to his creation of humans in general. Examples of this use of *ʿśh* are common: see Gen 12:2; Exod 32:10; Num 14:12; Deut 9:14; 32:6, 15; Isa 43:7, 44:2, 46:4; Ezek 37:19, 22; Ps 95:6. Israel as the work (*mʿśh*) of YHWH's hands appears in Isa 29:23, 60:21, 64:7, and YHWH as the One who 'forms' (*yṣr*) Israel appears often in Isaiah: see 27:11; 43:1, 21; 44:2, 21, 24; 45:9 (2x), 11; 64:7. Since YHWH has created Israel (Ps 100:3), Israel belongs to him; Israel does not belong to Baʿal, Marduk, or any other deity, but rather to its own covenant God, YHWH. The emphasis throughout the verse is on this ownership of Israel. They belong to him (v. 3b) and are his people and the sheep of his pasture (v. 3c).

An alternative reading of *wlʾ* has been advanced by Lewis (1967), who read *lʾ* as an asseverative particle, 'indeed, surely', pronounced *lū* or *lā* (Nötscher 1953: 373; Richardson 1966). That an emphatic *lāmed* exists has been clear since Haupt first identified examples in 1892.[93] Smith (1905) and Haupt (1905–6: 201) first identified emphatic *lʾ* as a variant of emphatic *lāmed*, using Exod 8:22 as a prime example: 'if we sacrifice offerings abominable to the Egyptians before their eyes, surely (*lʾ-*) they will stone us'.[94] Nötscher (1953) presented the prime treatment of the phenomenon, and on pp. 374–75 he detailed uses of *lʾ*. The strongest examples he gave are Gen 23:11; Exod 8:22; 1 Sam 14:30; 20:9, 14; 2 Kgs 5:26; and Ruth 2:13. In each case, there is a definite problem with reading *lʾ* as a negative, and there is either manuscript evidence, or a proposed emendation, for an alternative reading of some type,[95] which is why Nötscher argued for use of emphatic *lʾ* in those verses.

Lewis's reading with an asseverative particle is attractive, and would render the verse as follows:

| | | | |
|---|---|---|---|
| 3a | Know that YHWH, | 5 | |
| 3b | It is he who is God! | 4 | 13 |
| 3c | It is he who has made us! | 4 | |
| 3d | And indeed, we are his people, | 7 | 12 |
| 3e | And the sheep of his pasture! | 5 | |

93. Casanowicz 1896: clxvii and n.; cf. Dahood 1952; 1970: 406–7.

94. Rather than 'they will not stone us' or, by adding an interrogative *h-*, 'will they not stone us?'

95. See also Andersen (1974: 102), who discerned an asseverative *lʾ* at Exod 6:3; and McCarter (1984: 482), who gives additional bibliography on this emphatic particle.

The verse breaks into two halves of 13 and 12 syllables, demarcated by the disjunction signaled by *wlʾ*. In this scheme, the second half of the verse is almost identical syntactically with Pss 79:13 and 95:7:

| | | | |
|---|---|---|---|
| Ps 79:13 | (1) *wʾnḥnw* | (2) *ʿmk* | (3) *wṣʾn mrʿytw* |
| Ps 95:7 | (1) *wʾnḥnw* | (2) *ʿm mrʿytw* | (3) *wṣʾn ydw* |
| Ps 100:3 | (1) *wlʾ ʾnḥnw* | (2) *ʿmw* | (3) *wṣʾn mrʿytw* |

In each case, as I noted in the discussion of Psalm 95 above, elements (2) and (3) consist of a noun or compound noun that carries a suffix referring to YHWH. The first elements (1) in Pss 79:13 and 95:7 are identical and are varied in Ps 100:3 only by an emphatic particle, with no real semantic change. When the first half of Ps 100:3 is compared with Ps 95:6b and 7a, the connection is even closer: each pair refers to YHWH both as Israel's God and as its Maker.

The differences in meaning between Lewis's interpretation and the MT *Qere* are not nearly as great as the differences between them and the MT *Kethiv* reading. In the former two, the emphasis is on YHWH's relationship to his people. In Lewis's reading, the fact that YHWH was Israel's Maker is emphasized by the particle *wlʾ*. In the *Qere* reading, the fact of YHWH as Maker is reinforced by a new fact, namely, that Israel belongs to him.[96]

However, while the above studies have adequately shown the existence of an emphatic *lāmed* (and asseverative *lʾ*), I judge that this particle is not present in Psalm 100. In the final analysis, I have a slight preference for the *Qere* reading because it maintains the balance in the verse. It divides into three fairly well-balanced lines of 9, 9, and 7 syllables. This fits well with the line lengths in the rest of the psalm. Lewis's reading divides the verse into five lines of varying lengths, and there is no real coherence to the poetic structure. Furthermore, although the two halves obtained from his analysis are balanced, they are not true poetic lines (colons). They are too long, and the break between lines c and d is merely an artificial one, since the thoughts in d and e flow directly from line c. I therefore concur with the majority of modern writers in reading 'and we are his', despite the difficulty of explaining why 'to him' was written *lʾ*, when eleven words later (v. 4c) the poet spelled it *lw*.

96. Based on this reasoning, I reject Dahood's reading of *lʾ* as *lēʾ* 'the Omnipotent' as unnecessarily intrusive here. The emphasis is not on YHWH's power but on his relationship with his people.

**100:3c.** ***ʿmw wṣʾn mrʿytw*** **"(We are) his people and the sheep of his pasture"**

The Old Greek's Codex Alexandrinus reads 'and we are his people' in v. 3cα. With this reading, Pss 79:13a, 95:7bc, and 100:3c would be identical syntactically.[97] Adding *wʾnḥnw* to *ʿmw . . .* produces a line of 11 syllables and 4 stresses, a syllabic and metrical pattern of 9:9:11 and 4:4:4. The verse's structure would be:

| | | | | | |
|---|---|---|---|---|---|
| 3a | *dʿw ky-YHWH* | 5 | 9 | 2 | 4 |
| | *hwʾ ʾlhym* | 4 | | 2 | |
| 3b | *hwʾ ʿśnw* | 4 | 9 | 2 | 4 |
| | *wlʾ ʾnḥnw* | 5 | | 2 | |
| 3c | *wʾnḥnw ʿmw* | 6 | 11 | 2 | 4 |
| | *wṣʾn mrʿytw* | 5 | | 2 | |

This is a well-balanced layout and is even more balanced if only *ʾnḥnw* (rather than Alexandrinus's *wʾnḥnw*) is accepted. This yields 5 + 5 syllables in line 3c, which balances the 5 + 4 // 4 + 5 pattern in 3a and b. The loss of *ʾnḥnw* could then easily be explained by haplography.

However, the semantic sense of the verse does not change, whether or not *ʾnḥnw* is explicitly read, since it is implicit in any case. If the MT is followed, the word *ʾnḥnw* in 3b is understood to carry over into 3c, and almost all versions and commentators render it this way. The MT is the preferred reading, because of the preponderance of the manuscript evidence (including the Old Greek's Codexes Vaticanus and Sinaiticus). The most symmetrical analysis (adding only *ʾnḥnw* and not *wʾnḥnw*) is completely unattested. The Alexandrinus reading yields a rather heavy third line (9:9:11), which is 3 syllables removed from the expected norm of 8 syllables per line, whereas the MT reading is also unbalanced (9:9:7) but yields a third line much more in keeping with the expected poetic pattern (and, indeed, the actual pattern of the psalm).

## Form-Critical Genre and Structure

Psalm 100 is universally classified as a hymn. Many (including Gunkel, Dahood, Anderson, and Kraus) classify it as a processional or entry hymn associated with some aspect of Temple worship. This is a reasonable assumption, given the references to Temple precincts in v. 4 and the verb of

97. See the diagram above, at Ps 100:3b.

motion ($b^{\supset}$) in vv. 2b and 4a. Mowinckel (1962: 3) discussed it in connection with other festival psalms, including the Enthronment of YHWH psalms. It does fit well with the preceding Kingship of YHWH psalms as a concluding doxology (Westermann 1981b: 255), but there is nothing in the psalm that compels the judgment that it is a Kingship psalm per se. It is general enough to fit almost any Israelite festival or occasion for thanksgiving (see also Anderson 1972: 698). In fact, most arrangements of the Kingship of YHWH group end with Psalm 99 (see above, p. 21).[98]

The heart of the psalm is v. 3. The general language of praise and thanksgiving in vv. 1–2 and 4–5 gives way in v. 3 to affirmations of YHWH's position as God and as Creator of his people. The only non-imperative verb form (*ᶜśh*) occurs in v. 3. Verse 3 is further set off by the inclusio formed by the use of the word *b*ᵓ*w* in both 2b and 4a.

On a structural level, we find that the word or clause in the exact midpoint of the psalm is significant, as is also the case in Psalm 95. In the discussion of Psalm 95 above, I noted that the clause *ky hw*ᵓ ᵓ*lhynw* 'for he is our God' in v. 7a is positioned precisely in the structural midpoint of the psalm. In Psalm 100, the word *ᶜmw* '(We are) his people' stands in the same position. It is both preceded and followed by 20 words (excluding the title). It comes immediately after the great assertion in v. 3b: YHWH has created his people and as a result they belong to him. In fact, v. 3 contains the core of the message of Psalm 100, and *ᶜmw* summarizes this message in one word. The word *ᶜmw* reinforces the statements of 3a and b and carries them further by introducing the next thought, that YHWH's people are also the sheep of his pasture (3c).

The syllable and word counts for the sections are:

| | | |
|---|---|---|
| I | (vv. 1–2) | 25 (MT 26) syllables and 11 words |
| II | (v. 3) | 25 (MT 25) syllables and 12 words |
| III | (v. 4) | 23 (MT 23) syllables and 9 words |
| IV | (v. 5) | 18 (MT 18) syllables and 9 words |

The threefold call to worship (using three imperatives) in vv. 1–2 is balanced by the fourfold call (also using three imperatives) in v. 4. Both call sections are similar in length: vv. 1–2 contain 25 (MT 26) syllables and 11 words, and v. 4 contains 23 (MT 23) syllables and 9 words.

The conclusion in v. 5 follows the second call section, and contains the reasons for praise, and fittingly enough, speaks of the end of time. Because it follows the call to praise in v. 4, giving the reasons for praise (introduced by *ky*), it pairs well with v. 4, and many scholars group the two verses together (e.g., Delitzsch, Briggs, Weiser, Kraus). However, v. 5 contains a

98. On the psalm's relation to the thank offering, see above, on the title (pp. 90–91).

liturgical formula that is repeated (in varied forms) in other psalms (Pss 106:1; 107:1; 118:1–2; 136 *passim*). Consequently, the line can be seen as the conclusion to the entire psalm. It may well have been repeated as a congregational response, in the same manner in which Psalm 136 was undoubtedly read. Because of this, I separate v. 5 from v. 4, despite the connections between the two. This analysis of v. 5 is confirmed by the structure of the psalm. Verse 5 contains the only bicolon in the psalm; it is preceded by three tricolons. Thus, v. 5 is unique within the psalm, in structure as well as in content and function.

The only divine name used is *YHWH*, which occurs in three of the four sections, vv. 1a and 2a; 3a; 5a. However, the entire psalm repeatedly refers to him by means of pronouns and suffixes distributed throughout all three sections.

# *Chapter 4*
# *The Texts in Context*

## Introduction

In this chapter, I shall dissect the internal structure of the section comprised of Psalms 93–100 by analyzing each psalm's links, lexical and otherwise, with every other psalm in the section. This is a chapter devoted primarily to presenting the raw data of connections within the section. A more coherent picture of the relationships will be described in the overall summary in chapter 5. In the summary, the outlines of the structure of the section as a whole will be drawn sharply, the salient features highlighted, and the section's place in Book IV considered. However, the summary in chapter 5 is based on the exhaustive treatment in chapter 4, which results in 28 individual analyses. I have laid out the material in such a manner that readers need not read through the entire chapter in consecutive order—although reading the entirety would yield the most coherent picture of the data—but they may consult the data on any psalm pair in which they are interested.

One feature that should prove helpful in this regard is that I have summarized each psalm's primary relationships with the other 7 psalms in separate, concluding sections before I consider the next psalm. Thus, the reader may obtain a preliminary understanding of the contours of the structure of Psalms 93–100 by perusing the individual summary discussions. A more comprehensive and coherent summary follows in chapter 5.

The data are presented in different fashions in chapters 4 and 5. In chapter 4 the discussion is forward-looking (and more detailed). For example, the relationship of Psalm 93 with each of the psalms following it is discussed in sequence. As a result, the section on Psalm 93 consists of eight separate treatments (one for each of the seven following psalms and a special section on "Psalm 93 and Psalms 96–99"), plus a concluding summary. By contrast, the section on Psalm 99 consists of only one treatment, its links with Psalm 100, because its links with preceding psalms have been discussed previously. There is, then, no separate section devoted to Psalm 100, because its connections have all been discussed in previous sections.

In chapter 5, however, the discussion of each psalm is of a more summary nature, and it is both forward- and backward-looking. More emphasis is placed on each psalm's relationships with *preceding* psalms than in chapter 4, but the overall place and function of each psalm is also summarized, with attention given to both preceding and following contexts.

It should be stressed that the editors of the Psalter did not approach their task in the same manner that I am pursuing in chapter 4, and they certainly did not consciously use every connection noted below in arranging their material. My approach is intentionally exhaustive, describing relationships between psalms that have not previously been noticed. The most obvious connections between psalms *are* noted in every technical commentary. However, these observations are usually random in nature,[1] whereas, my approach in this chapter is systematic: it confirms the major connections previously noted, and it also uncovers numerous other significant connections.

In the discussions below, each section devoted to a psalm pair follows a similar outline. After introductory comments about the general relationships between two psalms, I list the raw data showing the various connections in chart form. The connections have been analyzed according to three categories: lexical, thematic, and generic/structural. Following the presentation of this data, detailed consideration will be given to "key-word links," "thematic connections," and, occasionally, other considerations.

### *The Data*

In this section, the raw data of every lexical repetition is presented, along with thematic and structure/genre similarities. The total number of repeated words is given in parentheses, and every one of these words then appears in one of the three indicated subcategories (key-word links, thematic word links, or incidental links). Repeated phrases, clauses, and verses are listed in full and, since some words occur more than once in these cases, the total number of words listed may be higher than the total number of repeated words found in the parentheses. In other words, the latter represents the number of *different* words or lexemes[2] common to both psalms.

1. Significant exceptions are now beginning to appear, as I noted in chapter 1: see especially the commentaries by Tate (1990), Hossfeld and Zenger (1993), Mays (1994a), and McCann (1996).

2. Lexemes are the minimal units of semantic meaningfulness. They are essentially the same as words, although words are more specific than lexemes. To illustrate, *šāpaṭ* and *mišpāṭ* are two different words, but they are from the same lexeme: *špṭ*. In the discussion of Psalms 93 and 94, *gēʾût* and *gēʾîm* are different words based on one lexeme—in fact, there are nine words in all that are based on this one lexeme (see the discussion below on Psalms 93 and 94). In this work, usually *word* is used, unless using *lexeme* is helpful

The lexical repetitions between psalms are the most important of all of the links. My analysis of lexical repetitions is exhaustive: *every* word or lexeme that recurs in each pair of psalms is listed. Each of them is then sorted into one of the three categories already mentioned.

Key-word links are the most important of the lexical repetitions. Thematic word links are less important words that recur in any given psalm pair. Incidental links are words common to two psalms that have little or no significance in the psalms' positioning or that are not used in any significantly similar way. These include most particles and many common words. They are included in the data listings but are not discussed further.

### *Key-Word Links*

The key words are the *Leitwörter*, the important words that were undoubtedly present in the editors' thinking as they made decisions about bringing the Psalter together.[3] Sometimes these links encompass entire repeated clauses (e.g., Pss 98:4 and 100:1) or even entire verses (e.g., Pss 96:13 and 98:9). Sometimes the links are not identical repetitions but are complexes of identical words and ideas (e.g., Pss 95:6–7c and 100:3). Sometimes the links are repetitions of single words that are significant structurally by virtue of their semantic importance in both psalms (e.g., *ʿnn* and *ṣywn* in Psalms 97 and 99). Sometimes the words are significant structurally because they are juxtaposed in two adjacent psalms and seldom (or never) elsewhere (e.g., *gʾwt*/*gʾym* in Pss 93:1; 94:2).

### *Thematic Connections*

Thematic connections between psalms are of two types. First, many themes are elaborated via repeated words or lexemes that I call "thematic word links." These are words or lexemes found in any two psalms that show connections between the two, but that are not as significant as the key-word links. These usually are words that are part of the general vocabulary of praise, or, more specifically, that are common to the Kingship of YHWH psalms. However, their significance is limited to showing general similarities of outlook and theme between the psalms under consideration, and not in highlighting any significant structural relations within Psalms 93–100 or Book IV.

in clarifying the issue at hand. See Lyons 1969: 194–98 for a discussion of words and lexemes in a standard work on general linguistics.

3. For our purposes, it makes no difference whether the editors involved were the *final* editors or earlier ones. My task is a synchronic description of the connections that are visible, as I noted in chapter 2.

A second type of thematic connection is broader than simple repetitions of words or lexemes, in that the ideas may be similar, even though the vocabulary is not identical. Thus in some cases, I discuss "thematic similarities,"[4] even though the words are not the same. For example, *ᶜdwt* and *twrh* in Psalms 93 and 94 are both expressions of YHWH's will or decrees. Similarly, YHWH's sovereignty may be a theme in two psalms, though the specific words used are not the same.[5]

### *Structure/Genre Similarities*

Structural comparisons of psalms are of two types, and the types may overlap at times. One type of analysis that I have done is to compare the internal structures of the two psalms under consideration; the best example of this is found in the similarities of structure of Psalms 96 and 98. The second type of analysis is a comparison of the function of two psalms within the larger group of eight psalms; the best example of this is the bracketing function of Psalms 95 and 100.

I have also noted similarities of genre (following modern form-critical categories), although I have not usually discussed them in great detail, since most of the psalms among Psalms 93–100 are of the same form-critical genre.[6] Concerning the importance of the ancient genres (*maśkîl*s, *mizmôr*s, etc.), however, Wilson has concluded (1985a: 161–62) that genre "does not constitute a primary editorial principle for the organization of the Psalter" (p. 161).

On the other hand, many scholars do point out significant clusterings of modern form-critical genres. Note, for example, Westermann's insight (1981b: 252, 257)[7] that clusters of laments of the individual occur toward the beginning of the Psalter, whereas praises of the community predominate toward the end. See also Brueggemann's lengthy note (1991: 79 n. 2), which includes the following statement: "It is clear that a canonical approach to the Psalter must pay attention to genre analysis." In a similar vein, McCann has noted (1993a: 96) that "most of the community laments in the Psalter appear in Book III." Thus, the fact that Psalms 93–100 consist of an unbroken string of community psalms, bounded by two psalms of the individual (Psalms 92 and 101), may be somewhat

4. As opposed to "thematic word links."

5. Whenever the distinction between "thematic word links" and "thematic similarities" is not helpful or significant, I have not divided the "thematic connections" section into subcategories.

6. The form-critical genres of Psalms 94 and 95 will be of some interest, however (see below, pp. 119–22).

7. Wilson (1993b: 81 n. 1) discusses other scholars who make the same point.

significant. More significant are the similarities in genre between Psalms 94 and 95 and their surroundings, however, which will be noted below.

### *Summary*

Finally, we should note that, while there are 28 sets of relationships within the present group of psalms, not all are of equal importance. As a rule, adjacent psalms tend to exhibit significant links with each other of one type or another. In every case but one, significant concatenation of terms or subject matter is evident. By "concatenation," I mean the occurrence of key-word links between adjacent psalms (see Barth 1976).

Many key-word links are also discernible between nonadjacent psalms. Beyond key-word links, the majority of connections between nonadjacent psalms are thematic. Thematic connections are of two types: those that are characteristic of the Kingship of YHWH genre in particular (see on Watts 1965, below, pp. 110–11); and those that are common to almost every psalm (these themes focus particularly on covenantal and Jerusalem traditions, as well as various attributes of YHWH).

In some cases, links between psalms are of structural significance: the relationships between Psalms 95 and 100 are the most striking examples of this type, but there are a number of others that I shall discuss below.

## Psalms 93–100 and Superscriptions

Before I begin the discussion of specific inter-psalm links, one further topic deserves discussion: the matter of superscriptions. It is well to discuss it in a separate section in advance, since it affects almost every one of the psalms under study here.

Gerald Wilson (1985a), in laying a framework for the study of the editorial processes of the Psalter, has focused most of his attention on the psalm superscriptions, noting the significance of such matters as groupings of titles of authorship and of genre.[8] As part of his study, he analyzes the matter of untitled psalms in some detail;[9] the patterns he has demonstrated have some significance for considering the editorial juxtaposition of the psalms in this grouping, and especially Psalms 94 and 95, which are not categorized by modern scholars as Kingship of YHWH psalms, as are the others.

8. By *genre*, Wilson means the ancient genres, such as *maśkîls*, *maᶜălôt* psalms, and so on.

9. Wilson 1985a: 131–32, 135–36, 173–81. See also Wilson 1984 and 1985c.

Wilson begins his discussion of the untitled psalms by noting that in Books I–III there is good evidence that the juxtaposition of an untitled psalm with a preceding titled one is an editorial device to signal the latter psalm's association with the preceding one. In some cases—most notably Psalms 9–10 and 42–43—the second psalm was originally almost certainly a unified part of the preceding psalm.[10] In several cases, however, psalms that are almost universally judged to have been originally independent compositions now appear in the MT as "pairs" in which the first is titled and the second is untitled.

In Book I, only four psalms are untitled: Psalms 1, 2, 10, and 33. Since the first two function as a heading for the entire book, Psalms 10 and 33 stand out as the only two within Book I without titles (and, we should note, all the others are Davidic, as well). The case of Psalm 10 is clear: it is an acrostic with Psalm 9. Psalm 33, while probably not originally composed with Psalm 32, nevertheless exhibits numerous connections with the latter. Some manuscripts actually join the two, and the Old Greek adds a title that makes Psalm 33 a Davidic psalm.[11] Furthermore, Psalm 33 begins in the same way that 32 ends: in 32:11, the righteous and upright in heart are exhorted to rejoice (*rnn*), be glad, and shout for joy in YHWH; 33:1 contains similar encouragement of the righteous and upright in heart, including an exhortation to rejoice (*rnn*).[12]

In Books II and III, Psalm 71 is the only untitled psalm, aside from Psalm 43, already mentioned. Again, various pieces of evidence combine to suggest the close connections between Psalms 70 and 71, including substantial manuscript evidence and the Old Greek's ascription of a Davidic title, which Psalm 70 already has, to Psalm 71.[13]

10. The absence of a title in Psalms 10 and 43—while Psalms 9 and 42 do carry titles—confirms this judgment, which is made on other grounds: (1) the broken acrostic across Psalms 9 and 10 and the repeated refrain across Psalms 42 and 43, (2) the string of Korahite psalms from 42 to 49, (3) and the unity of theme in both sets of psalms. Later manuscript evidence also supports this (Wilson 1985a: 173–76; 1985c: 405–7).

11. On the special significance of titles of authorship for joining purposes and the particularly disjunctive effect when a string of them ends, see Wilson 1984: 339; 1985a: 155–58.

12. On the other connections between Psalms 32 and 33, including the manuscript evidence, see Wilson 1985a: 174–76; 1985c: 405–7. It is interesting to observe that Dahood also observed that both the lack of a superscription in Psalm 33 and the concatenation of the two psalms was editorially significant: these indicate "that Ps xxxiii is not a later addition and at the same time [explain] its lack of superscription" (Dahood 1966: xxxi).

13. Wilson 1985a: 131–32, 177; 1985c: 408. The apparatus in BHS is cognizant of the manuscript evidence as well.

In Books IV–V, the logic behind psalms with superscriptions is not as clear, since there are many more untitled psalms than in Books I–III and many occur consecutively. Nevertheless, the same arguments obtain. Some manuscripts combine up to four consecutive psalms, and at least one combines five. Such large-scale combination occurs most frequently in two groupings: Psalms 90–99 and 114–19.[14] Such lengthy and complex combinations are not likely to have been composed together as single psalms originally, but rather, they are evidence of editorial activity.

The longest unbroken stretch of untitled psalms in the Hebrew Psalter is Psalms 93–97.[15] According to the argument above, this combination is evidence of a perceived unity by the editors of the tradition underlying the MT.[16] While no one would dispute the unity of outlook among Psalms 93, 96, and 97, the lack of superscriptions in Psalms 94 and 95 urges a reconsideration of the usual scholarly judgments about their supposed anomalous place among the others. The presence of the formulaic *YHWH mlk* at the beginning of the group (93:1) signals the initiation of a new composition here, after which the untitled psalms follow in succession. The subsequent absence of titles indicates a dependence of sorts of each psalm upon the preceding one. (It even can be argued, on the basis of titles alone, that the stretch of unified psalms extends further and consists of Psalms 93–99, although this does not materially affect my thesis.)[17] Thus, the group Psalms 93–97, and perhaps Psalms 93–99, is unified by the lack of superscriptions as well as by numerous other considerations (to be noted below).

14. Wilson 1985a: 177; 1985c: 409. See now also the evidence in Millard 1994: 12–15.

15. See Wilson's appendix C for a convenient tabulation of the superscriptions and postscripts of all the psalms (1985a: 238–44). Note that he includes clauses such as *hllw-yh* in his considerations; without them, the longest stretch of untitled psalms is Psalms 111–18, and Psalms 93–97 constitute the second longest.

16. Wilson takes pains in discussing Psalms 93–99 (1985a: 178–79; 1985c: 410–11) not to overemphasize this point, especially in view of the nature of Psalms 94 and 95 vis-à-vis Psalms 93 and 96–99. However, the section, if it does anything, lends support to his argument rather than undercuts it, particularly since Psalms 94 and 95 are more closely related to the others than is commonly supposed. (On the connections of Psalm 94 with Psalm 95 and the following psalms, see Auffret 1984: 69–72 and the relevant sections below, pp. 119–31, 172–75; for Psalm 95, see also the relevant sections on pp. 131–41, 175–76.)

17. The argument runs as follows. The only titled psalm among Psalms 93–99 is Psalm 98, simply called a *mizmôr.* Since 96:1 and 98:1 both contain the same call to praise—*šyrw lYHWH šyr ḥdš,* a formula that recurs exactly in Ps 149:1 and Isa 42:10 (and compare Pss 33:3, 40:3, 144:9; Rev 14:3)—the presence of this title in Psalm 98 likely serves to emphasize the "new beginning" (of a new song), mentioned within the psalm itself in v. 1. Thus, the presence of a simple title in Psalm 98 is only mildly disjunctive: it does not add any significant new information, and it is not nearly as disruptive

## Psalm 93 in Context

### *Psalm 93 and Psalm 94*

These two psalms contrast with each other in many ways. Psalm 94 is not considered to be a Kingship of YHWH psalm[18] or a praise psalm,[19] but Psalm 93 is both. However, two key-word links are significant, and several thematic connections highlight the contrasts in significant ways. Furthermore, Psalm 94 does echo themes found in the Kingship of YHWH psalms, including Psalm 93, but I shall discuss this fact in connection with Psalm 94.

*The Data*

| | |
|---|---|
| Lexical Repetitions (8): | |
| Key-word links:[20] | *gʾwt/gʾym* |
| | *dky/dkʾ* |
| Thematic word links: | *mwṭ* |
| | *ksʾ* |
| | *nśʾ* |
| Incidental repetitions: | *YHWH, ywm, rb(ym)* |
| Thematic Similarities: | YHWH's sovereignty (over rebellious waters and people) |
| | YHWH's secure, high position |
| | *ʿdwt/twrh* (93:5, 94:12) |
| Structure/Genre Similarities: | |
| Community psalms | |
| Anadiplosis (93:3, 94:3) | |

*Key-Word Links*

The most important links between Psalms 93 and 94 are the two key-word pairs: *gʾwt/gʾym* and *dky/dkʾ*. They also provide examples of concatenation between two adjacent psalms. The use of *gēʾût* ('proud

as a title of authorship would be (see n. 11). The numerous connections Psalm 98 has with its neighboring psalms (see below) confirms the perceived unity among Psalms 93–99 indicated by their lack of titles. (The clause beginning Psalms 97 and 99—*YHWH mlk*—also signals a "new beginning" of sorts, although it also is not nearly as disruptive as a psalm title, especially a title of authorship, would be.)

18. See the comments below (p. 130), however, on "Psalm 94 as a Kingship of YHWH Psalm."

19. It is a lament.

20. In the two sets of key words here, the roots are closely related to each other and can be considered as repeated roots or identical lexemes (see the discussion above, on *gʾwt* at Ps 93:1a, and the assessment of KB[3] [*sub dkh*] that *dkh* and *dkʾ* are allomorphs).

majesty',[21] 93:1) and *gēʾîm* ('proud ones', 94:2) is a case in point. Within Psalm 93, YHWH's proud majesty in v. 1 stands in opposition to the rebellious waters of vv. 3–4. Externally, however, it stands in opposition to proud, arrogant people (the *gēʾîm*, 94:2) in Psalm 94. Throughout Psalm 94, what is at issue is human pride and arrogance. The fact that YHWH himself is clothed with proud majesty and strength in Psalm 93 reduces the pride of the wicked in Psalm 94 to insignificance or absurdity. In fact, the use of *gēʾût* in Psalm 93 contributes to the psalm's overall picture of YHWH's strength: as one who is powerful (v. 1), whose throne is secure (v. 2), and who is mightier than the waters (vv. 3–4). Confidence in YHWH's sovereignty provides justification for calling on him to intervene on the people's behalf in Psalm 94.

The other key-word link between the psalms is the use of the roots *dky* (93:3) and *dkʾ* (94:5), both meaning 'to crush, oppress'. The sound of crushing by the rebellious waves in opposition to YHWH in Ps 93:3 is of a piece with the oppressive crushing of YHWH's people by the rebellious evil-doers in Ps 94:4–5. Both are examples of rebellion against YHWH. Anything or anyone that rebels against YHWH or crushes his people is an enemy of both. Again we can see that the confidence in YHWH that is expressed in Psalm 93—in this case, the fact that he was victorious and sovereign over his enemies—forms the basis for the request in Psalm 94 that YHWH assert himself over the psalmist's enemies, as well as a basis for confidence that he will do as requested.

These two sets of roots—*gʾwt/gʾym* and *dky/dkʾ*—form the most direct contrasts between Psalms 93 and 94, and this contrast accounts in large part for the roots' significance. Their significance is further highlighted by the infrequency of their use in the Psalms.

The word *gēʾût* occurs 8 times in the Hebrew Bible, 3 times in the Psalms.[22] The word *gēʾeh* (pl., *gēʾîm*) also occurs 8 times but only twice in the Psalms.[23] Furthermore, 93:1 and 94:2 are the only verses in all of Book IV where either of these 2 roots or of any of the 7 related roots occurs.[24] Thus, out of 9 cognate terms—terms that occur 95 times in the Hebrew Bible, 14 times in the Psalms—the only 2 times any of these is used in Book IV is in these adjacent psalms: in 93:1 and 94:2. In fact, in only one other case in the entire Psalter do any of these roots appear in adjacent psalms: *gaʾăwāh* (46:4) and *gāʾôn* (47:5).

21. See chapter 3 at 93:1a for this translation of the term.

22. Pss 17:10, 89:10, 93:1; Isa 9:17; 12:5; 26:10; 28:1, 3.

23. Isa 2:12; Jer 48:29; Pss 94:2, 140:6; Prov 15:25, 16:19; Job 40:11, 12.

24. *Gēʾ* (1×), *gāʾah* (5×), *geʾah* (1×), *gaʾăwāh* (19×), *gāʾôn* (49×), *gaʾăyôn* (1×), *gēwāh* (3×).

This juxtaposition in adjacent psalms of a relatively common root that is otherwise missing in Book IV and that otherwise appears in only one other psalm pair, thus lends credence to the identification of the root as a key word in these two psalms.

There are four related roots in BH used for crushing/oppressing. (1) The verb *dkʾ* ('to oppress'), the most common of these (it occurs 18 times),[25] is the one found in Psalm 94. The root occurs 3 times in noun form, as *dakkāʾ*.[26] (2) The root *dkh* ('to crush') occurs 5 times as a verb[27] and once as a noun.[28] (3) The adjective *dak* ('crushed, oppressed') occurs 4 times.[29] (4) *Dokî* ('crushing'), the word in Psalm 93, occurs only once.[30] What is significant from these data is that out of 32 occurrences, 15 of which are in the Psalms, only 3 occur in Book IV.[31] Besides the two verses under consideration (93:3, 94:5), the only other place where the lexeme is used in Book IV is 90:3, where the object is dust, which is somewhat removed semantically from the more violent crushing and oppressing usually associated with these terms.

In Psalms 93 and 94, the juxtaposition of two forms of a somewhat rarer term, which is otherwise found only once in Book IV and is likewise seldom used as a link in any psalm pair, is a clue that it too is a key word.

*Thematic Connections*

As I noted at the outset, Psalms 93 and 94 are, for the most part, dissimilar in tone and content. However, some thematic connections can be observed, both among the repeated words ("thematic word links") and among the more general motifs ("thematic similarities"). "Thematic word links" (repetitions of words that are not key words) are generally contrastive, whereas "thematic similarities" (similar motifs) generally correspond more closely to each other.

*Thematic Word Links.* The use of *mwṭ* and *ksʾ* in Psalms 93 and 94 is contrastive, showing the radical distinctions between YHWH's position and humanity's condition. In Ps 93:1, the root *mwṭ* 'to waver, stagger' (with *bl* 'no, not') refers to the stable condition of the world (*tbl*) that YHWH has

25. Isa 3:15; 19:10; 53:5, 10; 57:15; Jer 44:10; Pss 72:4; 89:11; 94:5; 143:3; Job 4:19; 5:4; 6:9; 19:2; 22:9; 34:25; Prov 22:22; Lam 3:34.

26. It means 'crushed, contrite' in Ps 34:19 and Isa 57:15, and '[pulverized] dust' in Ps 90:3.

27. Pss 10:10; 38:9; 44:20; 51:10, 19.

28. Deut 23:2.

29. Pss 9:10, 10:18, 74:21; Prov 26:28.

30. Ps 93:1.

31. The roots for crushing and oppressing appear in *adjacent* psalms only one other time, in two psalms that were originally one: *dkh* (10:10) and *dk* (9:10, 10:18).

established, whereas in Ps 94:18, it refers to the unstable condition of a human foot. In a similar manner, in 93:2 *ksʾ* speaks of YHWH's eternal and secure throne, in contrast to 94:20, where it speaks of an ephemeral 'throne' of destruction.

The use of *nśʾ* in both psalms is also contrastive, although not as directly. In the one case (93:3), it refers to angry waters lifting up a roar, and in the other (94:2), it is part of a (liturgical) plea for YHWH to rouse himself. However, because of the mythopoeic background of Ps 93:3–4,[32] *nśʾ* can be seen in both psalms as speaking of deity asserting itself and thus as a link of at least some significance.

*Thematic Similarities.* General thematic similarities between Psalms 93 and 94 are relatively few, but some do exist. First, in both, YHWH is the sovereign God who is above rebellious waters (93) or rebellious evildoers (94).[33] Second, YHWH's high position is featured in both psalms: 93:4c portrays him as mighty in the heights; 94:2a and 16a imply that he can arise on behalf of the psalmist, and 94:22a describes him as a secure high retreat and a mountain of refuge. Third, both psalms picture YHWH as a secure, well-established God: in 93:2, YHWH's throne is firmly established; 94:17, 18, and 22 likewise picture him as a source of security. The motifs of YHWH's sovereignty and secure, high position are common throughout the Psalter, of course, but the specific expression of the themes varies, and in this sense some limited connections are apparent here.

A final example of general thematic similarities between the psalms is the link formed by YHWH's decrees in Psalm 93 (v. 5a) and his Torah in Psalm 94 (v. 12b). The term *ʿdt* (*ʿēdōt*) (or *ʿdwt* [*ʿēdôt*]) 'decrees', 'testimonies', 'warnings' always carries the connotation of "divine testimonies or solemn charges" (BDB, s.v.). It occurs 32 times in BH, 25 times in the Psalter (of which 21 times are in Psalm 119), referring to the Torah. Its related root *ʿdwt* (*ʿēdût*) is used similarly. In Ps 19:8, for example, it is parallel with the Torah. The echoes of the Sinai experience implicit in these terms are especially common in Book IV of the Psalter, as I have noted in chapter 1. In later periods, these terms came to be associated with the wisdom movement. Psalm 94 resumes the use of wisdom motifs present in Psalm 92. These motifs further help to explain the presence of Psalm 94 in Book IV, especially in light of the fact that no other laments in Books IV and V have any wisdom sections equivalent to the interlude in 94:8–15.[34] Thus, as a wisdom-flavored lament echoing Psalm 92, Psalm 94 is uniquely suited to its position.

32. See the notes on these verses in chapter 3.

33. This picture in Psalm 94 is not explicit, but it is implicit, since YHWH is appealed to as the One who could put the wicked in their place if he so chose.

34. See below, in chapter 5, for significant wisdom-related links between Psalms 94 and 92 (pp. 172–73).

*Structure/Genre Connections*

The only meaningful connection between the two psalms on the level of genre is that they are both psalms of the community.[35]

## *Psalm 93 and Psalm 95*

Psalms 93 and 95 are both hymns. As such, Psalm 95 resumes the note of praise of YHWH that was suspended in Psalm 94. Furthermore, it serves well as a re-introduction to the Kingship of YHWH psalms that follow. However, it is a very different type of hymn from Psalm 93. Psalm 95, primarily in vv. 1–7c, contains much of the standard praise vocabulary found throughout the rest of the Psalter, whereas Psalm 93 does not (even though it is certainly honorific in nature). Nevertheless, the Kingship of YHWH motif binds these two psalms together as an appropriate bracket around Psalm 94, in which the motif is not as readily apparent as elsewhere.[36]

*The Data*

Lexical Repetitions (5):

| | |
|---|---|
| Key-word links: | *YHWH, mlk* |
| Thematic word links: | *ym* |
| Incidental links: | *qwl, ywm* |

Thematic Similarities:

- YHWH's kingship
- YHWH's sovereignty (over nature)

Structure/Genre Similarities:

- Both are Kingship of YHWH hymns

*Key-Word Links*

The only key-word link between the two psalms is the repetition of the kingship terms *YHWH* and *mlk*. In 93:1, it is found in the standard cry, *YHWH mlk*, and in 95:3, YHWH is described as a *mlk gdwl* 'a great king'. Thus Psalm 95 resumes the Kingship of YHWH theme that is subordinated in Psalm 94 (as we have noted).

*Thematic Connections*

*Thematic Word Links.* The only other lexical connection of any note between the two psalms is contrastive: in Ps 93:3 the sea (*ym*) is rebellious, whereas in Ps 95:5 it is not; the point is explicitly made in Psalm 95 that it was YHWH who created this sea.

35. Despite the composite make-up of Psalm 94, see the arguments in chapter 3 for defining it as a lament of the community. See also the comments above (pp. 101–2) on the significance of similarities in form-critical genres.

36. But see below, p. 130.

*Thematic Similarities.* Beyond the obvious connection of YHWH's kingship, his sovereignty is affirmed in the allusions to him as Creator in both psalms. In Psalm 95, his sovereignty is implicit, since there is no reference to any rebellious tendencies in the elements he created (vv. 4–5). He created the various elements of nature and is absolute over them. His sovereignty is affirmed in Psalm 93 in a slightly different manner, in the emphasis on his distance above the rebellious waters (vv. 3–4) and on his secure rule, extending into time immemorial in the past (vv. 1–2, 5).

### *Psalm 93 and Psalms 96–99*

Since Psalms 93 and 96–99 are *the* paradigmatic psalms used by Mowinckel and others in establishing the Kingship of YHWH genre (a subcategory of the hymnic genre), it is not surprising that the many prominent links among them have been discussed at length in the many scholarly studies of these psalms. Many lexical and thematic connections exist, as well as some structural ones. The thematic connections can be divided between those that are characteristic of the genre and are found clustered in these psalms (such as YHWH's kingship, YHWH as Creator, and a certain universal outlook) and those that are more characteristic of the Psalter as a whole and also occur in other psalms outside this section (such as the centrality of Zion and the Temple, Israel as God's covenant people, and the sapiential contrasting of the ways of the righteous and the wicked and the attendant emphasis on the Torah).

Watts's study (1965) is foundational in isolating themes characteristic of the Kingship of YHWH genre, and his results are worth repeating here.[37] He began with the core group of *YHWH mālak* psalms identified by Mowinckel (Psalms 47, 93, 96, 97, 99) and adduced five characteristic motifs from them (1965: 342–43):

A. The characteristic and unique expectation that all the earth, all peoples, or the nations should be present
B. References to other gods
C. Signs of exaltation and kingship
D. Words showing characteristic acts of Yahweh, including creating, making, establishing, sitting, doing wonders, judging, doing righteous acts, and saving
E. Words indicating an attitude of praise before this heavenly king

37. Mays's recent study (1994b) sees the *YHWH mlk* psalms as the key to identifying a theological "center" of the Psalter, and he too studies the most important motifs associated with this central theme.

From our group of psalms, Watts identified Psalms 96 and 97 as containing all five motifs. Psalms 98 and 99 contain four of the five (A, C, D, E), as does Psalm 95 (B, C, D, E). Psalm 100 contains three of the five (A, D, E), and Psalm 93 has two (C, D).

Watts's categories are rough and mechanical, as he himself emphasized. For example, one could argue that E should also be seen in Psalm 93. Watts based his judgment on the presence of actual praise terms, but certainly the psalm exudes praise for YHWH, even though it lacks specific praise vocabulary. One could also wish that Watts had further divided his fourth group (D), which is rather all-encompassing as it now stands. Creation, one of the motifs in (D), is certainly important enough to merit separate consideration. It could be defined as YHWH's creating activity per se[38] or as YHWH's sovereignty over other gods.[39] Related to YHWH's sovereignty as Creator, but not mentioned by Watts, is YHWH's sovereignty over the elements of nature.[40] YHWH's judgment is another prominent theme that perhaps deserves separate treatment.[41] The list could go on.

Mowinckel's work (1922, 1962) also dealt with common motifs, although his focus was a great deal different (and more exhaustive) from Watts's or mine. Combs (1963) discerned the creation motif in the "Enthronement psalms" but likewise with different emphasis. However, my interest in these links is not in the motifs per se (contrary to most of the scholarly studies), but rather in the function of the repeated motifs in elucidating the structure of the section.

The unique link among the five psalms is the divine kingship motif, expressed in the clause *YHWH mlk*, that appears at 93:1, 96:10, 97:1, and 99:1, and the identification of YHWH as King in 98:6. This exact verbal clause, *YHWH mlk*, occurs nowhere else in the Hebrew Bible, and the only variant is found in Pss 47:9, 146:10, and Exod 15:18.

Psalm 93 is related to Psalms 96–99 primarily in form-critical genre and similar themes. It is the least like the others of the group in inclusiveness of themes and length.[42] The internal ordering of Psalms 96–99 is not dependent on any significant links with Psalm 93 but is due to connections among the four psalms themselves. Nevertheless, significant key-word links

38. Ps 96:5b is the best example of this in the core group, but see also 93:1c = 96:10b, and possibly 96:3b and 98:1b; outside the core group, compare 95:5, 6b, and 100:3b.

39. Watts's second category: see 96:4b, 5a; 97:7, 9b; cf. 95:3b.

40. See 93:3–4; 96:11–12; 97:1, 4–6; cf. 95:4–5; 98:7–8.

41. See 96:10c, 13; 97:2b, 8b; 99:4; and cf. 98:9.

42. It is most likely the earliest of the group, as well (see appendix 1, on psalm dating).

do exist between Psalm 93 and 96–99, in effect binding it closely to them despite its distance two psalms removed from the group. Also, probably significantly, its closest connections are with the first psalm in the group, Psalm 96.

## *Psalm 93 and Psalm 96*

The connections between these two psalms are the strongest of any pairing between Psalm 93 and Psalms 96–99. The two share 14 words. Both are Kingship of YHWH hymns; both contain the *YHWH mlk* clause (93:1a, 96:10a); and both contain an exact, 5-word repetition: *ᵓp-tkwn tbl bl-tmwṭ* (93:1, 96:10). Surely it is significant that Psalm 96—the first psalm after Psalm 93 to contain the exact clause *YHWH mlk*—has stronger connections with Psalm 93 than any of the following psalms. Psalm 95 functions as an appropriate transition back to the Kingship of YHWH motif (see above), while Psalm 96 reminds us again of the motif in even stronger terms, harking back specifically to Psalm 93 in the process.

*The Data*

Lexical Repetitions (14):

| | |
|---|---|
| Key-word links: | *YHWH mlk* |
| | *ᵓp-tkwn tbl bl-tmwṭ* |
| Thematic word links: | *ᶜz* |
| | *ym* |
| | *qdš* |
| | *mᵓd* |
| Incidental repetitions: | *nšᵓ*, *ywm*, particles (*ᵓz*) |

Thematic Similarities:
YHWH's kingship
YHWH's sovereignty (over gods, nature)

Structure/Genre Similarities:
Both are Kingship of YHWH hymns

*Key-Word Links*

Both Psalms 93 and 96 contain the *YHWH mlk* clause (93:1, 96:10), which is not found in this form either in Psalm 94 or 95. However, after this, the most significant link between the two psalms is the verbatim repetition of 93:1c in 96:10b, accounting for 5 of the 14 repeated words: *ᵓp-tkwn tbl bl-tmwṭ* 'Surely the world is established! It will not be moved'. Psalm 96:10 functions as a bridge, standing independent of the material both preceding and following, and yet binding them together, as I have already noted in chapter 3. Since Psalm 93 was probably earlier than Psalm 96,[43] it is easy to imagine that 96:10b was modeled after 93:1c.

YHWH's kingship is inextricably bound up with the establishment and fixity of the world in both psalms. At the same time, the ideas of 93:1 are adapted to the new environment of Psalm 96: (1) the prose statement in 96:10a, *ᵓmrw bgwym* 'Say among the nations', is added before *YHWH mlk*, linking it with the imperatives of vv. 7–9; and (2) the last clause in v. 10, *ydyn ᶜmym bmyšrym* 'He will judge peoples with equity' ties *YHWH mlk* in both psalms with 96:13, where YHWH as righteous Judge also appears.

*Thematic Connections*

*Thematic Word Links.* Several, more general word links exist between Psalms 93 and 96. One is the repetition of the root *ᶜz* 'strength'. This is an attribute of YHWH in 93:1 and 96:6, 7. Second, YHWH is above the waters (*ym*) and other elements of nature in both psalms. In Psalm 93, the seas are loud, rebellious waters (vv. 3–4), whereas in Psalm 96, the sea roars with joyful praise (v. 11); nevertheless, YHWH is exalted over the seas in both.[44] Third, holiness (*qdš*) appears in the context of the Temple in both psalms (93:5, 96:9). And finally, the psalms are linked by the use of *mᵓd* 'Mighty One',[45] in 93:5 and 96:4. The word only occurs once more in Psalms 93–100, at 97:9.

## *Psalm 93 and Psalm 97*

None of the connections between Psalms 93 and 97 have any structural significance for the ordering of Psalms 93–100 or Book IV. However, the key-word links between them show their general relatedness. The other links are mostly thematic in nature.

*The Data*

| | |
|---|---|
| Lexical Repetitions (8): | |
| Key-word links: | *YHWH mlk* |
| | *kwn* |
| | *ksᵓ* |
| Thematic word links: | *qdš* |
| Incidental repetitions: | *tbl*, *ᵓth*, *rb* |

43. See appendix 1.

44. In 96:1, 11–13, YHWH is to receive praise from the other elements of nature, as well, over which he also is sovereign.

45. On this translation of *mᵓd*, see the translation note in chapter 3, at 93:5a.

Thematic Similarities:
YHWH's kingship
YHWH's sovereignty (over nature)
YHWH's abode: Temple/Zion, Judah

Structure/Genre Similarities:
Both are Kingship of YHWH hymns

*Key-Word Links*

The two psalms begin identically, with *YHWH mlk*. Psalm 97 is the first psalm since Psalm 93 to begin this way, and thus the link is a significant one. Another key-word link—connected with *YHWH mlk*—is YHWH's kingly throne (*ksʾ*), which is 'firmly established' (*kwn*) in each psalm (93:2, 97:2). His throne is mentioned only one other time in Book IV, in Ps 103:19,[46] a fact that highlights its importance in Psalms 93 and 97. Other connections between the two psalms are more generally thematic.

*Thematic Connections*

As Kingship of YHWH hymns, the two psalms are similar in several respects. Beyond the key words noted above, they are similar in that YHWH is sovereign over elements of nature in both (93:3–4; 97:1, 4–6). Second, both psalms refer to the earthly place where YHWH is especially identified, 93:5 referring to the Temple and 97:8 mentioning Zion and Judah. Third, YHWH's holiness (*qdš*) is mentioned in 93:5 and 97:12.

### *Psalm 93 and Psalm 98*

The connections between Psalms 93 and 98 are important in binding Psalm 93 together with the Psalm 96–99 group. Beyond this, however, there is little about their links that is of structural significance for the shape of Psalms 93–100 or of Book IV.

*The Data*

Lexical Repetitions (8):

| | |
|---|---|
| Key-word links: | *YHWH, mlk* |
| | *ym* |
| | *nhrwt* |
| Thematic word links: | *tbl* |
| | *qdš* |

46. Where it is established in the heavens.

Incidental repetitions: *qwl, byt*

Thematic Similarities:
YHWH's kingship
YHWH's sovereignty (over nature)
YHWH's relationship with Israel

Structure/Genre Similarities:
Both are Kingship of YHWH hymns

*Key-Word Links*

YHWH's kingship is linked in the two psalms by the use of the key words *YHWH* and *mlk.* In the 93/98 pair (as in the 93/95 pair), the words are not identical, since 93:1 begins with a verbal clause, *YHWH mlk* 'YHWH reigns!' whereas 98:6 ends with a nominal reference, *hmlk YHWH* 'the king, YHWH'. Nevertheless, the links are obvious.

Psalm 98 is the closest of Psalms 96–99 to Psalm 93 in its emphasis on YHWH and the waters. In Ps 93:3–4, the sea (*ym*) is rebellious, while in 98:7, it is urged to praise YHWH (as in Psalm 96). More important than the references to the sea, however, are the references to the floods (*nhrwt,* literally 'rivers'). They appear in both psalms (93:3 [3×], 98:8), but the word *nhrwt* appears nowhere else in Psalms 93–100.

The occurrences of *nhrwt* deserve closer attention. As a singular noun, *nhr* appears 75 times in BH, meaning 'river', and it is often used in narratives to designate the Euphrates and other rivers. The feminine plural (*nhrwt*) occurs 34 times (a masculine plural form occurs 7 times), most often in poetic contexts. The feminine plural form, which occurs in Psalms 93 and 98, carries mythopoeic or cosmological overtones, usually referring to underground streams (BDB; $KB^3$, s.v.). *Nhrwt* occurs 15 times in the Psalter, but only in 93:3 and 98:8 in the Psalms 93–100 group and again in Book IV only in 105:41. Most significantly, the four occurrences of *nhrwt* in 93:3 and 98:8 are the only times in Psalms that *nhrwt* appears as a grammatical subject and the only uses in the Hebrew Bible where *nhrwt* as a subject has anything to do with God. Elsewhere, for example, the rivers overwhelm humans or merely flow. This key-word link is thus important in binding Psalm 93 to Psalms 96–99.[47]

47. The significance of the link is that it is used with God as subject, rather than in having any greater, structural connection. That is, *nhrwt* does not link Psalms 93 and 98 in the same way that other connections do. For instance, Psalms 95 and 100 form a "frame" around the group of Psalms 96–99. Nevertheless, *nhrwt* does show another connection between Psalm 93 and Psalms 96–99, despite its distance from the group.

*Thematic Connections*

*Thematic Word Links.* Other lexical connections between the two psalms refer to YHWH and various elements of nature. He is to be praised by hills, floods (98:7–8), and the world (*tbl*), and he is the One who has established the world (93:1). The fact that he is King appears in both psalms (93:1, 98:6), and holiness (*qdš*) attaches to him in both (93:5, 98:1).

*Thematic Similarities.* In addition to YHWH's kingship and sovereignty in both psalms, which has already been mentioned, one final connection can be seen in the focus on Israel. In 93:5, YHWH's decrees (to Israel) and a reference to the Temple appear, and YHWH's relationship to Israel is emphasized in 98:3 by references to the fact that he remembers his *ḥsd* and his *ʾmwnh*.

## *Psalm 93 and Psalm 99*

Psalms 93 and 99 are the first and last in the string of Kingship of YHWH psalms, and their strongest connections center on YHWH's kingship. The two psalms also contain the only references to YHWH's decrees in Book IV. As in the case of the Psalm 93/98 pair, however, there is little of structural significance for the shape of Psalms 93–100 or of Book IV beyond this reference to his decrees.

*The Data*

Lexical Repetitions (9):

| | |
|---|---|
| Key-word links: | *YHWH mlk* |
| | *ʿdt* |
| Thematic word links: | *ʿz* |
| | *mrwm/r(w)m* |
| | *kwn* |
| | *qdš* |
| Incidental repetitions: | *ʾth, nśʾ* |

Thematic Similarities:
- YHWH's kingship
- Temple/Zion
- YHWH's throne/YHWH's footstool
- YHWH's sovereignty
- YHWH as Creator

Structure/Genre Similarities:
- Both are Kingship of YHWH hymns

*Key-Word Links*

These two psalms begin identically, with *YHWH mlk* (as does Psalm 97). Beyond this, the most striking key-word link between the psalms is the occurrence of YHWH's *ᶜdt* 'decrees'. As noted above (p. 108), the term recalls the Torah and the covenant with Israel, and within Psalms 93–100, or indeed any of Book IV, it only occurs in 93:5 and 99:7. Apart from the 21 occurrences in Psalm 119 (the Torah psalm par excellence), this lexeme otherwise only occurs again in the Psalter in Pss 25:10 and 78:56. Psalm 99 emphasizes Zion a great deal, as well as YHWH's relationship with his people, those in Jacob (v. 4) who obey him (vv. 6–8). Likewise, Psalm 93 ends by affirming YHWH's covenantal decrees, as well as his Temple, which is located on Zion.

*Thematic Connections*

Most of the thematic word links and similarities revolve around YHWH's kingship and exaltation. Aside from the opening acclamations (93:1, 99:1), both psalms ascribe strength (*ᶜz*) and exalted position to him. He has girded himself with strength in 93:1 and is called the Strong (= Victorious) One in 99:4. He is mighty on high (*mrwm*) in 93:4 and exalted (*rm*) above the peoples in 99:2. In addition, the refrain in 98:5, 9 urges people to exalt (*rwm*) YHWH.

YHWH the King is Creator, One who establishes (*kwn*) the world (93:1) and equity (99:4). Zion and the Temple figure in both psalms: the Temple in Ps 93:5 and Zion in 99:2a (Zion is also referred to in vv. 5 and 9). The reference to YHWH's throne in 93:2 also is echoed in the appearance of his footstool in 99:5. As in the other Kingship psalms, YHWH's holiness (*qd*[*w*]*š*) also figures in both psalms (93:5; 99:3, 5, 9).

## *Psalm 93 and Psalm 100*

There are almost no direct lexical or thematic links between these two psalms. Psalm 100's strongest links are with Psalm 95, not 93. Both Psalms 93 and 100 are hymns and both celebrate YHWH in one way or another, but their individual themes are quite different. Furthermore, they have only two words in common: *ᶜwlm* (93:2, 100:5) and *YHWH*. This paucity is due to their different themes and also no doubt to the fact that they are both relatively short.

*The Data*

Lexical Repetitions (2):

| | |
|---|---|
| Key-word links: | none |
| Thematic links: | none |
| Incidental repetitions: | *YHWH*, *ᶜwlm* |

Thematic Similarities:
- Temple
- Covenant references

Structure/Genre Similarities:
- Both are hymns
- They are the first and last of a string of community psalms
- Length
- Bicolon-tricolon structure

*Thematic Connections*

*Thematic Similarities.* Both psalms exhibit the theme found in all the other Kingship psalms: a concern with the Temple or Zion and with Israel as YHWH's people. The mention of the Temple in 93:5 is echoed by reference to its gates and courts in 100:4. References to YHWH's covenant people in 100:3 and especially to his covenantal attributes of steadfast love and faithfulness in 100:5 recall his covenantal decrees in 93:5.

*Structural Similarities*

Psalms 93 and 100 are the beginning and end of a string of community psalms; Psalms 92 and 101 are (formally, at least) psalms of the individual. This difference may have had some role in the shaping of this section of the Psalter, but its significance should not be over-emphasized.[48]

Structurally, the psalms are very close in length. Furthermore, their internal structures are analogous. Psalm 93 opens with a bicolon that is followed by four tricolons, while Psalm 100 opens with three tricolons and closes with a bicolon. However, it is doubtful that either of these facts is significant to the structure of the group as a whole.

## *Summary of Psalm 93 in Context*

Psalm 93 opens the Kingship of YHWH section of the Psalter with a great burst of praise for YHWH, the sovereign King and Creator. It is the first of eight psalms of the community. Consonant with the notes of despair or skepticism sounded at the end of Book III and the beginning of Book IV, the praise in this psalm is tempered somewhat by the lengthy lament in Psalm 94. The confidence in YHWH nevertheless shines through in both Psalms 93 and 94. Two important key-word links highlight the contrasts between YHWH and those who rebel against him in both psalms. In the end, we see that Psalm 94 has much stronger connections with Psalm 93 than is generally assumed.[49]

48. See the comments above, pp. 101–2, on the role of form-critical genres in the shaping of the Psalter.

49. And see further the discussion on Psalm 94, pp. 129–31, 173–75, below.

Psalm 95 reintroduces the great Kingship of YHWH motif, and it does so with more of the vocabulary of praise than we find in Psalm 93. There are not many connections between Psalms 93 and 95 beyond the Kingship of YHWH motif. A prophetic warning is sounded at the end of Psalm 95, keeping alive some of the more somber perspectives found earlier in Book IV. Psalms 93 and 95 bracket Psalm 94 well, "softening" some the discontinuities with its surrounding psalms.

Psalms 96–99 burst forth with the unfettered praise of YHWH as sovereign King and Creator that first appears in Book IV in Psalm 93, but they go far beyond it in their praise. Significantly, Psalm 93 matches up most strongly with the first psalm of that group, especially in the identical assertion in both psalms that YHWH firmly established the world, a statement that also binds Psalm 93 to the rest of the group of which Psalm 96 is the first. The connections of Psalm 93 with Psalms 97–99 are primarily thematic, but a few specific key-word links (to Psalms 98 and 99) serve to bind it more closely to the group than is generally imagined.

The section concludes with Psalm 100. Like Psalm 93, it is another hymn of praise, and it is the last of the string of community psalms.

## Psalm 94 in Context

### *Psalm 94 and Psalm 95*

Psalms 94 and 95 exemplify the juxtaposition of two very different form-critical genres, just as do Psalms 93 and 94. Psalm 94, a complex lament, is adjacent to Psalm 95, a complex liturgy composed of a hymn and a prophetic oracle. Psalm 95 is actually closest in structure and genre to Psalm 81, but within the 93–100 group, its closest affinities are with Psalm 100.[50]

There are at least 3 connections between the two psalms, however, that are significant in the positioning of the two psalms together. Indeed, among Psalms 93–100, Psalm 94 is most closely connected to Psalm 95, both lexically and structurally. First, the two share a large number of common words (20), more than Psalm 94 shares with any other psalm in the present group.[51] Among these, the key-word *ṣwr* is the strongest link between the

50. The few commentators who mention connections between Psalms 94 and 95 (e.g., Delitzsch, Alexander) usually have noted only the occurrence of *ṣwr* ('rock', 'mountain') in 94:22 and 95:1. Wilson (1985a: 217) also mentions the function of Psalm 95 to act as a transition back to the Kingship of YHWH motif.

51. Psalm 94 shares but 8 words with Psalm 93, 16 with Psalm 96, 16 with Psalm 97, 14 with Psalm 98, 17 with Psalm 99, and 11 with Psalm 100.

psalms. Second, a number of thematic connections present themselves, many building on the shared vocabulary. Third, structurally, the two psalms contain the most prominent nonhymnic sections in all of Psalms 93–100.

*The Data*

Lexical Repetitions (20):

| | |
|---|---|
| Key-word links: | *ṣwr* |
| Thematic word links: | *ʿm* |
| | *ʾlhym* |
| | *ʾl ('God')* |
| | *ʾrṣ* |
| | *yṣr* |
| | *pʿl* |
| | *ydʿ* |
| | *lb(b)* |
| Incidental links: | *ʾmr, rʾh, šmʿ, ywm, hm(h)*, YHWH, particles (*ʾm, ʿl, kl, ʾšr, lʾ*) |

Thematic Repetitions:
- Covenantal motifs
- YHWH's sovereignty (over people)
- YHWH as Creator

Structure/Genre Similarities:
- Both are community psalms
- Major nonhymnic portions
- Hortatory admonitions to God's people

*Key-Word Links*

The strongest lexical link between Psalms 94 and 95 is the use of *ṣwr* in 94:22 and 95:1 as a concatenation linking two adjacent psalms. In both cases, *ṣwr* is an epithet of YHWH ('Mountain' or 'Rock'), depicting him as a secure place of retreat and salvation. These are the only occurrences of the term in Psalms 93–100. The only other place it is used in Book IV to refer to YHWH is 92:16, a repetition that reinforces the links between Psalms 94 and 92 I shall note in chapter 5. This confidence in YHWH apparent in the second half of Psalm 94 is reiterated and magnified in the opening of Psalm 95.

*Thematic Connections*

The thematic connections between these two psalms are found intermixed among specific word links with more general thematic similarities, so the two sets of connections will be considered together here. YHWH's relationship with his people (*ʿm*) is significant in both psalms. Every occurrence of *ᶜm* in the two psalms (94:5, 8, 14; 95:7, 10) refers to Israel, never to the nations.[52] Furthermore, in these two psalms *ᵓlhy*(*m*) only refers to Israel's or the psalmists' God, as opposed to, more generally, the God of the nations or the cosmos. In 94:7 the reference is to the 'God of Jacob', while in 94:22 it is to 'my God'. In both Pss 94:23 and 95:7, the reference is to 'our God'. The divine name *ᵓēl* is also found only in 94:1 (2×), 95:3, and in Psalm 99.

YHWH's relationship with his people also forms the subtext for all of Psalm 94: precisely because YHWH is his people's God, the psalmist wonders where God is during this time of trouble. In Psalm 95, this relationship is more explicit, in the great language of praise of vv. 1–7c (and especially in vv. 6–7c), as well as in the entire prophetic oracle of Ps 95:7d–11.

YHWH's sovereignty is linked to the use of the word *ᵓrṣ* 'earth', as well as to other words. He is Judge of the earth (94:2) and holds the earth in his hand (95:4). In Psalm 95, his sovereignty is over all gods (v. 3), elements of nature (vv. 4–5), and his own people (vv. 6–7). In Psalm 94, his sovereignty over evil-doers is evident in the fact that he is capable of vindicating the psalmist, of standing up for him, and even of exterminating the wicked. Furthermore, the basis for the prophetic warning in 95:7d–11 is that YHWH was sovereign over his covenant people as the Creator of the nation. It is this that gives him the right, so to speak, to upbraid the nation so harshly.

Related to the theme of sovereignty is the theme of YHWH as Creator in both psalms. He is the One who 'forms' (*yṣr*) the eye (94:9) and dry land (95:5), as well as the One who 'plants' the ear (94:9) and 'makes' the sea (95:5). In 95:6, he is also the Maker of his people.

The contrasts between the psalms are numerous, given the difference in genre and content. Several of the repeated words are used in ways that signal these contrasts. The verb *pᶜl* 'to do, make' in 94:4 and 16 refers to doers of *evil*, while in 95:9 it refers to YHWH's *gracious* deeds on behalf of his people. The verb *ydᶜ* 'to know' in 94:11 refers to YHWH's knowing (and caring about) the thoughts of fragile humanity, whereas in 95:10 it refers to the fact that his people do *not* know (or care about) his ways. The *lb*(*b*) 'heart' in 94:15 is an upright heart, whereas in 95:10 it is an errant heart.

*Structural Connections*

Structurally, Psalms 94 and 95 contain the only sustained nonhymnic material among Psalms 93–100. Virtually all of Psalm 94 sounds a note of lament, and Ps 95:7b–11 sounds a hortatory note. On closer examination,

52. This exclusive sense of *ᶜm* in Psalms 93–100 is found again only in Psalm 100.

we find that the wisdom interlude in Psalm 94 (vv. 8–11, 12–15) is somewhat related to the prophetic oracle in Psalm 95 (vv. 7d–11). Both open with admonitions to the people to hear (95:7d) or to understand and gain wisdom (94:8), and both consist of hortatory messages from YHWH or his representative, the psalmist.

### *Psalm 94 and Psalms 96–99*

The links between Psalms 93 and 96–99 are primarily thematic and generic, and there are few specific structural links between Psalm 93 and any of the others. This is even more true of the links between Psalms 94 and 96–99. Psalm 94 has significant ties to Psalm 92, and it has important connections with Psalms 93 and 95, but it is related to Psalms 96–99 only via isolated repeated words and a few related themes. The related themes are primarily of a piece with those found throughout the Psalter, namely, a concern for YHWH's covenant people and the ways of wisdom, and are not peculiar to the Kingship of YHWH genre. Accordingly, the following remarks will not belabor individual relationships.

### *Psalm 94 and Psalm 96*

Psalms 94 and 96 are the two longest poems of Psalms 93–100. Because of their length, we find more common words in them (16) than in many other psalms that are more closely related, but shorter. Some of the repeated words are representative of the common themes mentioned above and many are merely incidental.

The placement of Psalm 94 is primarily due to its relationships with Psalms 92, 93, and 95; the placement of Psalm 96 has more to do with its relationships with Psalms 95 and 97–99 (and even Psalm 93) than with Psalm 94.

*The Data*

Lexical Repetitions (16):

| | |
|---|---|
| Key-word links: | none |
| Thematic word links: | *špṭ* |
| | *ʾrṣ* |
| | *ṣdq* |
| | *gwym* |
| | *mwṭ* |
| | *ʿlz* |
| Incidental links: | *YHWH, nśʾ, ʾmr, ywm, ʿm, hwʾ*, particles (*kl, ky, ʿl, ʾšr*) |

Thematic Similarities:

YHWH's sovereignty (over earth, nations)

Structure/Genre Similarities:

Both are community psalms

*Thematic Connections*

YHWH's sovereignty over the earth and the nations is again witnessed in both psalms. He is Judge (*špṭ*) of the earth (*ʾrṣ*) in 94:2 and 96:13. He is the One who instructs nations (*gwym*) in 94:10, and his glory is to be declared among the nations in 96:3, 10.

Several of YHWH's attributes are found in both psalms. His position as Judge in 94:2 and 96:13 has been mentioned above, and his justice (*mšpṭ*) is celebrated in 94:15. His righteousness (*ṣdq*) is mentioned in 94:15 and 96:13, both times parallel to his judging activity. The unmovable condition of the world that he established (96:10) contrasts with the unsteadiness of human footsteps (94:18); the common root is *mwṭ*.[53]

Besides the obvious contrasts in genre—Psalms 94 is a lament, whereas Psalms 96 is a hymn—and in the use of *mwṭ*, another contrast involves the term *ʿlz* 'to exult'. It has negative overtones in 94:3, speaking of the attitudes of the wicked over the misfortune of the righteous. In 96:12, however, the elements of nature are urged to exult in YHWH. These are the only times that the root occurs in all of Book IV.[54]

## *Psalm 94 and Psalm 97*

These psalms, like Psalms 94 and 96, have 16 words in common. Again, this is primarily due to the length of the poems (especially Psalm 94) and due to miscellaneous lexical and thematic connections, not to connections of major significance to the larger grouping of psalms. However, the presence of a significant wisdom section in both psalms does serve to bind Psalm 94 in a significant way to the Psalms 96–99 group.[55]

53. See also above, on the use of *mwṭ* in Psalms 93 and 94 (pp. 107–8).

54. The word *ʿlz* is a relatively rare word, occurring only 16 times, 7 in the Psalter; consequently, there is not much that can be said about the relationship of Psalms 94 and 96 on the basis of the number of occurrences. However, its use does confirm the picture of contrasts between the psalms. Ps 94:3 contains the only such negative use in the Psalter; the other 6 times, the word is used positively, to encourage exulting in YHWH.

55. Psalm 94 is bound to Psalms 96–99 by the presence of a wisdom section in the same way that Psalm 93 is bound to Psalms 96–99 by specific (but somewhat random) key-word connections such as *YHWH mlk* (all psalms), *ksʾ* and *kwn* (93 and 97), *ʿdt* (93 and 99), and especially *nhrwt* (93 and 98).

*The Data*

Lexical Repetitions (16):
  Key-word links: none
  Thematic word links:
    *Wisdom motifs*:
      *rš*ᶜ*(ym)*
      *r*ᶜ
      *yšr lb*
      *mšpṭ*
      *ṣdq*, *ṣdyq(ym)*
    *Nonwisdom motifs*:
      *ks*ᵓ
      *npš*
      ᶜ*m*
      ᵓ*rṣ*
  Incidental links: *r*ᵓ*h*, *šm*ᶜ, *rb*, *YHWH*, particles (*kl*, *ky*)

Thematic Similarities:
  Wisdom motifs
  YHWH's faithfulness
  YHWH's sovereignty (over earth)

Structure/Genre Similarities:
  Both are community psalms
  Roughly tripartite structure
  Discrete wisdom sections

*Key-Word Links*

Strictly speaking, we find no true key-word links between these two psalms. However, 5 lexical repetitions occur between the two wisdom sections of the psalms, to which I now turn.

*Thematic Connections*

*Thematic Word Links (Wisdom Vocabulary).* The primary thematic connections between Psalms 94 and 97 are the wisdom sections (Ps 94:8–15 and Ps 97:10–12). Five lexical repetitions can be observed, and the general language of the sections is sapiential. Each section has clear connections to its own context within its psalm, as I noted in chapter 3, but each one also changes the mood and focus within that context. In addition to these lexical repetitions within the wisdom sections, the two psalms also share 2 other lexemes from wisdom vocabulary, though they occur outside of the wisdom sections.

*The Wisdom Sections.* In Psalm 94, the wisdom interlude answers the derisive questions of the evil-doers with reminders of YHWH's instruction and faithfulness to his people. In Psalm 97, YHWH's faithful followers are instructed and his faithfulness to them is also emphasized. The psalms have 5 lexemes in common: *rš*ᶜ*(ym)* 'wicked (ones)' (94:13, 97:10; cf. also 94:3); *r*ᶜ 'evil' (94:13, 97:10); *yšr lb* 'upright in heart' (94:15, 97:11); and *YHWH*. YHWH's preservation of his people is prominent in both psalms, in 94:12–15 and 97:10–11.

*Additional Wisdom Vocabulary.* In addition to the wisdom vocabulary found in the wisdom sections in each psalm, we find other wisdom terms occurring in both psalms, in the wisdom section of one or the other (but not in both). YHWH's judgments/justice (*mšpṭ*) and his righteousness (*ṣdq*) are paralleled in 94:15, part of that psalm's wisdom section, and also parallel to each other in 97:2, not in this psalm's wisdom section.[56] In Psalm 97, reference to the righteous one(s) (*ṣdyq*[*ym*]) appears in the wisdom section (vv. 11, 12), whereas in Psalm 94 the term appears outside of it, in v. 21.

*Thematic Word Links (Nonwisdom).* General, nonwisdom thematic links are few, and not very specific, between these two psalms. Some words are used in the same way in both psalms: *npš* 'life, soul' occurs in 94:17, 19, 21; 97:10, in each case referring to the life of the righteous. Furthermore, YHWH is over the earth (ᵓ*rṣ*) in both psalms, as he is in almost every psalm. The term ᵓ*rṣ* occurs in 94:2; 97:1, 4, 5, and 9.

Some thematic connections are contrastive. Just as the word *ks*ᵓ 'throne' was contrasted in Psalms 93 and 94, so also it is contrasted in Psalms 94 and 97. In 97:2, YHWH's throne is firmly based on righteousness and judgment, whereas in 94:20, it is an ephemeral throne of destruction, opposed to YHWH. The use of ᶜ*m* 'people' also is different in each psalm, since, as noted above, it refers to Israel in Psalm 94 (vv. 5, 8, and 14), whereas it includes all peoples in Psalm 97 (v. 6).

### *Psalm 94 and Psalm 98*

These two psalms have 14 words in common, but none has any special significance for the structure of Psalms 93–100. The thematic connections are similar to those found elsewhere throughout the section.

56. They are also found in 97:8 (*mšpṭ*) and 6 (*ṣdq*).

*The Data*

Lexical Repetitions (14):

Key-word links: none

Thematic word links: *špṭ*, *ṣdq*, *ʾrṣ*, *gwym*, *ḥsd*, *ʾlhym*

Incidental links: *rʾh*, *ʿm*, *ʿyn*, *ydʿ*, *YHWH*, particles (*ky*, *kl*, *ʾt*)

Thematic Similarities:

YHWH's sovereignty (over earth, nations)
Covenantal motifs

Structure/Genre Similarities:

Both are community psalms

*Thematic Connections*

YHWH's sovereignty as Judge (*špṭ*) is present in both psalms (94:2, 15; 98:9[2×]), and his righteousness (*ṣdq*) is coupled with his judgments (94:15, 98:9). YHWH is sovereign over the earth in both (*ʾrṣ*: 94:2; 98:3, 4, 9) and also over the nations (*gwym*: 94:10, 98:2). In both psalms, YHWH appears as Israel's covenant God: he is 'our God' (*ʾlhynw*) in 94:23 and 98:3, and his *ḥsd* 'steadfast love' (a covenantal term) appears in 94:18 and 98:3.

## *Psalm 94 and Psalm 99*

The two psalms share 17 words, 9 of them particles or divine names or titles. Most of the rest are random or general thematic connections. However, 2 words—*ʾl* and *nqm*—contribute to a key-word connection, and the emphasis in both psalms on YHWH's covenantal relationship with his people Israel is likewise significant (as opposed to the more universal outlook elsewhere in this section).

*The Data*

Lexical Repetitions (17):

Key-word links: *ʾl* ('God'), *nqm*

Thematic word links: *ʾrṣ*, *ṣdq*(*h*)

*mšpṭ*
*twrh*/*ᶜdt*, *ḥq*
*ᵓlhym*

Incidental links: *ᶜm*, *nśᵓ*, *dbr*, *rgl*, *hwᵓ*, *hyh*, *YHWH*, particles (*ᶜl*, *kl*, *ky*)

Thematic Similarities:
YHWH's sovereignty (over earth, peoples)
Covenantal motifs

Structure/Genre Similarities:
Both are community psalms

*Key-Word Links*

The most important key-word links between these psalms are *ᵓēl* and *nqm*. YHWH is a vindicating God in both: *ᵓēl* occurs in 94:1 (2×) and 99:8, and *nqm* occurs alongside of it in each case. It serves to bind Psalm 94 with the viewpoints expressed in Psalm 99, the last of the Kingship of YHWH psalms, just as the wisdom connections do so in Psalms 94 and 97. This key-word link stands out in bolder relief when we note that these 2 words are otherwise only linked in the Psalter twice, in Ps 18:48 and 149:7 (and nowhere else in Book IV), despite the fact that the root *nqm* occurs 77 times in the Hebrew Bible (including 9 times in the Psalter) and *ᵓēl* appears almost 200 times (including 76 times in the Psalter).

*Thematic Connections*

*Thematic Word Links.* The remaining word repetitions are generally thematic. YHWH is over the earth (*ᵓrṣ*) in 94:2 and 99:1. His judgment/justice (*mšpṭ*) and righteousness (*ṣdq*[*h*]) appear in both psalms (94:15, 99:4). The Torah plays a role in the wisdom interlude in Ps 94:12, as does YHWH's instruction (vv. 10, 12). In Psalm 99 his instruction is implicit in his speaking to Moses and Aaron (v. 7a); his decrees (*ᶜdt*) and 'law' (*ḥq*) in v. 7 also recall the Torah.[57]

The two psalms share several divine names (see appendix 3). The most significant for the purposes of this monograph is *ᵓlhynw* ('our God') in 94:23;[58] 99:5, 8, and 9 (2×). The possessive suffixes indicate YHWH's special relationship with his covenant people, Israel.

57. The word *ḥq* occurs in 94:20 as well, but there it does not refer to YHWH's statutes.

58. And note 'my God' in v. 22.

*Thematic Similarities.* The special covenantal relationship to Israel indicated by *ʾlhynw* is also seen in some of the terms used in the wisdom section in Ps 94:8–15 and the references to his decrees and law in 99:7. It is seen in other ways throughout most of Psalm 99 (especially vv. 2, 4, and 6–9), as well as in the references to his people and his inheritance in Psalm 94 (vv. 5, 14) and the reference to the God of Jacob (v. 7).

Beyond this covenantal emphasis, YHWH's sovereignty over all things is present in both psalms (as it is throughout the section): it is implicit in Psalm 94's appeal to him to judge and deliver; it is explicit in Psalm 99's view of him as King over the peoples and the earth.

## *Psalm 94 and Psalm 100*

These two psalms have 11 words in common, but none has any special significance for the structure of Psalms 93–100. There are few thematic connections, and they are similar to the others found throughout the section. No true structural relationship exists between Psalms 94 and 100.

*The Data*

Lexical Repetitions (11):

| | |
|---|---|
| Key-word links: | none |
| Thematic word links: | *ʾlhym* |
| | *ʿm* |
| | *ḥsd* |
| | *ʾrṣ* |
| Incidental links: | *ydʿ*, *hwʾ*, *YHWH*, particles (*kl*, *ky*, *ʾt*, *ʿd*) |

Thematic Similarities:

YHWH's sovereignty (over earth)
Covenantal motifs

Structure/Genre Similarities:

Both are community psalms

*Thematic Connections*

The connections between Psalms 94 and 100 center around the covenantal relationship between YHWH and his people.[59] He is the God (*ʾlhym*) of *Israel* in both psalms (94:7, 22, 23; 100:3). The people (*ʿm*) referred to in both are YHWH's own people (94:5, 14; 100:3). His steadfast love (*ḥsd*) figures in both (94:18, 100:5). Besides this, YHWH is sovereign over the earth (*ʾrṣ*) in both psalms (94:2, 100:1).

59. As we have already seen, this is also true between Psalms 94 and 99 (p. 127).

### *Summary of Psalm 94 in Context*

The place of Psalm 94 among the Kingship of YHWH psalms has puzzled scholars more than the place of any of the others. However, it does indeed fit its context well, as I have demonstrated in the sections above.[60] In addition, I shall add three more observations that support the placement of Psalm 94 in the 93–100 group and then conclude by summarizing all of the evidence.

*Psalm 94 and Superscriptions*

I have noted above[61] that (1) the presence or absence of superscriptions is a factor in analyzing connections between psalms and that (2) untitled psalms can often be shown to be linked with the psalms that precede them. I noted that the longest unbroken stretch of untitled psalms in the Hebrew Psalter occurs precisely in our group: Psalms 93–97. This fact alone is evidence that the editors of the tradition underlying the MT perceived a unity among them and that the presence of the untitled Psalm 94 within a series of similarly untitled psalms is significant. By subject matter, it is somewhat misplaced, since the group is largely composed of laudatory Kingship of YHWH psalms. However, the lack of a title serves to "soften" the disjunction and highlights its affinities with neighboring psalms, especially with the preceding psalm, Psalm 93.

*Psalm 94 as an Untitled Lament Psalm*

Psalm 94 is not only an untitled psalm, it is also an untitled *lament* psalm. Gunkel identified 47 complete psalms and parts of at least 20 others as individual and communal laments, in his foundational form-critical work, thus showing that almost half of the Psalter consists of laments (Gunkel 1933: 117, 172).[62] Among the 67 laments identified by Gunkel, there are only *three* lament psalms that lack a superscription, of which Psalm 94 is one. When we add to this the fact that one of the other 2, Psalm 43, is almost universally considered to be an originally unified composition with Psalm 42, and the other, Psalm 71, is very possibly Davidic and was linked with Psalm 70,[63] then Psalm 94 emerges as the *only* lament in the entire Psalter that is untitled.[64]

60. And see below, pp. 130–31.

61. Chapter 4, pp. 102–4.

62. In his recent form-critical work, Gerstenberger (1988) essentially agrees with Gunkel's classifications, although he acknowledges both the "concordance and divergence among [more recent] form critics" (1988: 14).

63. See the discussion above in chapter 4, p. 103, for more details on the links between Psalms 42 and 43 and Psalms 70 and 71.

64. In any case, it stands as the only untitled lament in Books IV–V (there are 11 in these two books).

If there is any validity in the observations above about the links of untitled psalms with the psalms preceding them, then certainly Psalm 94 stands out as the only logical choice in the present canon of a lament psalm for insertion among a string of untitled praise psalms. This fact alone may not have been sufficient for the placement of the psalm, but it undoubtedly was a convenient one for the editors of Book IV.[65]

*Psalm 94 as a Kingship of YHWH Psalm*

Even though Psalm 94 is not usually considered to be a Kingship of YHWH psalm, there are at least two reasons for arguing that its perspective on YHWH is similar to the perspective in the other Kingship psalms. First, in 94:1 YHWH is seen as the God of 'vengeances' (*nqmwt*). George Mendenhall has pointed out that the function of this 'vengeance' is a royal one, a function of a king or of YHWH, in exercising his legitimate executive power (Mendenhall 1973: 70–104). By calling forth YHWH's avenging power, his imperium, Psalm 94 recognizes his royal authority and easily assumes its place among the Kingship of YHWH psalms (Tate 1990: 489–90).

Second, Psalm 94:1–2 calls for a theophany, for YHWH to appear and act. Watts has pointed out (1965) that "words showing characteristic acts of Yahweh, including creating, making, establishing, sitting, doing wonders, judging, doing righteous acts, and saving," are another feature of the Kingship of YHWH psalms. This is another reason, then, that Psalm 94 fits well among the Kingship of YHWH psalms.

*Summary of Psalm 94 in Context*

The placement of Psalm 94 should no longer be seriously questioned. Its strongest connections are with the two preceding psalms and the one following it.[66] It is like Psalms 93 and 95 in that it too is a psalm of the community and it lacks a superscription. However, Psalms 92 and 93 abound with praise of YHWH, whereas Psalm 94 changes the mood, introducing a lament, but it does so in terms reminiscent of the psalms preceding it (even harking back to questions raised in Psalm 90).

The links between Psalm 94 and Psalm 95 are the key-word concatenation of *ṣwr*, much shared vocabulary centering around YHWH's relationship with his people, the shared genre of psalms of the community, and the structural phenomenon of lengthy "intrusive" sections (94:8–15; 95:7d–11). The fact that two Kingship of YHWH psalms bracket Psalm 94 and have several connections to it serves to "anchor" it firmly in place.

65. As to why a lament of *any* type is found there, see the remarks below, on pp. 174–75.

66. See below, pp. 172–73, for the primary links between Psalm 94 and Psalm 92, and above, pp. 105–9, 119–22, for the links between Psalm 94 and Psalms 93 and 95.

Psalm 94's connections with Psalms 96–99 are mostly thematic. A significant structural link can be seen between Psalms 94 and 97, since both have a wisdom section (94:8–15, 97:10–12). Psalms 94 and 99 are linked by the significant key-words *ʾēl* and *nqm*. These links serve primarily to bind Psalm 94 to the entire group (96–99), not to highlight specific connections between the individual psalm pairs.

## Psalm 95 in Context

### *Psalm 95 and Psalm 96*

There are several ways in which Psalm 95 links with Psalm 96. Most notably, the reference to YHWH as a great king (*mlk gdwl*) in 95:3 provides justification for its classification with the other Kingship of YHWH psalms (including Psalm 96). Furthermore, the hymnic character of the first two sections is very similar to Psalm 96's. The psalms have 18 words in common, including particles. The significant lexical links are in the vocabulary of praise, the root *mlk*, and the phrase *ʿl-kl-ʾlhym* 'above all gods'. Beyond this, there are also two significant connections on the structural level.

*The Data*

Lexical Repetitions (18):

| | |
|---|---|
| Key-word links: | *YHWH, mlk* |
| | *ʿl-kl-ʾlhym* |
| Thematic word links: | *rnn* |
| | *gdwl* |
| | *ḥwh* |
| | *ʿśh* |
| | *ym* |
| | *bwʾ* |
| Incidental repetitions: | *ywm, ʾmr, ʿm, hwʾ,* particles (*ky,* [*l*]*pny, ʾšr*) |

Thematic Similarities:

YHWH's kingship
Praise motifs
YHWH's sovereignty (over nature, gods)
YHWH as Creator

Structure/Genre Similarities:

Both are Kingship of YHWH hymns
Opening praise structure
Parallelism between 95:3 and 96:4

*Key-Word Links*

Two sets of key-word links bind Psalms 95 and 96 together in a pattern of concatenation. These are stronger links than the links between most other adjacent psalm pairs in the 93–100 group. These two key-word sets undoubtedly were among the primary reasons for the Psalter's editor(s)' juxtaposing these two psalms. The first set—and the most obvious—are the words *YHWH* and *mlk*, which occur in 95:3 and 96:10. Both psalms are Kingship of YHWH psalms, and these words make that clear. The second set of links is the repeated phrase *ᶜl-kl-ᵓlhym* 'above all gods' in 95:3 and 96:4. This phrase describes YHWH: in Psalm 95, he is a 'great King above all gods', and in Psalm 96 he is 'to be feared above all gods'.

*Thematic Connections*

Both psalms are rich with the vocabulary of praise. They both speak of singing for joy (*rnn*: 95:1, 96:12) and worshiping (*ḥwh*: 95:6, 96:9). YHWH is great (*gdwl*) in both psalms; in fact, *gdwl* is found in the *ky* clause in both psalms, giving reasons for praise (95:3, 96:4). Both psalms include a liturgical use of *bwᵓ* 'come', calling worshipers to come and worship YHWH (95:6, 96:8). Other specific hymnic terms are not repeated, but joyful singing, praising, and worshiping / doing obeisance are an integral part of both psalms.

YHWH's sovereignty over nature is present in Psalms 95 and 96, as it is in the other psalms of the genre. He is Creator (*ᶜśh*: 95:5a, 96:5b), and he is sovereign over the sea (*ym*: 95:5, 96:11) and other elements of nature (95:4–5; 96:5, 11–12). He is above the gods, as well (95:3, 96:4–5).

*Structural Connections*

*Overall Structure.* The first unit of Psalm 95 (vv. 1–7c) is somewhat similar structurally to the first unit of Psalm 96 (vv. 1–9). Both units open with calls to praise (95:1–2, 96:1–3) and are followed by reasons for praise (95:3–5, 96:4–6). Each of the reasons-for-praise sections opens by speaking of YHWH's greatness and mentions YHWH's sovereignty over the gods and nature. Both units then continue with a second call-to-praise section (95:6, 96:7–9). Psalm 96 does not have a second section of reasons for praise to parallel 95:7a–c (though it does have one later, in v. 13).

*The Structures of 95:3 and 96:4.* A significant structural link exists between 95:3 and 96:4. In each verse, the word *gdwl* describes YHWH, as I noted above. Also, each verse claims that YHWH is above all gods (*ᶜl-kl-ᵓlhym*). But these word links are not as significant as the fact that the entire structure of each verse is similar to the other's:

Psalm 95
3a *ky ʾl gdwl* Yhwh
b *wmlk gdwl ʿl-kl-ʾlhym*

3a For a great God is Yhwh,
b And a great King above all gods!

Psalm 96
4a *ky gdwl* Yhwh *wmhll mʾd*
b *nwrʾ hwʾ ʿl-kl-ʾlhym*

4a For great is Yhwh, and worthy of praise is the Almighty One;
b To be feared is he above all gods.

Each verse begins with a clause, part of the reasons for praise (introduced by *ky*), stating that Yhwh is great: *ky ʾl gdwl* Yhwh 'for a great God is Yhwh' (95:3a) and *ky gdwl* Yhwh *. . .* 'for great is Yhwh . . . ' (96:4a). Each continues with another affirmation of Yhwh's position and worthiness, introduced by *wāw*: *wmlk gdwl* 'and a great King' (95:3b) and *wmhll mʾd* 'and worthy of praise is the Almighty One' (96:4a). Ps 96:4b adds a second clause of affirmation (*nwrʾ hwʾ* 'to be feared is he'), and then both verses finish identically, with *ʿl-kl-ʾlhym* 'above all gods'.

*Final Remarks.* The major difference in structure and content between the two psalms is that Psalm 96 does not have a section parallel to 95:7d–11, nor even to 7a–c, where the focus is exclusively on Yhwh's people Israel. Psalm 96 is much more universal in outlook than Psalm 95.[67] Psalm 95:7d–11 especially differs from anything in Psalm 96, both in genre and in content, but 95:7a–c also has no counterpart in Psalm 96. However, these differences highlight the connections of Psalm 95 with other psalms: (1) its function as a well-placed transitional psalm between the lament in Psalm 94 and the glorious praises in Psalm 96 and following psalms; and (2) its function with Psalm 100 as a frame around the four intervening Kingship of Yhwh psalms.

### *Psalm 95 and Psalm 97*

Psalms 95 and 97 are only generally related lexically and thematically. They have 15 words in common, including particles, and the links occur

67. Psalm 96 does show itself to be Temple-oriented, since vv. 6b, 8b, and 9a refer to the Temple precincts and Yhwh's appearance there, and Psalm 95 does exhibit a universal outlook (vv. 3–5); nevertheless the overall differences in outlook are clear.

only among random words (except for *YHWH* and *mlk*). There are no repeated phrases or extended thoughts, but there is one striking structural connection.

*The Data*

Lexical Similarities (15):

| | |
|---|---|
| Key-word links: | *YHWH, mlk* |
| Thematic word links: | *ʾlhym* ('gods') |
| | *ʾrṣ* |
| | *ḥwh* |
| | *rʾh* |
| | *šmʿ* |
| | *lb(b)* |
| Incidental repetitions: | *yd, ʿm, hr,* particles (*lpny, kl, ʿl, ky*) |

Thematic Similarities:
- YHWH's kingship
- Praise motifs
- YHWH's sovereignty

Structure/Genre Similarities:
- Both are Kingship of YHWH hymns
- Nonhymnic sections
- Hortatory admonitions to God's people

*Key-Word Links*

The primary key words in Psalms 95 and 97 are *YHWH* and *mlk*, which reveal both psalms to be of the Kingship of YHWH genre.

*Thematic Connections*

As a Kingship of YHWH hymn, Ps 97:1–9 parallels Ps 95:1–7c. Both units contain the root *mlk* (95:3, 97:1). Both open with calls to joyful praise. However, Psalm 97 focuses on the awe and fear associated with worship of YHWH more than Psalm 95 does. Both speak of him as sovereign over the gods (95:3; 97:7, 9) and nature (95:4–5; 97:1, 4–6). The idea of YHWH's works or glory as a testimony to his power is present in the use of *rʾh* 'to see' in 95:9 and 97:4, 6.

One link between the prophetic oracle in Psalm 95 (vv. 7d–11) and the hymn in Psalm 97 (vv. 1–9) is the use of *šmʿ* 'to hear'. In both cases, its subject is the covenant people. In 95:7d, the people are urged to listen to YHWH's words, and in 97:8, Zion is said to hear of YHWH's judgments and be glad.

*Structural Connections*

Although the hymnic portions of the two psalms are not very similar structurally, there is one important respect in which the final forms of the psalms are much alike: in the parallels between 95:7d–11 and 97:10–12. Neither of these sections is a hymn like the rest of the psalm in which it is found.

Psalm 95:7d–11 is a prophetic oracle addressed to Israel, the covenant people, and 97:10–12 is a hortatory admonition that is also addressed to the covenant people, the faithful lovers of YHWH. Both sections express thoughts that differ greatly from the thoughts immediately preceding them, and they may have been independent units at one time. However, as I argued in chapter 3, they have been logically linked with these preceding thoughts, if, in fact they were separate originally. These two sections speak much more directly to the covenant community than the hymnic portions do. Ps 97:10–12 speaks much more hopefully and encouragingly than does 95:7d–11, but both do speak directly to God's people.

## *Psalm 95 and Psalm 98*

Psalms 95 and 98 have more in common than Psalms 95 and 97; they compare in a way that is similar to Psalms 95 and 96, where the vocabulary of praise forms the basis for many links. Because there are strong connections between Psalms 96 and 98, the similarities between Psalm 95 and both of them should not be surprising. Psalms 95 and 98 share 19 words, many of which reflect the common praise vocabulary found in the Kingship of YHWH psalms.

*The Data*

| | |
|---|---|
| Lexical Repetitions (19): | |
| Key-word links: | *YHWH, mlk* |
| Thematic word links: | *rwʿ* |
| | *rnn* |
| | *zmr* |
| | *ʾrṣ* |
| | *ym* |
| | *hrym* |
| | *ʾlhym* |
| | *yšwʿh / yšʿ* |
| Incidental repetitions: | *ʿśh, bwʾ, ʿm, qwl, rʾh, ydʿ*, particles (*ky, kl,* [*l*]*pny*) |

Thematic Similarities:

YHWH's kingship

Praise motifs
YHWH's sovereignty (over nature)
Covenantal motifs

Structure/Genre Similarities:
Both are Kingship of YHWH hymns
Hymnic structure

*Key-Word Links*

The primary key-word links between Psalms 95 and 98 are again the words *YHWH* and *mlk*. The most important connections between Psalm 95 and all of Psalms 96–99 are related to this Kingship of YHWH motif.

*Thematic Connections*

The first section in Psalm 95 and the second in Psalm 98 open with calls to praise, sharing some of the same vocabulary (*rwᶜ* 'to raise a glad cry', 95:1, 2; 98:4; *rnn* 'to sing for joy', 95:1; 98:4; *zmr* 'to sing praises', 95:2; 98:4, 5 [2×]). The object of the acclamation is YHWH, the King (95:3, 98:6).

YHWH's sovereignty is a common theme in both psalms. He is over the earth (*ᵓrṣ*: 95:4; 98:3, 4), the sea (*ym*: 95:5; 98:7), the mountains (*hrym*: 95:4; 98:9), and other elements of nature (95:5; 98:7, 8).

Furthermore, YHWH is presented as the covenant God of Israel in both psalms. He is referred to as 'our God' (*ᵓlhynw*) in 95:7 and 98:3. And, as noted earlier, Ps 95:6–7c and especially 7d–11 focus on his relationship to Israel; Ps 98:1–3 focuses specifically on YHWH's faithfulness to Israel. In a related vein, YHWH's salvation (*yšwᶜh*; verb *yšᶜ*), his deliverance of Israel, is mentioned in 95:1 and 98:1, 2, 3.

### *Psalm 95 and Psalm 99*

Psalms 95 and 99 have 15 words in common, but more than half are particles or divine names or titles. The lexical relationships are only general, except for *YHWH* and *mlk*. The greater correspondences are thematic and structural.

*The Data*

Lexical Repetitions (15):

| | |
|---|---|
| Key-word links: | *YHWH*, *mlk* |
| Thematic word links: | *gdwl* |
| | *ᵓrṣ* |
| | *ḥwh* |
| | *ᶜśh* |
| | *ᵓl* ('God') |

Incidental repetitions: *ᶜm*, *hr*, *hwᵓ*, *ᵓlhym*, particles (*ᶜl*, *kl*, *ky*, *ᵓl* ['to'])

Thematic Similarities:
- YHWH's kingship
- YHWH's sovereignty (over earth, nature, gods, peoples)
- YHWH as Creator
- Praise motifs
- Covenantal motifs

Structure/Genre Similarities:
- Both are Kingship of YHWH hymns
- Length
- Hymnic structure of first two sections
- Allusions to the Exodus in the final sections

*Key-Word Links*

YHWH as King naturally appears in both psalms, in 95:3 and 99:1, 4. As was true in the connections between Psalm 95 and two other psalms, Psalms 97 and 98, YHWH as King is also the only key-word connection between Psalms 95 and 99.

*Thematic Connections*

*Thematic Word Links.* YHWH's sovereignty and status as Creator are revealed by means of other word links. For example, YHWH is a great God (*gdwl*: 95:3 [2×], 99:2), exalted above all gods (95:3) and all peoples (99:2). He is a God who is sovereign over the earth (*ᵓrṣ*: 95:4, 99:1) and other parts of nature (95:4–5). He is to be worshiped (*ḥwh*: 95:6; 99:5, 9). He is the One who has made (*ᶜśh*) the sea (95:5), his people (95:6), and justice and righteousness in Jacob (99:4).

*Thematic Similarities.* Thematically, both psalms contain general hymnic vocabulary, although the tone of Psalm 99 is more somber, less joyous (more like Psalm 97 than Psalms 95, 96, or 98). Psalms 95 and 99 also both mention YHWH's covenant people. Ps 95:6–7c and 7d–11 focus on his relationship with them, as does Ps 99:6–8. The first sections of Psalm 99 also draw attention to Zion (v. 2) and Jacob (v. 4).

*Structural Similarities*

The psalms are of similar length, and they consist of several sections that are roughly analogous to each other. The first two sections in each psalm are hymnic exaltations of YHWH, and the next sections hark back in one way or another to the Exodus period: the third section in Psalm 95 is a prophetic oracle harking back to the wilderness period, and the third and fourth sections in Psalm 99 speak of Moses and Aaron and the pillar of cloud. They differ, however, in that Psalm 95 has no repeated refrain like the one in Psalm 99 (*qdwš hwʾ*). The overall relationship between the two psalms is only a general one, based on common genre and themes.

### *Psalm 95 and Psalm 100*

Although Psalm 95 is roughly twice as long as Psalm 100, the two are very closely related in several ways. As psalms that share several important themes and are similar structurally, they form an inclusio or frame around Psalms 96–99, which are all Kingship of YHWH psalms. The psalms share 15 words, including particles.

*The Data*

| | |
|---|---|
| Lexical Repetitions (15): | |
| Key-word links: | *YHWH, hwʾ, ʾlhym, ʿśh* |
| | *ʾnḥnw, ʿm, mrʿyt, ṣʾn* |
| Thematic word links: | *rwʿ* |
| | *rnn(h)* |
| | *twdh* |
| | *bwʾ* |
| | *d(w)r* |
| | *ʾrṣ* |
| Incidental repetitions: | *ydʿ* |

Thematic Similarities:
- YHWH's close relationship with Israel
- YHWH as Creator
- Praise motifs

Structure/Genre Similarities:
- Both are hymns
- Both function as an inclusio around Kingship of YHWH group
- Opening hymnic structure
- Middle affirmations
- Closing addresses

*Key-Word Links*

Pride of place among the links between these psalms must be given to those between 95:6b–7c and 100:3b–c. More than half of the words that these psalms share fall into the key-word category (8 of 15), making the connections between these two psalms among the strongest between any two psalms in Book IV. Beyond the 8 key words, an additional 6 display more general thematic connections between the psalms.

The key-word links between the psalms have been discussed in depth in the treatment of Psalm 100 in chapter 3, but I will review them here briefly for convenience.

Psalm 95:6b–7c
6b *nbrkh lpny-YHWH ʿśnw*
7a *ky hwʾ ʾlhynw*
b *wʾnḥnw ʿm mrʿytw*
c *wṣʾn ydw*

6b Let us kneel before YHWH our Maker!
7a For he is our God,
b And we are the people of his pasture,
c And the sheep of his hand.

Psalm 100:3b–c
3b *hwʾ-ʿśnw wlʾ ʾnḥnw*
c *ʿmw wṣʾn mrʿytw*

3b It is he who has made us, and we are his!
c (We are) his people, and the sheep of his pasture!

These two sections are the heart of both psalms. As I noted in chapter 3 in the respective discussions, *ky hwʾ ʾlhynw* 'for he is our God' in 95:7a and *ʿmw* '(We are) his people' in 100:3c stand at the exact structural midpoints of their respective psalms. That is, structure and content converge in both of these psalms to highlight certain important—and similar—themes.

Furthermore, the syntactical structures of Pss 95:7b–c and 100:3bβ–c are identical:

| | | | |
|---|---|---|---|
| Ps 95:7b–c | (1) *wʾnḥnw* | (2) *ʿm mrʿytw* | (3) *wṣʾn ydw* |
| Ps 100:3bβ–c | (1) *wlʾ ʾnḥnw* | (2) *ʿmw* | (3) *wṣʾn mrʿytw* |

Ps 95:7b And we are the people of his pasture,
Ps 95:7c And the sheep of his hand.

Ps 100:3bβ and we are his!
Ps 100:3c (We are) his people, and the sheep of his pasture!

As I pointed out in the discussion of Psalm 100 in chapter 3, in each psalm, elements (2) and (3) consist of a noun or compound noun carrying a suffix that refers to YHWH. Element (1) is identical in Pss 79:13 and 95:7 and is only varied in Ps 100:3 by an emphatic particle (*lʾ*), but there is no real semantic change in any case. When all of Ps 100:3b–c is compared with Ps 95:6b–7a, the connection is even closer: each psalm asserts that YHWH is Israel's God and that he made it into the nation it became. This is affirmed by 95:7a ('for he is our God') and 100:3b ('it is he who has made us, and we are his!'). The close relationship is further illustrated by the shepherd imagery: Israel is dependent on God in the same way that sheep depend on their shepherd in both passages.

*Thematic Connections*

*Thematic Word Links.* The first half of Psalm 95 is a hymn, as is Psalm 100, and hymnic vocabulary accounts for most of the remaining word links between the psalms. The word *rwᶜ* 'to raise a glad cry' opens each psalm: 95:1, 2; 100:1. Joyful singing (*rnn*[*h*]) is described: 95:1, 100:2. The noun for thanksgiving (*twdh*) occurs only in Psalms 95:2; 100:1, 4, in all of Book IV, although the verbal form (*ydh*) occurs more frequently. The liturgical imperative of *bwʾ* 'come!' occurs in 95:6 and 100:2 and 4.

*Thematic Similarities.* Psalm 100 poses a contrast to the negative picture drawn at the end of Psalm 95. There, YHWH loathed the generation (*dwr*) of rebellious Israelites of Moses's day (95:10); in 100:5, by contrast, YHWH's faithfulness (and steadfast love) is extended to all generations (*dr wdr*) of Israel.

*Structural Connections*

Structurally, the psalms are both similar and dissimilar. They are dissimilar because Psalm 100 has no obvious counterpart to the prophetic oracle at the end of Psalm 95. All of the lexical links (except for the one concerning *dwr / dr* just noted) exist only in the hymnic sections. Psalm 100 also concludes with a call to praise (v. 4) and reasons for praise (v. 5) that are not paralleled in Psalm 95.

On the positive side, the hymnic structures are somewhat similar. Both open with calls to praise (95:1–2, 100:1–2), although Psalm 95 follows up this section with a section of reasons for praise speaking of YHWH's sovereignty over nature (vv. 3–5) that lacks a counterpart in Psalm 100. The sections that are most closely linked (95:6b–7c; 100:3b–c) are both preceded by imperatives of *bwʾ* (95:6a, 100:2b).

The structural similarities of the three sections can be defined further. The first section in each psalm (95:1–5, 100:1–2) is an introductory, generalized call to praise. The second section in each contains statements about the close relationship of YHWH to his people Israel (95:6–7c, 100:3). The third sections (95:7d–11, 100:4–5), while on the surface very different, are both introduced by imperatives addressed to Israel (95:8a, 100:4a) to remember its covenant with YHWH. Psalm 95 does this by reflecting back to the wilderness experiences and the rebellious generation there; Psalm 100 does this by reflecting on YHWH's continuing *ḥesed* and faithfulness to every generation of his people.

### *Summary of Psalm 95 in Context*

Psalm 95 functions in important ways in the shaping of Psalms 93–100 and Book IV. As a hymn in praise of YHWH's kingship, it doubles with Psalm 93 to bracket the lament in Psalm 94. It also resumes the notes of praise begun in Psalm 93 (and, actually, earlier, in Psalms 91 and 92).[68] Yet, it is also similar to Psalm 94, as well: the prophetic oracle in 95:7d–11 sounds a warning reminiscent of the somber notes in Psalms 90 and 94, and key-word link (*ṣwr*) between Psalms 94 and 95 further binds the two together.

Psalm 95 is a transitional (or pivot) psalm to the great string of Kingship of YHWH psalms found in Psalms 96–99, since it looks both backward and forward. In particular, its specific links with Psalm 96—the first in the following group—contrast with its lack of links with Psalms 97–99; in fact, Psalm 96 is the most suited among Psalms 96–99 to follow immediately after Psalm 95. The connections of Psalm 95 with Psalms 97–99, however, are primarily thematic. The internal structure of Psalms 96–99 is governed by other considerations and is not greatly affected by the presence of Psalm 95, except for its important links with Psalm 96.

The most important function of Psalm 95, in the shaping of Book IV, however, is to anticipate themes in Psalm 100 and with it, to bracket Psalms 96–99 as a discrete unit, forming a clear inclusio or "frame" around these Kingship of YHWH psalms. Psalms 95 and 100 are among the closest of all the psalms in the 93–100 group in common vocabulary, themes, and structure. Psalm 100 answers the question that might arise from the end of Psalm 95, which is "Has YHWH rejected succeeding generations?" The answer in Psalm 100 is "No!"

## Psalm 96 in Context

### *Psalm 96 and Psalm 97*

Psalms 96 and 97 share more words not found elsewhere in Psalms 93–100 than any other two psalms in the group. As Kingship of YHWH psalms, they also have a great deal in common, as one would expect. They are the

68. See chapter 5 (pp. 169–70).

only two psalms in the group that have all five of the themes that Watts (1965) identified as characteristic of the Kingship of YHWH genre. They have 22 words in common, most of which are significant in one way or another.

*The Data*

Lexical Repetitions (22):

| | |
|---|---|
| Key-word links: | *YHWH mlk* |
| | *tgl hʾrṣ* |
| | *ʾlylym, šmym, kbwd, gyl, ḥyl* |
| Thematic word links: | *mʾd* |
| | *tbl* |
| | *ʿmym* |
| | *(m)špṭ* |
| | *yšr / myšrym* |
| | *ṣdq* |
| | *ḥwh* |
| | *ʾlhym* ('gods') |
| | *šm / zkr* |
| | *qdš* |
| | *śmḥ* |
| Incidental repetitions: | particles (*kl, lpny, ʿl*) |

Thematic Similarities:
- YHWH's kingship
- YHWH's sovereignty (over nature, peoples, gods)
- Praise motifs

Structure/Genre Similarities:
- Both are Kingship of YHWH hymns

*Key-Word Links*

There are several key words that link Psalms 96 and 97 together by concatenation, the most important being *YHWH mlk* (96:10, 97:1) and *tgl hʾrṣ*. *YHWH mlk* links the two psalms together as Kingship of YHWH psalms, and it is at once the most significant and the most obvious of the connections between the psalms.

The clause *tgl hʾrṣ* 'let the earth be glad' is identical in the second half of both 96:11a and 97:1a, constituting another important example of concatenation. More than this, the larger complex of ideas is identical in 96:11–12 and 97:1: both passages exhort the elements of nature to participate in the joyful worship of the King. Ideas, not specific words, are concatenated in this case. All of these connections show that the two psalms are closely related—that Psalm 97 begins where Psalm 96 leaves off.

Five additional key words link the two psalms. They are key words either because their appearances in Psalms 96 and 97 are (1) the only appearances in Psalms 93–100 or (2) the only appearances in all of Book IV, or (3) the only appearances in the entire Psalter. The most important of these 5 key words is *ʾlylym* 'worthless idols': its occurrences in Pss 96:5 and 97:7 are the only 2 occurrences of the word in the entire Psalter. In each case, the psalms draw a strong contrast between the absurdity of the idols and the sovereignty of YHWH, the true God.

Four key words are part of the vocabulary of praise: *šmym* 'heavens' (96:5, 11; 97:6) and *kbwd* 'glory' (96:3, 7, 8; 97:6) occur only here among Psalms 93–100. Both 96:11 and 97:6 refer to the heavens as exulting in YHWH or proclaiming his righteousness. His glory is something to behold and to proclaim in both psalms. Two honorific words are similarly unique here: *gyl* 'to rejoice' occurs only in 96:11 and 97:1, 8, and nowhere else in Book IV; *ḥyl* 'to tremble' (96:9, 97:4) occurs again in Book IV only in 90:2. Both words convey something of YHWH's awesomeness, which inspires both rejoicing and trembling at the same time.[69]

It is unlikely that any one of these words can be singled out as *the* key word responsible for placing the two psalms adjacent to each other. However, Psalms 96 and 97 are unique among Psalms 93–100 in sharing so many terms that are not used elsewhere in the group. At the very least, this fact shows the close relationship between the two psalms; it confirms Watts's results noted above, which show these two psalms (along with Psalm 89) as the Kingship of YHWH psalms most closely related to each other thematically. The cumulative effect resulting from so many key words uniquely held in common very likely did influence the editor(s)' decision to position the two psalms side by side. I shall demonstrate below that Psalm 96 shares more words with Psalm 98 than with 97 and that 96 and 98 are more closely related in other ways, as well, but even they do not share as many words that are unique only to them as Psalms 96 and 97 do.

*Thematic Connections*

Psalms 96 and 97 share many words that are an indication of general thematic connections. Three lexemes and one word pair all coalesce around the motif of worship. (1) 'Rejoicing' (*śmḥ*) is prominent at the end of Psalm 96 and the beginning of Psalm 97 (96:11; 97:1, 8, 11, 12).[70] (2) YHWH's holiness (*qdš*) elicits responses of praise and worship (96:9,

69. A further word that could easily be included here is *śmḥ* 'to rejoice'. See the comments under "Thematic Connections" (next section) and in n. 70.

70. This prominence could very well influence us to classify *śmḥ* as a key-word link, and it would be a further example of concatenation between the psalms. However,

97:12). (3) YHWH's 'name' is to be worshiped (*šm* in 96:2, 8; *zkr* in 97:12). (4) Worship itself is the subject of contrast in the two psalms: YHWH is to be worshiped (*ḥwh*) in his holy splendor in 96:9, whereas worshipers or idols are put to shame in 97:7; indeed, the idols themselves worship (*ḥwh*) YHWH.

YHWH's sovereignty over nature and peoples is emphasized in both psalms. In addition to including the general exhortations that elements of nature should praise YHWH noted above, the psalms also portray YHWH as Lord of all the earth (*ʾrṣ*: 96:1, 9, 11, 13; 97:1, 4, 5, 9; *tbl*: 96:10, 13; 97:4). The heavens (*šmym*) are under him and testify to him (96:5, 11; 97:6), and he is over all the peoples as well (*ʿmym*: 96:3, 5, 7, 10, 13; 97:6).

Both psalms affirm the fact that YHWH is greater than the gods and the idols that represent the gods. Pss 96:4b–5a and 97:7a–c, 9b all emphasize this, using such terms as *ʾlhym* 'gods' (96:4, 5; 97:7, 9) and (as noted above) *ʾlylym* 'worthless idols' (96:5; 97:7).

We may also note that the divine epithet *mʾd* 'the Mighty one' occurs only in these two psalms (96:4, 97:9) and in 93:5 among Psalms 93–100. In Psalms 96 and 97, *mʾd* also occurs in the context of affirming the Almighty's sovereignty over the gods.[71]

YHWH's sovereignty includes his right to judge (*špṭ*): 96:13b–c; compare this with his *mšpṭ* in 97:2, 8. Indeed, YHWH's justice is expressed in various ways. He is a righteous (*ṣdq*) judge (96:13, 97:2);[72] he judges with equity (*myšrym*: 96:10); and he gives joy to the upright (*yšr*) in heart (97:11).

## *Psalm 96 and Psalm 98*

Most commentators have pointed out the many strong connections between Psalms 96 and 98. They share 25 lexemes, more than any other psalm pair in the 93–100 section, and most of them are important in some way. There are more important key-word links between these two psalms than between any other psalm pair; indeed, they are more closely related to each other than any pair under study. They are part of an alternating pattern of closely related psalms, 96/98 and 97/99, the four of which

---

the key-word links highlighted above are so numerous and so unique (in occurring only between these two psalms) that I have placed *śmḥ* in this second, more general category. Regardless of how we classify it, however, its use still reinforces the strong ties between the two psalms.

71. In Psalm 93, *mʾd* occurs in a different context but immediately follows a passage affirming his sovereignty over unruly waters (vv. 3–4).

72. In addition, the heavens proclaim his righteousness (*ṣdq*)in 97:6, and the righteous person (*ṣdyq*) is mentioned in 97:11.

are bracketed by two other psalms that are themselves closely related, Psalms 95/100.

The thematic connections are also very close, the only difference being that Psalm 98 does not specifically mention other gods or idols, whereas Psalm 96 does. However, if the waters of Psalm 98 are understood as "gods" (mythopoeically),[73] the connections are even closer than normally imagined. The two psalms are even closely related structurally.

*The Data*

Lexical Repetitions (25):

Key-word links: *šyrw lYHWH šyr ḥdš*

*lpny YHWH ky bᵓ*
*[ky bᵓ] lšpṭ hᵓrṣ*
*yšpṭ-tbl bṣdq*
*wᶜmym b- . . .*

*YHWH, mlk*
*nplᵓwt*
*yrᶜm hym wmlᵓw*

Thematic word links: *yšwᶜh*
*gwym*
*rnn*
*ᵓmwnh*
*myšrym*
*kl-hᵓrṣ*
*dyn lšpṭ*
*qdš*

Incidental repetitions: *bwᵓ, ᶜśh*

Thematic Similarities:
YHWH's kingship
YHWH's sovereignty (over nature, earth, peoples, nations)
Praise motifs

Structure/Genre Similarities:
Both are Kingship of YHWH hymns
Poetic (hymnic) structure:
Opening calls to praise and reasons for praise
Renewed calls to praise
"YHWH is King!"
Closing (calls to) praise and reasons for praise

73. See above, on *nhrwt* in Psalms 93 and 98, pp. 39–40 and 115.

*Key-Word Links*

*Repeated Clauses.* We encounter an embarrasment of riches in key-word links between Psalms 96 and 98. Several identical clauses occur in their entirety in both psalms. Pride of place goes to the two opening calls to worship, which are identical: *šyrw lYHWH šyr ḥdš* 'sing to YHWH a new song!' (96:1, 98:1).

Second, the psalms end almost identically, with an even more extensive duplication: Ps 98:9 almost exactly replicates 96:13:

Psalm 96:13
13a *lpny YHWH ky bʾ*
b *ky bʾ lšpṭ hʾrṣ*
c *yšpṭ-tbl bṣdq*
d *wʿmym bʾmwntw*

13a Before YHWH, for he comes,
b For he comes to judge the earth;
c He will judge the world with (his) righteousness,
d And the peoples with his faithfulness!

Psalm 98:9
9a *lpny-YHWH ky bʾ*
b [*ky bʾ*] *lšpṭ hʾrṣ*
c *yšpṭ-tbl bṣdq*
d *wʿmym bmyšrym*

9a Before YHWH, for he comes,
b [For he comes] to judge the earth;
c He will judge the world with righteousness,
d And the peoples with equity.

The only difference between the two verses[74] is in the word used for the instrument of YHWH's judgment: in 96:13, it is 'his faithfulness' (*ʾmwntw*), whereas in 98:9, it is 'equity' (*myšrym*).

A third identical clause is found in Pss 96:11b and 98:7a: *yrʿm hym wmlʾw* 'let the sea roar, and all that fills it!' This clause is the most important link between 96:11–12 and 98:7–8 and will be explored further below, under "Structural Connections" (pp. 148–49).

*Repeated Key Words.* Even beyond the exact repetitions of significant

74. In the MT there is one other difference between these two verses: *ky bʾ* 'for he comes' occurs only once in 98:9, whereas it occurs twice in 96:13. However, in chapter 3, I have restored *ky bʾ* in 98:9 on textual grounds, and consequently, the difference between the verses amounts to only one word. Nevertheless, even if the MT is followed, the congruity between the two verses is strikingly obvious.

clauses, the vocabulary of the two psalms still has a great deal in common. First, YHWH as King appears in both psalms, with the phrase *YHWH mlk* 'YHWH reigns!' embedded in 96:10 and the phrase *hmlk YHWH* 'the King, YHWH' appearing in 98:6.

Second, YHWH works wonders (*nplʾwt*) in both psalms (96:3, 98:1). This is a particularly significant pair of occurrences, since the term *nplʾwt* is not otherwise found in Psalms 93–100, and elsewhere in Book IV it is found only in Psalms 105 and 106, two psalms that are also closely related to each other.

A third, very significant repetition appears in the sections on YHWH's judgment, in 96:10c and 98:9c. Both verses affirm that YHWH will judge the peoples with equity (*myšrym*). The verbs of judging are different—in 96:10 the verb is *dyn*, whereas in 98:9 it is *špṭ*—but the ideas are the same.

Fourth, YHWH's faithfulness (*ʾmwnh*) in 96:13 is echoed in 98:3. The contexts are slightly different, but YHWH's righteousness (*šdq*[*h*]) is poetically parallel with his faithfulness in both cases, strengthening the connections (96:13, 98:2).

*Thematic Connections*

Psalms 96 and 98 are also closely related thematically. Both are rich in imperatives of praise (96:1–3, 7–9;[75] 98:1, 4–6[76] ). Both speak of YHWH's characteristic acts, such as salvation, judgment, doing wonders (Watts's thematic category D). Both show YHWH's sovereignty over elements of nature (96:11–12, 98:7–8) and over the earth, peoples, and nations (96:1–3, 7, 9, 13; 98:2–4, 9). For example, YHWH's salvation (*yšwʿh*) is made known in both psalms: by the worshipers in 96:2 and by YHWH in 98:2, 3. Second, the nations (*gwym*) and the peoples (*ʿmym*) receive the revelation of YHWH's power and righteousness (*gwym*: 96:3, 10; 98:2; *ʿmym*: 96:3). They are involved in worship of him (96:7) and receive his judgment (96:10, 13; 98:9).

The phrase *kl-hʾrṣ* 'all the earth' conveys an idea common to all the Kingship of YHWH psalms, including 96 and 98 (96:1, 9; 98:4).[77] As I mentioned above, "the characteristic and unique expectation of these Psalms that *all the earth*, all peoples, or the nations should be present" is one of the five characteristic motifs of the Kingship of YHWH psalms (Watts 1965: 343, emphasis mine).[78]

75. And see also the jussives in vv. 11–12.

76. See also the jussives in vv. 7–8.

77. And compare Ps 98:3c: *kl-ʾpsy-ʾrṣ* 'all the ends of the earth'.

78. Pss 96:1b and 98:4a go beyond merely containing the phrase *kl-hʾrṣ*. They are almost identical, differing only in the verb of praise employed:

96:1b: *šyrw lYHWH kl-hʾrṣ*
98:4a: *hryʿw lYHWH kl-hʾrṣ*.

Another set of thematic connections is apparent in the complex of words and ideas communicating YHWH's ways of dealing with the world and its peoples in righteousness, faithfulness, and equity. There are four loci for these connections: 96:10c, 13c–d; 98:2b–3a, 9b–c. I have already pointed out two of these connections, 96:13 and 98:9, but the presence of 96:10 and 98:2–3 highlights the thematic connections even more. Each passage is linked with each other one by repeated words or phrases:

Psalm 96
10c *ydyn ʿmym bmyšrym*
c He will judge peoples with equity.

13c *yšpṭ-tbl bṣdq*
d *wʿmym bʾmwntw*
13c He will judge the world with (his) righteousness,
d And the peoples with his faithfulness!

Psalm 98
2b *lʿyny hgwym*
c *glh ṣdqtw*
3a *zkr ḥsdw [lyʿqb]*

2b In the eyes of the nations—
c He has revealed his righteousness.
3a He has remembered his steadfast love [to Jacob]

9b *[ky bʾ] lšpṭ hʾrṣ*
c *yšpṭ-tbl bṣdq*
d *wʿmym bmyšrym*

9b [For he comes] to judge the earth.
c He will judge the world with righteousness,
d And the peoples with equity.

YHWH's judgments, righteousness, covenant faithfulness, equity, and sovereignty over the nations are all emphasized in these verses.

*Structural Connections*

*Individual Psalm Sections.* I have already described above (p. 146) the virtually exact structural repetition of Ps 96:13 in Ps 98:9. It is also striking that the sections immediately preceding them, Pss 96:11–12 and 98:7–8, are similar. They express essentially identical ideas, since they are both exhortations to the various elements of nature to join in the joyful worship of YHWH. This repetition is expressed lexically by the verb *rnn* 'sing for joy' in 96:12 and 98:8. The elements of nature instructed to praise YHWH are the heavens, earth, sea, field, and trees in 96:11–12, and they are the sea, world, floods, and mountains in 98:7–8. Thus, both psalms end with significant sections that urge nature to praise YHWH and affirm YHWH's coming to judge all things (96:11–13, 98:7–9).

*Overall Psalm Structure.* Structurally, the two psalms might appear at first glance to be dissimilar. As analyzed in chapter 3, Psalm 96 divides into two main units (vv. 1–6, 7–13), composed of five sections: I (vv. 1–3); II (vv. 4–6); III (vv. 7–9); IV (v. 10); V (vv. 11–13). By contrast, Psalm 98 separates into only three sections: I (vv. 1–3); II (vv. 4–6); III (vv. 7–9). Closer analysis, however, reveals the structure to be quite similar:

| | |
|---|---|
| Call to praise (I) | 96:1–3 // 98:1a |
| Reasons for praise | 96:4–6 // 98:1b–3 |
| Call to praise (II) | 96:7–9 // 98:4–6 |
| Bridge | 96:10 // ——— |
| Call to praise (III) | 96:11–12 // 98:7–8 |
| Reasons for praise | 96:13 // 98:9 |

The major structural difference between the psalms is in the presence of Ps 96:10, which has no counterpart in Psalm 98. As I observed in the discussion of Psalm 96 (above, pp. 64–66), this verse serves as a bridge between the earlier and later portions of the psalm. It repeats motifs mentioned earlier, and it also introduces a new motif, that of YHWH's kingship. Ps 96:11–13 then elaborates on the implications of YHWH's kingship, urging the elements of nature to praise him. However, the motif of YHWH as King is already present in Psalm 98 (v. 6b), at precisely the same juncture where it appears in Psalm 96, namely, immediately before the concluding sections that exhort nature to praise YHWH.

Thus, structurally, the two psalms are indeed very much alike. The first set of reasons for praise is different in each case. In 96:4–6, the reasons are YHWH's status as Creator and sovereign over other gods and, in 98:1b–3, they are his status as Israel's covenant God, worker of wonders, and salvation. There are other variations in content as well, but the overall structural similarities are striking nevertheless.

*Excursus: A Note on Composition*

The close correspondence in content and structure argues against entirely independent composition for Psalms 96 and 98. However, the question of dependence—that is, whether Psalm 98 was condensed from Psalm 96 or Psalm 96 was expanded from Psalm 98—is impossible to answer with any certainty.[79] There is not enough evidence to determine whether one was significantly earlier than the other. It is easier to explain additions to a text than omissions, however, and one can speculate that Psalm 98 was the (earlier) basis for Psalm 96, for this reason.

### *Psalm 96 and Psalm 99*

Psalms 96 and 99 are the first and last in the core string of Kingship of YHWH psalms in the 93–100 section. They have less in common with each other than they do with the others in the core string, however. The strongest connections of Psalm 96 are with Psalms 97 and 98, and the strongest connections of Psalm 99 are with the same two psalms. Psalms 95 and 100 bracket the section as a discrete unit. Psalms 96 and 99 have 18 words in common, but most of these merely relate to the general perspectives of the Kingship of YHWH psalms or of other praise psalms.

*The Data*

Lexical Repetitions (18):

| | |
|---|---|
| Key-word links: | *YHWH mlk* |
| | *nwrʾ, šm* |
| Thematic word links: | *ʾrṣ* |
| | *ʿmym* |
| | *gdwl* |
| | *qdš* |
| | *ʿz* |
| | *ʿśh* |
| | *ḥwh* |
| | *myšrym* |
| | *(m)špṭ* |
| Incidental repetitions: | *nśʾ, kwn, hwʾ,* particles (*kl, ʿl*) |

Thematic Similarities:
- YHWH's kingship
- YHWH's sovereignty (over earth, peoples)
- Worship motifs

Structure/Genre Similarities:
- Both are Kingship of YHWH hymns
- Parallelism between 96:10 and 99:4

79. One scholar who contended that they came from the same hand was Briggs (1907: 296–313). Indeed, he theorized that Psalms 93 and 96–100 were originally one long, unified composition (presumably composed by one person or group), to which numerous glosses were added to produce the present final forms.

*Key-Word Links*

The clause YHWH *mlk* naturally binds these two psalms together (Pss 96:10, 99:1),[80] and it is the most important (and perhaps the only) key-word link between them.

Two terms that may be considered key words occur only in Psalms 96 and 99 out of the 93–100 group.[81] First, the participle *nwrᵓ* 'awesome, fearsome, frightening' occurs in 96:4 and 99:3, describing YHWH or his name. This is the only occurrence of the form in Psalms 93–100; it occurs again in Book IV only in Ps 106:22, describing acts of YHWH.[82] Second, the name (*šm*) of YHWH is particularly visible here. It occurs 4 times in these two psalms: 96:2, 8; 99:3, 6.[83] In the first 3 cases, YHWH's name is to be acclaimed; in the 4th instance (99:6), Moses and Aaron called upon YHWH's name.[84]

*Thematic Connections*

As in most psalms of the genre, YHWH's sovereignty over the earth and the peoples or nations is prominent in Psalms 96 and 99. Pss 96:1, 9, 10, 11, 13, and 99:1 depict his sovereignty in relation to the earth (*ᵓrṣ, tbl*), while 96:3, 5, 7, 10, 13 and 99:1, 2 reveal his sovereignty over the peoples (*ᶜmym*) or nations (*gwym*). However, Psalm 99 does not contain the specific theme of YHWH's sovereignty over other gods and idols that is contained in Psalms 96 and 97.

There are also other lexical correspondences that, though they are somewhat random, nevertheless represent similar themes. (1) *Gdwl* 'great' occurs in both 96:4 and 99:2 to describe YHWH and in 99:3 to describe his name. (2) YHWH or his appearance is holy (*qdš*) in 96:9 and 99:3, 5, 9. (3) Strength (*ᶜz*) belongs to YHWH in 96:6, 7, and he is called the Strong (= Victorious) One in 99:4. (4) YHWH is the Creator of the heavens (96:5) and of justice and righteousness (99:4); the common root is *ᶜśh* 'to make'. (5) The root *ḥwh* 'to worship, prostrate oneself' occurs in 96:9 and 99:5, 9. None of these terms occurs in any identical phrases or clauses, however, and none in identical or related structural positions; they are significant only in showing the general thematic correspondences between the two psalms.

All of these connections show the overlapping themes of the psalms. However, the general tone and mood of the psalms are different. Psalm 96 consists of more purely hymnic elements, and a note of joy runs through

80. Ps 99:4 also refers to YHWH as King.

81. Their function in structuring the section, however, was probably negligible.

82. None of the related words formed from *yrᵓ* 'to fear' occurs at all in Psalms 93–100.

83. The word *šm* occurs again among Psalms 93–100 only in Ps 100:4.

84. *Zkr* (rendered 'name' in context) is found in 97:12, so the idea is not exclusive to these two psalms; however, the term *šm* is found especially concentrated here.

it. Psalm 99 acclaims YHWH as King but emphasizes his awe-inspiring qualities.

*Structural Connections*

Two facts stand out about the structure of Psalms 96 and 99. First, Pss 96:10 and 99:4 are similar in some ways. As noted above, 99:4 introduces the second section of its psalm, and it roughly parallels 99:1, which is linked to 96:10 by the clause *YHWH mlk*. Both 96:10 and 99:4 contain the following ideas: (1) YHWH is King; (2) YHWH is Judge (he judges in 96:10c and loves and creates justice in 99:4a, c); (3) YHWH is concerned with equity (he judges with equity in 96:10c and establishes equity in 99:4b); and (4) YHWH firmly establishes things (he establishes the world in 96:10b and equity in 99:4b). It is doubtful that one psalm was consciously drawn from the other, however, since the ideas they express are common to most psalms of the genre.

Psalm 96:10
10a *ʾmrw bgwym YHWH mlk*
b *ʾp-tkwn tbl bl-tmwṭ*
c *ydyn ʿmym bmyšrym*

10a Say among the nations, "YHWH reigns!
b Surely the world is established! It is unmoveable.
c He will judge peoples with equity."

Psalm 99
4a *wʿz mlk mšpṭ ʾhb*
b *ʾth kwnnt myšrym*
c *mšpṭ wṣdqh byʿqb*
d *ʾth ʿśyt*

4a Indeed, the Victorious One is King! He loves justice!
b You have established equity;
c Justice and righteousness in Jacob—
d You have wrought (them).

The second fact about the structure of the two psalms is that 99:6–8 is only marginally related to the rest of the psalm, departing as it does from the adulatory themes concerning YHWH the King (as I noted in the discussion of Psalm 99 [pp. 88–89]). This analysis is supported by the fact that all of the connections between this psalm and Psalm 96 appear in vv. 1–5, 9 (with the exception of *šm* in v. 6). The themes that make this psalm characteristic of the Kingship of YHWH genre are also advanced in vv. 1–5 and 9. Verses 6–8 do fit the overall scheme of the psalm (as noted), but the links with Psalm 96 occur mainly in the other parts of the psalm.

### *Psalm 96 and Psalm 100*

Because of its general hymnic nature, Psalm 96 has many links with Psalm 100 (another hymn), even though Psalm 100 is not a Kingship of YHWH psalm. The two psalms have 15 words in common, which is striking, since the body of Psalm 100 only has a total of 32 different words. Aside from particles, the words shared are part of the common vocabulary of praise. However, their connections do not significantly contribute to the structuring of Book IV.

*The Data*

Lexical Repetitions (15):

| | |
|---|---|
| Key-word links: | none |
| Thematic word links: | *brkw šmw* |
| | *bʾw . . . ḥṣr(w)t* |
| | *hll* / *thlh* |
| | *rnn(h)* |
| | *kl-hʾrṣ* |
| | *ʿśh* |
| | *ʾmwnh* |
| Incidental repetitions: | *ʿm*, *YHWH*, *hwʾ*, particles (*lpny*, *ky*) |

Thematic Similarities:
- Praise motifs
- YHWH's sovereignty (over earth)
- YHWH as Creator

Structure/Genre Similarities:
- Both are hymns
- Hymnic structure (initial and final calls to praise and reasons for praise)

*Key-word Links*

No true key-word links exist between these two psalms. Several words are repeated—including the clause *brkw šmw* 'bless his name!'—but all of these words are part of the general vocabulary of praise.

*Thematic Connections*

The clause *brkw šmw* 'bless his name!' appears in 96:2 and 100:4. The vocabulary of praise (*hll*: 96:4; *thlh*: 100:4) and joyful singing (*rnn*:

96:12; *rnnh*: 100:2) is found in both. Liturgical instructions to enter (*bwʾ*) his courts (*ḥṣr*[*w*]*t*) are found in 96:8 and 100:4a–b. All the earth (*kl-hʾrṣ*) is instructed to join in the praise at the outset of both psalms (96:1 and 100:1).

The roots *ʿm* 'people', *ʿśh* 'to make', and *ʾmwnh* 'faithfulness' are found in both psalms, but in different contexts. In Psalm 96, YHWH is over the peoples (vv. 3, 5, 7, 10, 13) and he is the Creator of the heavens (v. 5). In Psalm 100, *ʿm* refers to Israel and *ʿśh* to YHWH's creation of Israel as a nation. YHWH's faithfulness is to the peoples in 96:13 and to all generations (of his people) in 100:5.

### *Summary of Psalm 96 in Context*

Psalm 96 is one of the most important psalms for the structure of Psalms 93–100. Its assertion in v. 10—*YHWH mlk* / *ʾp-tkwn tbl bl-tmwṭ* 'YHWH reigns! Surely the world is established! It is unmovable'—echoes three clauses from 93:1 verbatim and serves as a strong tie between the first Kingship of YHWH psalm and the rest, which are somewhat removed from it in their present position. It combines the short assertions of YHWH's majesty in Psalm 93 and the joyful praise in Ps 95:1–7c to form the first psalm of completely unfettered praise in the group.

Psalm 96 dominates the group of four Kingship of YHWH psalms that appears between the frame of Psalms 95 and 100. In this group joyful, unfettered praise in Psalms 96 and 98 alternates with more restrained praise in Psalms 97 and 99, psalms that focus to a greater extent on YHWH's awesome and terrible majesty.

The strongest links between Psalm 96 and another psalm are with Psalm 98. Of the 25 words that they share, only 2 have no true significance structurally. Large complexes of words are repeated verbatim, most notably in the first and last verse of each psalm. In addition to these repetitions, several other key-word links bind the two psalms: *YHWH mlk*, *nplʾwt*, *dyn*/*špṭ*, *ʾmwnh*, and *ṣdq*[*h*]. The two psalms are even closely related structurally.

Psalm 96 also has important ties with the psalm immediately following it. This is significant because it has fewer ties with the last psalm in the 96–99 group; since the group is arranged in an alternating A-B-A′-B′ pattern, the placement of each psalm is important. Several important concatenations link Psalms 96 and 97; Psalms 96 and 98 are most strongly linked; Psalm 96 has fewest links with Psalm 99. However, Psalm 99 has stronger links with its adjacent psalm (98) and especially with its partner in the alternating pattern (97).

Because of the concluding, bracketing function of Psalm 100, Psalm 96 has no important ties with it, beyond the general vocabulary of community praise.

## Psalm 97 in Context

### *Psalm 97 and Psalm 98*

As one would expect between two psalms of the Kingship of YHWH genre, Psalms 97 and 98 share many words and themes, although not as many as most other pairs of psalms in the 96–99 group. This is because Psalm 98 is most strongly linked to Psalm 96, whereas Psalm 97 is to Psalm 99. Psalms 97 and 98 have 14 words and several themes in common.

*The Data*

Lexical Repetitions (14):

| | |
|---|---|
| Key-word links: | *YHWH, mlk* |
| | *qdš, zkr, ḥsd* |
| Thematic word links: | *ṣdq(h)* |
| | *(m)špṭ* |
| | *kl-hʾrṣ* |
| | *tbl* |
| | *ʿmym* |
| | *rʾh* |
| | *ṣywn, yhwdh / byt yśrʾl* |
| Incidental repetitions: | particles (*ky, lpny*) |

Thematic Similarities:

- YHWH's kingship
- YHWH's sovereignty (over earth, peoples, nature)
- YHWH's work, power, glory displayed
- Covenantal motifs
- Praise motifs

Structure/Genre Similarities:

- Both psalms are Kingship of YHWH hymns
- Chiastic arrangement of themes

*Key-Word Links*

*YHWH* and *mlk* are the primary key-word links between Psalms 97 and 98 (97:1, 98:6). Along with the thematic links that accompany these words (see below), they function as a concatenation linking adjacent psalms. The word *qdš* occurs at the end of Psalm 97 and again at the beginning of Psalm 98, demonstrating this concatenation principle, as well. YHWH's holy (*qdš*) name and arm appear in 97:12 and 98:1. Two other words illustrating the concatenation principle are *ḥsd* and *zkr*. The first refers to devoted followers of YHWH in 97:10 and YHWH's steadfast love for his people in 98:3. The second appears as YHWH's 'name' (or 'memory') in 97:12 and as his activity of remembering in 98:3. A significant concatenation of structure and theme is also apparent (see below, "Structural Similarities").

*Thematic Connections*

*Thematic Word Links.* According to Watts (1965), Psalms 97 and 98 are closely linked thematically, since Psalm 97 contains all five themes that he isolated, and Psalm 98 lacks only a specific reference to other gods. For example, YHWH is a God of righteousness (*ṣdq*[*h*]) and justice ([*m*]*špṭ*) (97:2, 6, 8; 98:9), and both psalms state that these attributes are inextricably linked (97:2, 98:9). YHWH is sovereign over the earth and its peoples in both psalms. He is Lord of all the earth (*kl-hʾrṣ*: 97:5, 9; 98:3, 4); the earth and the world (*tbl*) are under him and respond to him (97:1, 4 [2×]; 98:7, 9 [2×]). He is over all peoples (*ʿmym*) as well (97:6, 98:9).

*Thematic Similarities.* In addition to the specific lexical links, YHWH's sovereignty is evident in the similar vocabulary of the praise sections in both psalms (marked by jussive and imperative verbs of praise): 97:1, 8; 98:4–6, 7–8. In these sections, all elements of nature are expected to praise him.

The idea of YHWH's display of power and glory is present in both psalms, associated with the root *rʾh* 'to see' and other terms. In 97:4, 6, and 98:3, his power, glory, and victory are seen by all peoples or all the earth, and this produces reactions of fear and awe. In Ps 98:2 YHWH's work on behalf of Israel is a testimony to him before the nations.

Israel, the covenant nation, is another explicit theme in both psalms, despite their universal outlook. Zion and Judah appear in 97:8 and the house of Israel in 98:3. Indeed, all of 98:1–3 focuses on YHWH's activities on behalf of Israel. This is one strand of the common thread running through every psalm in the section: YHWH's concern for his own people. The true followers of YHWH are also in view in 97:10–12, in the wisdom section.

*Structural Connections*

Psalms 97 and 98 are not organically linked, but there is a chiasm discernible between them that is striking. Both psalms include both universal sections and sections that focus on Israel. In the layout of the psalms, the sections on Israel are adjacent to each other and the universal sections are most distant. That is, in Psalm 97, the second and third sections (vv. 7–9, 10–12) focus most directly on Israel, and in Psalm 98, the first section (vv. 1–3) does. The universal themes in Psalm 97 are in the first section (vv. 1–6), and in Psalm 98 they are in the second and third sections (vv. 4–6, 7–9). Thus, there is a rough chiastic arrangement of themes between the psalms:

Psalm 97: (A) the world, (B) Israel;
Psalm 98: (B′) Israel, (A′) the world.

The significance of this chiasm goes beyond the repetition of a few words at the end of one psalm and the beginning of the next. There is a concatenation of themes between the psalms, as well. In the opening of Psalm 98 (vv. 1–3), YHWH's wondrous acts (*nplʾwt*) reveal his steadfast love and faithfulness to Israel. At the end of Psalm 97 (vv. 10–12), his steadfast love and faithfulness are not mentioned specifically, but they are certainly recalled by the language of the verses. The battle motifs behind references in 98:1–3 to his holy arm and to his salvation also are present in 97:10–11, in references to his preserving and delivering activities.

## *Psalm 97 and Psalm 99*

Psalm 97 is similar to Psalm 99 in a number of ways. However, they are not as striking as the links between Psalms 96 and 98. Psalms 97 and 99 have 19 lexemes in common, including particles. This is more than Psalm 99 shares with any other psalm and more than Psalm 97 shares with any except Psalm 96, though many of the repetitions between 97 and 99 are incidental and there are not a large number of strong links. While many of the repeated words are used in similar ways, we do not find the exact repetition of several clauses that we find in Psalms 96 and 98. Nevertheless, several key-word links and numerous other thematic word links do exist.

### *The Data*

Lexical Repetitions (19):

| | |
|---|---|
| Key-word links: | *YHWH mlk* |
| | *ʿnn* |
| | *ṣywn* |

Thematic word links: *ᵓrṣ*
*ᶜmym*
*(m) kwn*
*mšpṭ*
*ṣdq(h)*
*qdš*
*ydh*
*ḥwh*

Incidental repetitions: *šmr, ᵓhb, hr, myšrym, ᵓth,* particles (*kl, ᶜl*)

Thematic Similarities:
YHWH's kingship
YHWH's sovereignty (over earth, peoples)
Covenantal motifs
Zion motifs

Structure/Genre Similarities:
Both are Kingship of YHWH hymns

*Key-Word Links*

The clause *YHWH mlk* begins each psalm and obviously binds them closely together (even more closely than others of the Kingship of YHWH grouping, which may have the clause in the middle of the psalm [e.g., Psalm 96] or may not have exactly the same clause at all [e.g., Psalms 95, 98]). This clause sounds the keynote for Psalms 97 and 99.

Both introductory clauses are followed by two jussive clauses urging the hearer to employ a particular attitude that flows from the implications of YHWH's kingship. In Psalm 97, this attitude is joy (vv. 1a and b), which is echoed in vv. 8 and 12. In contrast, the attitude enjoined in Psalm 99 is fear or awe (vv. 1a and b), and it is carried through the psalm; there are no verbs of joyful worship such as *gyl, śmḥ, šyr,* or *rnn* in Psalm 99.

Besides the introductory kingship clause, two other lexical connections are worth mentioning: cloud and Zion. First, Ps 99:6–8 mentions Moses and Aaron as priests, and v. 7a recalls the pillar of cloud (*ᶜnn*), the symbol of the theophany in which YHWH spoke. Ps 97:2a also mentions a cloud (*ᶜnn*) and thick darkness surrounding YHWH, another theophanic vision. These two verses contain the only 2 uses of the term *ᶜnn* in Psalms 93–100. In fact, the term only occurs twice more in the entire Psalter (Pss 78:14, 105:39), both times specifically harking back to the Exodus cloud. Out of 87 occurrences of *ᶜnn* in Biblical Hebrew, BDB (s.v.) classifies 58 as references to the theophanic cloud, including several that do not refer specifically to the Exodus cloud: see especially the cloud associated with the dedication of the Temple (1 Kgs 8:10,

11 // 2 Chr 5:13, 14). The Temple and Zion are the later counterparts of the Tabernacle and Sinai: YHWH is present and his name dwells in them.

'Zion' occurs in both psalms, in 97:8 and 99:2. It is used in two different contexts, but in both it serves as a reminder of where YHWH is enthroned: (1) the theophanic vision in 97:2–6 can be understood as emanating from Zion, where YHWH reigns; and (2) Zion appears as his footstool and holy mountain in 99:5, 9.

These occurrences of 'cloud' and 'Zion' are the only ones in Psalms 93–100, and they function as key words linking the psalms.[85] They show that Zion is the earthly site of YHWH's throne and that he now reveals himself there.

*Thematic Connections*

Both psalms display the motif of YHWH's sovereignty over all the earth, lands, and peoples that is characteristic of the Kingship of YHWH group. The earth (*ʾrṣ*) appears in the context of his sovereignty in 97:1, 4, 5, 9 and 99:1; the peoples (*ʿmym*) in 97:6 and 99:1, 2; and coastlands (*ʾyym*: 97:1), mountains (*hrym*: 97:5), and gods (*ʾlhym*: 97:7, 9) are likewise under him in Psalm 97. A related motif is YHWH's secure position and the security that flows from it. The foundation (*mkwn*) of his throne is righteousness and justice in 97:2. His establishment (*kwn*) of equity is closely related to the justice and righteousness that he achieves in 99:4.

The themes of YHWH's justice/judgment (*mšpṭ*) and righteousness (*ṣdq*[*h*]) are present in both psalms. The word *mšpṭ* occurs only once in 97:2 and twice in 99:4. It also appears in 97:8c, where Zion and the villages of Judah are glad because of his judgments. Verse 97:8c is linked with 99:4c, which mentions Jacob (= Judah) as the location of YHWH's execution of justice. In 97:2 and 99:4, YHWH's justice is also parallel with his righteousness (*ṣdq*[*h*]).

YHWH's holiness is a theme in both texts. The root *qdš* occurs in 97:12 and 99:3, 6, and 9 (2×). Pss 97:12b and 99:3a–b are particularly closely related, because both urge giving praise (*ydh*) to YHWH's name. In 97:12b, it is YHWH's 'holy name' (*zkr qdšw*), and in 99:3, YHWH's name, the Great and Awesome One (*šmk gdwl wnwrʾ*) is the source from which holiness flows.

## *Psalm 97 and Psalm 100*

The connections between Psalms 97 and 100 are only general, reflecting common hymnic genre and certain common themes, as is true of the

85. The only place *ʿnn* 'cloud' occurs again in Book IV is in Ps 105:39, as just noted; 'Zion' occurs again only in Psalm 102 (vv. 14, 17, 22).

relationship of Psalm 100 with all of the psalms in the immediately preceding group (Psalms 96–99). There are 11 words common to both Psalm 97 and Psalm 100. There is no repetition of phrases or clauses except for *kl-hʾrṣ*.

*The Data*

Lexical Repetitions (11):

| | |
|---|---|
| Key-word links: | none |
| Thematic word links: | *śmḥ(h)* |
| | *ydh* |
| | *hll* / *thlh* |
| | *kl-hʾrṣ* |
| Incidental repetitions: | *YHWH*, *ʿbd*, *ḥs(y)d*, particles (*ʿm*, *lpny*, *ky*) |

Thematic Similarities:
- Praise motifs
- YHWH's sovereignty (over earth)
- Covenantal motifs

Structure/Genre Similarities:
- Both are hymns
- Final focus on YHWH and his followers

*Thematic Connections*

The vocabulary of praise is the most notable common feature. Rejoicing (*śmḥ[h]*) is found in both psalms (97:1, 8, 11, 12; 100:2), as are thanksgiving (*ydh*: 97:12; 100:4 [2×]) and praise (*hll*: 97:7; *thlh*: 100:4). Other words of praise are found in 97:1, 8, 12 and 100:1–2, 4.

YHWH is over all the earth (*kl-hʾrṣ*) in both psalms: 97:5, 9; 100:1. More specifically, however, he is Israel's God (97:7–9 and 10–12; 100:3, 4–5). Both psalms end by especially focusing on YHWH's relationship with his devoted followers and his attitudes of steadfast love and faithfulness to them.

## *Summary of Psalm 97 in Context*

In v. 1, Psalm 97 continues the joyful exuberance of Psalm 96, but it quickly turns sober as it affirms YHWH's awesome majesty. It concludes with a sapiential affirmation of YHWH's relationship with those faithful to him. Many similarities in theme—concerning YHWH's attributes and people's praise of him—are found in the two psalms.

Several key words combine to provide a strong link between Psalms 97 and 98: *YHWH mlk*, *qdš*, *ḥsd*, and *zkr*. Psalm 98 resumes the more typical joyful and unrestrained praise found in Psalm 96 and elsewhere in the Psalter. A chiastic structure of themes also links Psalms 97 and 98.

Several key words also combine in Psalms 97 and 99 to form strong links, most notably *YHWH mlk*, *ʿnn*, and *ṣywn*. The two share other, more general thematic outlooks, including a more sober tone than the praise found in Psalms 96 and 98.

The connections between Psalm 97 and Psalm 100 are minimal, restricted primarily to the general vocabulary of praise.

## Psalm 98 in Context

### *Psalm 98 and Psalm 99*

Psalms 98 and 99 are both hymns of the Kingship of YHWH genre, by virtue of the reference to YHWH as King in 98:6 and 99:4 and the *YHWH mlk* clause in 99:1. They have 13 words in common and several key-word and thematic links.

*The Data*

Lexical Repetitions (13):
  Key-word links: *YHWH, mlk*
    *ʾrṣ, ʿmym*
    (*ṣdq*[*h*], [*m*]*špṭ, myšrym*)
  Thematic links: *qdš*
    *byt yśrʾl* / *yhwdh, ṣywn*
    *ʾlhynw*
    *ʿśh*
  Incidental repetitions: *yšb*, particles (*kl, ky*)

Thematic Similarities:
  YHWH's kingship
  YHWH's sovereignty (over earth, peoples)
  YHWH as Creator
  Covenantal motifs

Structure/Genre Similarities:
  Both are Kingship of YHWH hymns
  Anadiplosis (98:5–6, 99:6–7)
  Length

*Key-Word Links*

The description of YHWH as king in 98:6 and 99:4 and the *YHWH mlk* clause in 99:1 again form the most obvious and significant key-word links and a further example of concatenation between adjacent psalms.

Several other words also come together at the end of Psalm 98 and the beginning of Psalm 99 to exhibit a concatenation of ideas between the two psalms. First, the earth (*ʾrṣ*) and the peoples (*ʿmym*) are mentioned together in both 98:9 and 99:1; these are the only two places—aside from 96:13, which is identical to 98:9—in Psalms 93–100 that these two words are juxtaposed in parallel (or complementary) lines. Second, the other prominent words in 98:9 relate to YHWH's actions in judging: *špṭ* 'to judge', *ṣdq* 'righteousness', and *myšrym* 'equity'. Strikingly, all three of these roots appear in 99:4, which is parallel to 99:1.

*Thematic Connections*

Like most psalms of the genre, Psalms 98 and 99 both speak of YHWH as sovereign over peoples, nations, or nature. All the earth and nature are urged to praise him in 98:4–6, 7–8 and the earth and the peoples are commanded to fear him in 99:1.

YHWH's righteousness (*ṣdqh*) is revealed by means of his works on Israel's behalf (98:2, 99:4), and he will judge the world righteously (*bṣdq*: 98:9). YHWH's mountain and his power (literally, his arm) are holy (*qdš*: 98:1, 99:9).

YHWH often appears as Creator in the Kingship of YHWH psalms. In Psalms 98 and 99, he is seen fashioning (*ʿśh*), not nature or the world, but wonders (98:1) and justice and righteousness (99:4) on behalf of Israel in both psalms.

YHWH's relationship to Israel is also prominent in both psalms. The basis for the praise of YHWH that is urged in 98:7–8 is that he will judge the world with righteousness and equity (v. 9), a promise to the world that can be relied on because of what he has done for Israel specifically (vv. 1–3). This activity on Israel's behalf in vv. 1–3 is also the direct basis for the praise urged in vv. 4–6.

In Psalm 99, YHWH's relationship with Israel is also visible, first of all, in v. 4, where his activity in 'Jacob' is mentioned; and second of all, in vv. 6–8, where Moses, Aaron, Samuel, the pillar of cloud, and YHWH's holy mountain all are mentioned. Further evidence of YHWH's relationship with his people in Psalm 99 is found in the commands to worship at Zion (vv. 2, 5, 9). The repeated use of the term 'our God' (*ʾlhynw*) is another confirmation of the relationship (98:3; 99:5, 8, 9 [2×]).

## *Psalm 98 and Psalm 100*

Psalms 98 and 100, both hymns, have 13 words in common. Both are characterized by similar hymnic vocabulary, including one identical imperatival clause concerning praise. They also are the only two psalms in the 93–100 group that have a superscription.

*The Data*

Lexical Repetitions (13):

| | |
|---|---|
| Key-word links: | *hryᶜw lYHWH kl-hᵓrṣ* |
| Thematic links: | *mzmwr* |
| | *rnn(h)* |
| | *ḥsd* |
| | *ᵓmwnh* |
| | *ᵓlhynw* |
| Incidental repetitions: | *ᶜśh, ᶜm, bwᵓ*, particles (*ky, ᵓt*) |

Thematic Similarities:
- Praise motifs
- YHWH's sovereignty (over earth)
- Covenantal motifs

Structure/Genre Similarities:
- Superscriptions (*mzmwr*)
- Both are hymns
- Parallel calls to praise (98:4–6, 100:1–2)
- Final reasons for praise (98:9, 100:5)

*Key-Word Links*

The most notable repetition between the psalms is the congruity between 98:4a and 100:1a: they contain identical imperatival calls to praise: *hryᶜw lYHWH kl-hᵓrṣ* 'Raise a glad cry to YHWH, all the earth!'[86]

*Thematic Connections*

The thematic connections occur in the vocabulary of praise and YHWH's attributes. *Rnn* 'to sing for joy' appears in 98:4, 8 and *rnnh* in 100:2. Other hymnic terms are found throughout both psalms, in 98:1, 4–6, 7–8, and 100:1–2, 4. The reference to *kl-hᵓrṣ* is typical of the genre, as noted previously.

Two of YHWH's attributes, his steadfast love (*ḥsd*) and his faithfulness (*ᵓmwnh*) are paired with each other in both psalms (98:3, 100:5), a pairing that is fairly common.[87] Each word occurs again in Psalms 93–100 only once. In Psalms 98 and 100, they refer to YHWH's goodness to Israel. The references to 'God' (*ᵓlhy*[*m*]: 98:3d, 100:3a) emphasize the fact that YHWH is Israel's particular God.

*Structure/Genre Connections*

Psalms 98 and 100 are the only two psalms among Psalms 93–100 that have a superscription. It is simply *mzmwr* 'a psalm' in Psalm 98, whereas

86. The imperative of *rwᶜ* occurs also in 98:6.

87. According to Jepsen (1977: 319), about one-third of the references to YHWH's *ᵓmwnh* in the Hebrew Bible occur parallel to his *ḥsd*.

in Psalm 100, it is longer, *mzmwr ltwdh* 'a psalm of thanksgiving'. Psalm 100 is the first of a short string of four psalms with superscriptions. The recurrence of *mzmwr* in Psalm 100 serves to bind 98 and 100 loosely together.

*Summary of Psalm 98 in Context*

As the Kingship of YHWH section (Psalms 96–99) draws to a close, the final thematic connections among them are visible between 98 and 99. A few key words link 98 and 99 by concatenation, and they also share some common themes. However, Psalm 98 has stronger links with Psalm 96, and so does 99 with 97, as I have mentioned above.

The two most important ties between Psalm 98 and Psalm 100 are (1) a repeated imperatival call to praise in 98:1 and 100:1 and (2) the presence of a superscription in each.

## Psalm 99 in Context

*Psalm 99 and Psalm 100*

Both Psalm 99 and Psalm 100 are most significantly related to psalms already discussed, most notably Psalm 95 with Psalm 100 and Psalm 97 with Psalm 99. Both Psalms 99 and 100 are hymns, and they share 10 words, but there are few significant links between them.

Psalm 100 functions with Psalm 95 to frame the core Kingship of YHWH group (96–99). It does share a Zion outlook with Psalm 99, but, otherwise, few strong links can be seen.

*The Data*

Lexical Repetitions (10):

| | |
|---|---|
| Key-word links: | none |
| Thematic links: | *šm* |
| | *YHWH*, *ʾlhym* |
| | *ydh* |
| Incidental repetitions: | *ʾrṣ*, *ʿm*, *ʿśh*, *hwʾ*, particles (*kl*, *ky*) |

Thematic Similarities:
- Praise motifs
- Covenantal motifs
- Zion/Temple

Structure/Genre Similarities:
- Both hymns
- Universal openings narrow to focus on Israel

*Key-Word Links*

No key-word links exist between Psalms 99 and 100, and they are the only two psalms in the 93–100 group that do not have a significant concatenation of key words. A concatenation of themes does obtain, however, in the emphasis in both psalms on worship on Zion.

*Thematic Connections*

From a lexical standpoint, the prominence of YHWH's name (*šm*) in the two psalms at least deserves notice (99:3, 6; 100:4), since the only other occurrence of the word in Psalms 93–100 is in Psalm 96.

Thematically, both psalms, as hymns, praise YHWH in similar ways: compare the refrains in Psalm 99 (vv. 6, 9, and even v. 3) with the calls to praise in Ps 100:1–2, 4. The most significant thematic link, however, is the focus on the covenant people, Israel, in both psalms: references to 'YHWH our God' (*YHWH ʾlhynw*) in Psalm 99 (vv. 5, 8, 9 [2×]) and a similar view of YHWH as Israel's God in 100:3. Furthermore, while both psalms open with a vision of YHWH as sovereign over all creation and peoples, each narrows its focus and recalls the period of the Exodus in one way or another (99:6–8, 100:3). However, as I noted in chapter 3 on Psalm 99, the narrower themes of the Exodus and related motifs are also fused with (or subordinated to) the Zion motif in the overall outlook of each psalm's final form. In Psalm 99, Moses and Aaron are important as men who called on YHWH and obeyed him, but these acts are now (at the time of the writing of the psalm) to be done at Zion, at YHWH's holy mountain. In Psalm 100, YHWH's people, whom he made (v. 3), are to worship him within his gates and his courts (which were on Zion). Thus, worship at Jerusalem emerges as a common motif in both.

## *Summary of Psalm 99 in Context*

Psalm 100 brings the middle section of Book IV (consisting of Psalms 95–100) to an appropriate close. Its strongest connections are with Psalm 95, and the two form a frame around four Kingship of YHWH psalms. The links of Psalm 100 with Psalm 99, as a result, are minimal. Both do praise YHWH, however, and they do focus on his covenantal relationship with his people, which is to be expressed through worship at Zion.

# *Chapter 5*
# *The Structure of Psalms 93–100*

At this point, I propose to draw the outlines of the Psalms 93–100 section in sharper relief, highlighting the most significant points made above. As I observed in chapter 1, Psalms 93–100 form a logically coherent grouping and yet, at the same time, a somewhat artificial one. It appears that the overarching contour of Book IV consists of a tripartite division made up of Psalms 90–94, 95–100, and 101–6.[1]

Despite the somewhat artificial nature of the Psalms 93-100 grouping, the arguments I advanced in chapter 1 (pp. 21–22) about the group's coherence are significant. Furthermore, we have now seen significant links (concatenations) between consecutive psalms in every case but one (Psalms 99 and 100) among Psalms 93–100. Also, significant links exist between several nonadjacent psalms, links that contribute to the shaping of the section. The thoughts expressed throughout the section alternate between hymnic praise motivated by joy and hymnic praise motivated by reverence, fear, or awe. The overall thought progression, however, is one of increasing confidence in YHWH.

In this chapter, I focus on the structure of the Psalms 93–100 section,[2] but I also consider, at least briefly, the larger context of Book IV (90–106). Thus, I shall begin with the end of Book III, giving more attention to the material preceding Psalms 93–100 than the material following them, because of the necessary background that Book III and Psalms 90–92 provide for the 93–100 group.

1. H. V. D. Parunak has stimulated my thinking in this direction. Zenger (1991), on the other hand, identifies Book IV's structure as follows: Psalms 90–92, 93–100, 101–4, 105–6 (or, in his 1994 work, as follows: Psalms 90–92, 93–100, 101–6). His observations are well taken (see also below, p. 181 n. 20), but they do not fully account for the tightly knit structure of Psalms 96–99 framed by the similar Psalms 95 and 100. Psalms 95–100 form the centerpiece for a "concentric," tripartite analysis. The observations I shall make below concerning the pivotal nature of Psalm 94 argue that its role is to bind Psalms 93–100 together as a unit, while echoing Psalms 90–92 (thus justifying both a tripartite cycle of 5–6 psalms per cycle and also a unity among Psalms 93–100).

2. My discussion here may also be supplemented by the individual summaries in each section of chapter 4.

## Psalms 73–89

McCann (1993a) and Wilson (1985a) have pointed out the emphasis on laments and problems with the Davidic Covenant[3] in Book III. As Book III draws to a close, Psalm 89 ends on an inconclusive note (Wilson 1985a: 212–14). The Davidic Covenant is strongly affirmed in the psalm (vv. 4–5, 20–38[3–4, 19–37]), but it is described as being in the distant past, v. 20[19], "in days of old you spoke in a vision," and v. 50[49], "your tender mercies of old." More importantly, it is shown to be broken (vv. 39–46[38–45]). Note especially vv. 39–40[38–39]:

> (39) But you: you have cast off and rejected, yes, you have been most angry with your anointed one. (40) You have renounced the covenant with your servant; you have defiled his crown in the dust.

As a result, the psalm ends with a classic lament form (vv. 47–52[46–51]). Notice v. 47[46], for example: "How long, O YHWH? Will you hide yourself for ever? How long will your wrath burn like fire?" This lament asks for deliverance from the present state of meaningless existence (see the root *šwʾ* 'futility, vanity', v. 48[47]) and restoration of YHWH's *ḥesed* of old (v. 50[49]).

Psalm 89 is not the only one that sounds such discordant notes. They begin in Psalm 73 (McCann 1993a). Psalm 89 itself is preceded by the starkest, bleakest expression of lament in the Psalter, Psalm 88. Book III thus begins on a questioning note and also ends with a pair of psalms in which the psalmists doubt or question God.

Within the larger contours of the Psalter, the juncture between Psalms 89 and 90 forms a significant turning point, since the mood changes dramatically after Psalm 90. Westermann has pointed this out, as has Wilson.[4] In fact, Westermann has noted that laments dominate the first half of the Psalter, psalms of praise dominate the second, and Psalm 90 functions as the pivot.[5]

## Psalms 90–92

Psalms 90–92[6] precede Psalm 93 in Book IV, and they are of mixed genres: Psalm 90 is a community lament, Psalm 91 a complex liturgy, and Psalm

3. See further the comments on these problems in chapter 1 (pp. 9, 15), and my response in appendix 4 (pp. 200–207).

4. Westermann 1981b: 257; Wilson 1985a: 214–15.

5. Westermann 1981b: 252, 257. We may add that the outline of the Psalter as a whole, then, mirrors the outline of the lament itself: both end with movements toward praise.

6. Most of the material in this section on Psalms 90–92 first appeared in my "Contextual Reading of Psalms 90–94" (Howard 1993b). It is reproduced here with kind permission from Sheffield Academic Press.

92 a hymn or a thanksgiving of the individual. Westermann (1981b: 255) finds no apparent connection between these three psalms and Psalm 89 or 93–99.

Reindl, on the other hand (1981: 350–55), sees *many* internal links, most of them reflective of wisdom motifs (a wisdom speech form and a didactic tendency in each), and some of them of the key-word type. These wisdom images, used in psalms that are not usually classified as sapiential, form a remarkably visible combination. Reindl (p. 351) quotes Crüsemann, who observed this in Psalm 92: "Thus has a psalm emerged whose basic form represents the thanksgiving of the individual, but which has been recast into a new whole via hymnic and sapiential motifs and forms." In general terms, Reindl (p. 352) believes that the unifying themes center around the human condition: Psalm 90—humanity's general lot; Psalm 91—humanity under YHWH's protection; and Psalm 92—the differing destinies of the righteous and the evil-doers. A significant thread running through the psalms in the section is the theme of security in YHWH: he has been Israel's refuge in all generations (Pss 90:1; 91:1–4, 9–12, 14–16; 92:16).

Reindl's thesis is instructive, especially since other commentators on all three psalms have also mentioned the presence or influence of wisdom motifs (e.g., Anderson, Kraus). Wilson (1985a: 215–16) detects links among them of trust, protection, and security in YHWH motifs. He also describes Psalm 92 as "a transition from the 'Mosaic' theme of YHWH as refuge for those who trust in him to the central motif of the 'Enthronement['] pss: 'YHWH reigns!' " (1985a: 215). Likewise, Zenger, acknowledging Reindl's work, considers Psalms 90–92 to be "one composition" ("eine Komposition") of psalms that are linked by many key-word motifs and by questions in one psalm that are answered in a following psalm (Zenger 1991: 238–39).

## *Psalm 90*

Psalm 90, as a psalm of Moses, reminds us that YHWH's covenantal activity extended back not merely as far as David, but even back to Moses. It begins with a powerful assertion of YHWH's faithfulness as a refuge (*mā*$^{c}$*ôn*, v. 1) and his eternal existence (v. 2).[7] This sounds a keynote for the powerful affirmations of his sovereignty that will be heard throughout Book IV.

Psalm 90 also speaks of the ephemerality of humans in vv. 3–12, especially vis-à-vis the eternality of God mentioned in vv. 1–2. The language used is reminiscent of the wisdom tradition: portions of this section contain a cynical note—or, at the very least, a note of weary resignation (see

7. Compare 90:2 with 93:2, which makes essentially the same point.

especially vv. 3, 5–7, 9–10)—such as is found in Ecclesiastes. The psalm ends with a lament that calls for help in terms that are reminiscent of the lament at the end of Psalm 89.

Psalm 90 hints at the answer to the problem of humanity's condition. Verse 8 mentions sins twice: *ᶜwn* 'iniquities'; *ᶜlm* 'secret sins'.[8] Verses 7–12, especially vv. 7–8, show that God's wrath is due to human sins. Thus, the problems that humans have are not due to God's unfaithfulness or whim, but to their sins. The psalmist's answer to the human problem is v. 12: "So teach us to number our days // so that we may receive a heart of wisdom." In the context of the psalm, the verse recommends a positive attitude toward time that does not cynically or resignedly opt out of life, but sincerely tries to account well for one's days.

Psalm 90, then, serves as an effective bridge between the mixed message at the end of Book III and the towering affirmations in later parts of Book IV (and in almost all of Book V). The psalm echoes the petition in the lament at the end of Psalm 89, and its weariness of spirit in vv. 3–12 echoes the questioning of YHWH in 89:39–46[38–45] and in Psalm 88. However, the psalm also moves us forward to affirmations of YHWH. He is our eternal and faithful refuge (vv. 1–2). Psalm 90 tells us what Psalms 88 and 89 do not: that the poor human condition is due to sin (v. 8) and that the key to a well-lived life is to "number our days," to aspire to wisdom (v. 12).

## *Psalm 91*

Psalm 91 gives a much clearer answer to the human problem than Psalm 90 does. It echoes the idea of YHWH as refuge (see 90:1), specifically in 91:9 (*māᶜôn* 'refuge'),[9] and generally throughout the entire psalm. It too has a decided wisdom flavor. This time it is of the didactic sort, in which the psalmist instructs his listeners in the trustworthy ways of YHWH and the advisability of making him their security (vv. 3–13). The psalm ends with YHWH speaking (vv. 14–16), giving assurances of his presence and protection. The keys to a relationship with YHWH (v. 14) are loving God and "knowing his name," which means, being in covenantal relationship

8. The use of the word *ᶜlm* in 90:8 to refer to sin is a hapax legomenon; usually the verb of this root means 'to be hidden' (*Niphal*) or 'to hide, cover' (*Hiphil, Hithpael*).

9. The word is used elsewhere in this way only in 71:3 (Reindl 1981: 351). Compare the closely related root *ḥsh* in vv. 2, 4, 9, meaning 'refuge, shelter' or 'to seek refuge'. See also Creach 1996, which is a study of *ḥsh* and related roots and their structural implications for the shaping of the Psalter. (See pp. 93–97 for his treatment of "refuge" in Psalms 90–92 and 94.)

with him. The statement about human longevity in v. 16a ("With long life I will satisfy him") is particularly striking, in light of the thoughts on the ephemerality of life that are expressed in Psalm 90 (especially vv. 4–6, 9–10).

## *Psalm 92*

Psalm 92 is an individual psalm of thanksgiving. Read in conjunction with the preceding two psalms, it expresses the reader's/worshiper's response to the assurances of Psalms 90 and 91, especially Psalm 91. It is full of the trust and thanksgiving that are largely absent in Psalm 90. It is the first psalm in Book IV that contains the classic vocabulary of musical and joyful praise (vv. 2–5[1–4]). It is linked by a key word to Psalm 91 (by concatenation), YHWH's *šm* 'name' (91:14; 92:2[1]). Note also the references to *ᶜelyôn* 'Most High' (91:1 and 92:2[1]).[10]

Psalm 92 also echoes Psalm 90 in several ways. In Psalm 90, morning and night are terms used to emphasize human ephemerality (vv. 5–6); in Psalm 92, on the other hand, they symbolize the continuing praise to God for his *ḥesed* and faithfulness (92:3[2]). YHWH's eternality is also emphasized in both psalms (90:2; 92:9[8]). A striking key-word repetition is *ṣûṣ* 'flourish' in 90:6 and 92:8[7]; in both cases it refers to the quick flourishing of the grass, which just as quickly withers. In Psalm 92, the flourishing of the evil-doers is compared to the flourishing of the grass in a trenchant analogy.

In general terms, Psalm 92 contains the response to the petitions of Psalm 90, especially 90:13–17. Most noticeable are Ps 90:14a, which asks YHWH to 'satisfy us in the morning (with) your steadfast love' (*śabbĕᶜēnû babbōqer ḥasdekā*), and Ps 92:3a[2a], which replies that it is good 'to declare in the morning your steadfast love' (*lĕhaggîd babbōqer ḥasdekā*). Verse 90:14b continues by asking for these things "that we may rejoice (*rnn*) and be glad (*śmḥ*) all our days," and the psalmist replies in 92:5[4] that YHWH has indeed made him glad (*śmḥ*) and that he does rejoice (*rnn*).

I conclude with one final observation. Like Psalms 90 and 91, Psalm 92 contains a significant wisdom section. It is found in vv. 6–10[5–9] and vv. 13–16[12–15]).[11]

10. Auffret (1993: 315–17) has pointed out several more word links between the two psalms, including reference to the night (*lylh*) in 91:5 and 92:3[2], the wicked (*ršᶜym*) in 91:8 and 92:8[7], and YHWH's or his angels' hands (*ydym*) in 91:12 and 92:4[5].

11. Already in 1981, Reindl recognized the coherence of this unit of three psalms, focusing especially on wisdom motifs (pp. 350–55).

## Psalm 93

Psalm 93 is the first of eight psalms of the community. It changes the focus of praise in Book IV to the praise of YHWH as King, a motif that is sustained until Psalm 99. The groundwork for the shift in Psalm 93 has already been established in the general and joyful praises in Psalm 92, but Psalm 93 restricts its focus to YHWH's kingship and sovereignty; unlike Psalm 92, it does not focus on the effects on the people praising.

The best example of lexical and thematic links between Psalm 92 and 93 is found in 92:9 and 93:2. Ps 92:9 reads *wʾth mrwm lʿlm YHWH* 'But you are exalted/on high forever, O YHWH!' Ps 93:2 reads *nkwn ksʾk mʾz mʿwlm ʾth* 'Your throne was established from times past; // From long ago was you(r throne)!' Furthermore, *mrwm*, found in 92:9, is repeated in 93:4 and is followed by *YHWH* in both verses.

Despite the fact that Psalms 92 and 93 are of different form-critical genres, and despite the presence of a wisdom-flavored portion (vv. 7–10) in Psalm 92, this psalm nevertheless functions well in anticipating the predominant motif of the following psalms. They affirm YHWH's kingship, sovereignty, and everlasting presence. Psalm 92 casts an eye back to Psalms 90–91, but it also looks ahead to the following psalms. This is especially true since it also anticipates a number of ideas in Psalm 94, the most anomalous of the succeeding psalms.

Psalm 93, the shortest of the Kingship of YHWH psalms in the 93–100 group,[12] also heads the list. It is admittedly the most unlike the others: not only is it by far the shortest, but it does not share all of the themes that the others do.[13] However, it is one of the "core" group, since it begins with the paradigmatic clause, *YHWH mlk*, and it is thus well suited to open this section. It affirms the predominant motif to follow: YHWH is enthroned, and he has in fact been enthroned forever (v. 2). He is sovereign even over the rebellious waters (vv. 3–4). These facts provide the basis for the confidence in YHWH that is evident in Psalm 94 and most of the following psalms. In addition, the psalm affirms YHWH's decrees and his house, which are also of importance to all later generations and which are emphasized in several of the following psalms.

Psalm 93 has numerous individual links with Psalms 96–99, including some that stand out as key-word links. In particular, its strongest connections are with Psalm 96, the first of the four Kingship of YHWH psalms in that group (most notable are the repetitions of *YHWH mlk* and *ʾp-tkwn tbl bl-tmwṭ*). Key-word links with Psalms 98 (*YHWH*, *mlk*, *ym*, and *nhrwt*) and 99 (*YHWH mlk* and *ʿdt*) serve to bind Psalm 93 to the group as a whole.

12. And most likely the earliest (see appendix 1).

13. See Watts's categories (1965: 343).

## Psalm 94

In this section, I shall need to consider Psalm 94 under three subheadings, since it is the psalm most different from the others among Psalms 93–100.

### *Psalm 94 and Psalms 90–92*

Psalm 94, a complex community lament, echoes themes of discord that are found in Psalms 90 and 91, especially Psalm 90.[14] In this way, it brings the first section of Book IV to a close,[15] and it is appropriate in this location for several reasons. I noted above that Psalms 90–92 form a group of psalms that shares a common wisdom vocabulary, and they respond to each other in significant ways. Psalm 94 is also linked with them, by virtue of its wisdom interlude in vv. 8–15.

The connections are especially strong between Psalms 92 and 94. They share 20 lexemes, close to half of which are significant in one way or another. Most of the significant links are part of the wisdom vocabulary found in both psalms. For example, 92:6–10[5–9] speaks of the great gulf between YHWH on high and his enemies, who are described—in terms characteristic of wisdom—as dull, stupid, wicked, evil men; these motifs are echoed in 94:4, 8–11. Again, Psalm 92:7[6] is echoed in a remarkable way by 94:8:

92:7[6]:

> The dull man (*baʿar*) cannot know,
> the stupid one (*kĕsîl*) cannot understand (*bîn*) this.

94:8:

> Understand (*bîn*), O dull ones (*baʿar*) among the people!
> And, you stupid ones (*kĕsîl*), when will you become wise?

Furthermore, the 'wicked' in 92:8[7] (*rĕšāʾîm*) and the 'evil-doers' in 92:8, 10[7, 9] (*pōʿălê ʾāwen*) are prominent in Psalm 94, as well: the *rĕšāʾîm* are seen in 94:3 (2×), 13, and the *pōʿălê ʾāwen* in 94:4, 16.

Both Psalms 92 and 94 describe wicked and foolish people, who may flourish for a moment but ultimately will be overcome by YHWH, his righteousness, and his intervention on behalf of his own righteous people. As Marvin Tate notes (1990: 48),

> Ps 94 summons those with weak faith and lax commitment to a renewed perception of the work of Yahweh which would permit

14. Even more are found in Psalms 88 and 89.

15. See above p. 166 n. 1, on the division of Book IV into three groups of Psalms: Psalms 90–94, 95–100, 101–6.

them to join in the acclamation of his kingship. At the same time, both psalms . . . serve as a rebuke and warning to the wicked. . . .

Psalm 94 comes full circle in the first section of Book IV by echoing Psalm 90 as well as 92. The lament/petition comes at the end of Psalm 90 (90:13–17), leaving one with somewhat of a sense of irresolution. In Psalm 94, the lament/petition comes at the beginning (94:1–7), but it is followed by sustained expressions of trust in YHWH, leaving one with a sense of confidence that is fully of a piece with the trust expressed in all the Kingship of YHWH psalms surrounding it. These are the only two psalms in Book IV that contain a lament portion until Psalm 102.

Lexically, Psalms 90 and 94 have 21 roots in common. Most are incidental repetitions, but 3 are more significant. (1) In 90:2 and 94:2, YHWH is characterized as sovereign over the earth (*ʾrṣ*): as Creator in 90:2 and as Judge in 94:2. (2) In both psalms, the ability to know (*ydʿ*) is important: in 90:11, no human can know the power of YHWH's anger, while in 94:11, on the other hand, YHWH knows the very thoughts of humans. (3) The heart (*lbb*) is at the foundation of right living and desires: in 90:12, a heart of wisdom is to be desired, while in 94:15, the upright of heart are commended.

Both psalms emphasize the motif of the ephemerality of life (90:5–6, 9–10; 94:11). Psalm 94, however, speaks of it more positively, in a context of YHWH's benign sovereignty. This is in keeping with the more far more positive tone of the group of psalms of which Psalm 94 is a part. In this way, Psalm 94, while wrapping up the first section of Book IV, especially by echoing Psalm 90 (and Psalm 92), nevertheless advances the thoughts of Psalm 90 and echoes more of the confidence found in the Kingship of YHWH psalms around it.

### *Psalm 94 and Psalm 93*

After the great affirmations of joy and praise found in Psalms 92 and 93, Psalm 94 changes back to the mood found in several preceding psalms, although it does display confidence in YHWH and implicit affirmation of YHWH's sovereignty. It even assumes YHWH's kingship in v. 1, by crying for YHWH to rouse himself and take his own vengeance, a vengeance reserved to him as King.

The most striking link between Psalms 93 and 94 is the presence of rebellious waters in the one and rebellious people in the other, the common root being *dky/dkʾ*. YHWH's undisputed sovereignty over the rebellious waters in Psalm 93 assures the reader that he is also sovereign over those who persecute Israel in Psalm 94. The connections between YHWH's decrees (*ʿdt*) and his Torah form a second link between the two psalms.

Both terms hark back to the Mosaic period, but they have continuing relevance in the life of the nation in all periods.

The other word links between the psalms are contrastive. The contrasting pairs *gʾwt/gʾym* and *dky/dkʾ* are the best examples of concatenation of terms between the two psalms. They contrast YHWH's proud majesty with the arrogant pride of the wicked. Other contrasts include YHWH's secure throne in 93 and the ephemeral throne of destruction in 94 (*ksʾ*), the secure world that YHWH has established in 93 and the insecure footing of humans in 94 (*mwṭ*), and the waters that rise up roaring (93) and YHWH (94), whom the psalmist calls to rouse himself (*nśʾ*).

## *Psalm 94 in Its Present Context*

I observed briefly above (p. 110) that none of the other laments in Books IV and V has a wisdom section equivalent to the interlude in 94:8–15, which closely echoes part of Psalm 92. The reasons for the inclusion of a lament at this juncture in the Kingship of YHWH section remain somewhat puzzling.

A more limited question is what was the rationale for including *this particular* lament at this juncture. Certainly a significant part of this rationale was its links with Psalm 92 (and 90–91). Other factors must have been the uniqueness of the terms *dky/dkʾ* and *gʾwt/gʾym*, as well as the use of *ʿdt/twrh*, all links with Psalm 93. Additional factors were the community nature of Psalm 94, its lack of a superscription, and its assumption of YHWH's kingship.

This rationale does not tell us why a lament (of any type) appears in such a distinctive string of hymns as Psalms 93 and 95–100. The text presents no clear answer to this question, in this case. It does appear to be significant that four Kingship of YHWH psalms (96–99) are grouped together in immediate succession, but that one (93) is separated from them, at the beginning of the section. Wilson has pointed out (1985a: 212–14) that there are clear indications in Psalm 89 (just before the juncture between Books III and IV) that the Davidic covenant, although a prominent theme, is considered by the psalmist to be remote (89:20–21, 50[19–20, 49]) or even broken and failed (89:39–40, 45[38–39, 44]). Furthermore, the preponderance of the laments in the Psalter appear in Books I–III; thus, it is essentially a pessimistic view that obtains at this juncture in the Psalter.

Book IV then emerges as the " 'answer' to the problem posed in Ps. 89 as to the apparent failure of the Davidic covenant with which Books One–Three are primarily concerned" (Wilson 1985a: 215). However, as an "answer," Book IV begins slowly (Psalms 90–91), and Psalm 94 functions to remind the reader that YHWH's kingship is not yet fully experienced by his people. Within the section represented by Psalms 93–100, however, the trust in YHWH and praise of YHWH build to a climax, which is reflected in the unbroken notes of praise in Psalms 96–99 and also in the appropriateness of Psalm 100 as a conclusion to the group. Thus, from the perspective of the development of thought and motif, the location of the Psalm 94 lament early in the Psalms 93–100 section rather than later or at the end may itself have been significant. Also, the links between Psalm 94 and earlier psalms must be taken into consideration in trying to understand the logic behind the placement of Psalm 94 in its present location.[16]

## Psalm 95

Psalm 95 resumes the Kingship of YHWH motif clearly signaled in Psalm 93 but subordinated in Psalm 94. It functions as a "pivot" psalm, linking the psalms that follow with those that precede. It also functions in tandem with Psalm 100 to demarcate the second section of Book IV and to bracket the four Kingship of YHWH psalms between them. It is the third of the string of eight psalms of the community (Psalms 93–100).

It links backward most clearly with Psalm 93 and its Kingship of YHWH motif (93:1, 95:3). The first two sections of Psalm 95 (95:1–7c) are praise sections in the tradition of Psalms 92 and 93. However, its prophetic oracle in vv. 7d–11 echoes some of the somber notes of Psalms 90–91 and 94.

It also looks ahead, introducing the great, joyful Kingship of YHWH motifs in Psalm 96, including the general praise vocabulary, the emphases on YHWH's sovereignty, and his status as Creator. Psalm 95 functions especially well as a companion to Psalm 100, anticipating the themes of YHWH as Creator and Shepherd of his people.

Immediately preceding Psalm 95 is Psalm 94, whose closest companion among Psalms 93–100—significantly—is Psalm 95. It is closest to Psalm 95 in terms of number of shared words, similarity of outlook, and presence of significant nonhymnic material. The two psalms share more words than Psalm 94 does with any other psalm in the group. The presence of YHWH as Israel's source of security (*ṣwr*) at the end of Psalm 94 and the beginning of Psalm 95 (94:22, 95:1) is the most significant link and a prime example of concatenation. The divine name *ʾēl* is present in

16. Wilson also points out that Psalm 94 is part of a "Mosaic frame" in Book IV, along with Psalms 90–92, 102, and 105–6. The many links we have noted between Psalms 93 and 94 thus provide "an interlocking mechanism by which the YHWH-*mālak* group (with its 'frame') is bound together with the preceding group of Psalms 90–92 and 94" (1993b: 75–76).

both psalms, found again only in Psalm 99. The use of *ᶜm* to refer only to Israel is unique to these two psalms (and Psalm 100) among the group.

Finally, Psalms 94 in its entirety and Ps 95:7d–11 are the main non-hymnic sections in Psalms 93–100.[17] Indeed, the prophetic oracle section in Psalm 95, consisting as it does of a warning and exhortation to succeeding generations to avoid the sins of the wilderness generation, echoes the sapiential warning to fools and evildoers in 94:8–11. Even the affirmation of trust in YHWH's chastening in 94:12–15 forms a basis for assurance that YHWH's rejection is not forever and that his punishment is for positive purposes. This assurance informs 95:10–11, which could easily inspire a fear of YHWH's permanent rejection of all his people if read out of context.

Psalm 95's closest ties are with Psalm 100. In this way, the two psalms form an inclusio around the Kingship of YHWH group in Psalms 96–99. The close lexical correspondences between the hymnic portion of Psalm 95 and all of Psalm 100 are an indication that they were intended as an inclusio, as are the almost identical structure and content of Ps 95:6b–7c and 100:3b–c. The structure of each psalm as a whole is also parallel to the structure of the other (although they differ greatly in length): the opening hymnic structures are similar, as are the central sections of affirmation of YHWH's relationship to Israel, and the closing appeals to the faithful.

Of the two psalms, Psalm 95 is much more appropriately placed at the head of the group than Psalm 100 would have been, however. Its links with Psalm 94 confirm this, as do the links it has with Psalm 96 and its reference to YHWH as King (which is lacking in Psalm 100). Psalm 100 would not function nearly as effectively as a bridge between Psalm 93 and the Kingship of YHWH motif in Psalm 96. In addition, Psalm 95 includes more of the motifs found in Psalms 96–99 than Psalm 100 does (see Watts 1965).

## Psalm 96

The notes of joyful praise of YHWH's kingship that were resumed in Psalm 95 come to full expression in Psalm 96. This is the most purely praise-oriented of the eight psalms in the group. It contains all the major themes found in the other psalms of the Kingship of YHWH genre.

Psalm 96 links with Psalm 95 mainly in the Kingship of YHWH motif and the vocabulary of praise. However, there is a significant structural concatenation in 95:3 and 96:4, in the sections affirming YHWH's greatness.

Psalm 96 also echoes motifs from Psalm 93, the first of the Kingship of YHWH psalms in Book IV. Psalm 93 shares more words with Psalm 96

17. The other significant portion is Ps 97:10–12.

than with any other psalm in the group, including the *YHWH mlk* clause and the entire poetic line *ʾp-tkwn tbl bl-tmwṭ*, which speaks of the unshakeable condition of the world that YHWH the King has established.

Psalm 96 functions well at the head of the four closely related Kingship of YHWH psalms placed between Psalms 95 and 100. It functions as a preview of sorts of the material that is to follow. Its opening line ("Sing to YHWH a new song!") functions, in the context of Psalms 93–100 and Book IV, to draw attention to its function of resuming in earnest the Kingship of YHWH motif. As a "new song," it commences a new section of four related psalms. Furthermore, Psalms 96 and 97 both contain all of the major themes of the Kingship of YHWH genre. Psalm 96 is more purely praise oriented than Psalm 97 and more universal in its outlook; thus it is more appropriate at the head of the group of four psalms than Psalm 97 would be. The concatenation of clauses and ideas between the end and beginning of the two psalms also confirms the appropriateness of the present order.

## Psalm 97

Psalm 97 is closely bound to the preceding psalm by the concatenation of several clauses, phrases, and words. Two clauses from the end of Psalm 96 are found at the beginning of Psalm 97: *YHWH mlk* and *tgl hʾrṣ*. In addition, the ideas in 96:11–12 and 97:1 are identical: elements of nature are urged to participate in praise of YHWH the King. Psalm 97 has a more somber tone than Psalm 96, however. A theophany appears in 97:2–6, emphasizing YHWH's awesome nature, and in 97:10–12, the wisdom section is more hortatory and reassuring in nature than it is praise oriented.

Beyond this, Psalms 97 and 96 share a large number of words, including a striking number (5) that are unique to these two psalms out of the Psalms 93–100 group, all of Book IV, and the entire Psalter: *ʾlylym*, *šmym*, *kbwd*, *gyl*, and *ḥyl*. There are no other psalms in 93–100 that share so many words not found in other psalms of the group.

Psalm 97 also echoes earlier psalms, although not in any significant structural way. With Psalm 93, it is unique among Psalms 93–100 in emphasizing the establishment of YHWH's throne, and of course, it continues the Kingship of YHWH motif introduced in Psalm 93 and continued in Psalms 95 and 96. Psalm 97 shares a wisdom section with Psalm 94. This wisdom section links 97 with 95:7b–11, as well, since both are nonhymnic sections that serve as hortatory admonitions to YHWH's people.

Psalm 97 has significant ties with succeeding psalms, as well. Concatenations of key words between Psalms 97 and 98 include *YHWH*, *mlk*, *qdš*, *ḥsd*, and *zkr*. The psalms are closely related thematically, as should be expected. The placement of the two psalms adjacent to each other results in a chiastic structural arrangement with alternating themes of Israel and the world:

Psalm 97: (A) the world, (B) Israel;
Psalm 98: (B′) Israel, (A′) the world.

Psalm 99, a psalm that mentions YHWH's justice and Israel's wrongdoings, resumes the more restrained praises of Psalm 97, in contrast to the unbridled, joyful praises found in Psalms 96 and 98.

## Psalm 98

The keynotes of praise of YHWH the King that were sounded in Psalms 96 and 97 are continued in Psalm 98. It is very closely related thematically to both of them because it includes all of the same major themes except for specifically mentioning elements of nature. Like them (especially Psalm 96), Psalm 98 is dominated by praise; like them, it is universal in outlook. It also focuses on Israel as God's people, as does Psalm 97.

The concatenation of words at the end of Psalm 97 and beginning of 98 includes *qdš*, *zkr*, and *ḥsd*. Furthermore, a chiastic structure in the arrangement of themes is apparent in the two psalms: Psalm 97 opens with attention to the world and closes by focusing on Israel; Psalm 98 opens with an eye to Israel and closes by emphasizing the world.

Psalm 98's closest connections within the 93–100 group are to Psalm 96, and the reverse is also true. It appears likely that the one formed the basis for the other's composition, and they may even have come from the same hand. Psalm 98 resumes the more purely praise-oriented content found in Psalm 96. In general, it does this by repetition of almost all the themes in Psalm 96 and by its similarity in structure. The resumptive nature of Psalm 98 is explicitly seen in the presence of opening lines that are identical: *šyrw lYHWH šyr ḥdš* 'Sing to YHWH a new song!' As noted above, the presence of a brief superscription in Psalm 98 also contributes to the notion that Psalm 98 moves beyond Psalm 96, with a fresh start of sorts. For example, Psalm 98 more specifically emphasizes Israel and YHWH's relationship to it than Psalm 96 does. The two psalms are very similar in structure and thought progression, however. They both open with a call to praise followed by the reasons for praise, and they resume with a second call to praise. Both then affirm YHWH as King and conclude with a praise section that focuses on the elements of nature. The last verses of the psalms are essentially identical, emphasizing YHWH's coming as Judge of the world.

In addition to the specific repetitions 96:1a in 98:1a and 96:13 in 98:9 and the general structural similarities, there are other similar lines or verses. Psalm 96:11–12 closely parallels 98:7–8 as a praise section, and 96:11b is identical to 98:7a: *yrᶜm hym wmlᵓw* 'let the sea roar, and all that fills it!' Ps 98:9c–d echoes not only 96:13c–d but also 96:10c when it states that YHWH will judge the peoples with equity. The one word that is not shared by 96:13c–d and 98:9c–d *is* shared by 96:10c and 98:9c–d (*bmyšrym* 'with equity'). The praise vocabulary of 96:1b is almost identical to 98:4a, as well. Finally, the two psalms share the idea of YHWH as a worker of wonders (*nplᵓwt*), an idea that does not recur in Psalms 93–100.

Links between Psalm 98 and the psalms preceding Psalm 96 are only general. It is a hymn celebrating YHWH's Kingship, like Psalms 93 and 95, but there are few other significant links. The use of *nhrwt* in both Psalms 93 and 98 is noteworthy, however, since they are the only two texts in the entire Bible where "floods" take any action vis-à-vis God: they rebel against him in Psalm 93 and they are told to praise him in 98.

Psalm 98 projects forward into Psalm 99 by the concatenations of its words and ideas: *YHWH*, *mlk*, *ᵓrṣ*, *ᶜmym*, *špṭ*, *ṣdq*, and *myšrym*. Psalm 98 also anticipates Psalm 100 well, with an imperatival call to praise in 98:4a that is identical to the one in 100:1a: *hryᶜw lYHWH kl-hᵓrṣ* 'raise a glad cry to YHWH, all the earth!'

## Psalm 99

The "new song" (Psalm 96) that opens the concentrated section of Kingship of YHWH psalms is followed by a hymn (Psalm 97) that reveals YHWH's awesome nature and also gives assurance to YHWH's devoted followers. The second "new song" (Psalm 98) is likewise followed by a hymn (Psalm 99) that emphasizes YHWH's awesome attributes and provides assurance for those who call on YHWH's name. Psalm 99 closes this section of Kingship of YHWH psalms, echoing Psalm 97 and displaying links with 98 as well.

The primary links between Psalms 98 and 99 are the concatenation of key words at the end of Psalm 98 and beginning of 99. The words *ᵓrṣ* and *ᶜmym* are parallel to each other in both 98:9 and 99:1, displaying YHWH's sovereignty over them; this is the only place in Psalms 93–100 (aside from the duplicate 96:13) that these terms are paired in this way. Another verse that is parallel to 99:1 is 99:4; it contains three more of the roots found in 98:9: *špṭ*, *ṣdq*, and *myšrym*. Psalm 98 emphasizes the fact that YHWH's judging activity is cause for great rejoicing, because it is with righteousness and equity that he judges (v. 9), and it is on behalf of Israel that he displays his salvation (vv. 1–3). Psalm 99 also affirms that YHWH is an even-handed Judge (v. 4); this is the basis for confidence in him (vv. 6–8). However, Psalm 99 also emphasizes YHWH's holy and awesome nature.

The general A:B::A′:B′ pattern of Psalms 96–99 has been noted above in several places. However, the parallels between Psalms 97 and 99 have more to do with general outlook (less concentration of pure praise vocabulary, emphasis on YHWH's awesome nature, and so on) than specific lexical or structural links. The most significant lexical links are the theophanic references to YHWH in both (by the use of *ʿnn*) and the identification of YHWH with Zion.

The connections between Psalm 99 and the psalms preceding Psalm 97 are mainly thematic, but 99 does echo several of them in striking ways. For example, reference to YHWH's decrees (*ʿdt*) is found only in Psalms 93 and 99, and both psalms end by recalling motifs from the Mosaic period that are now identified with Zion. Because Psalms 93 and 99 begin and end the concentration of Kingship of YHWH psalms, their opening acclamations (*YHWH mlk*) likewise echo each other. Psalm 94 also displays an interest in YHWH's covenantal words: its use of *twrh* links it with the use of *ʿdt* and *ḥq* in Psalm 99. Furthermore, God as Vindicator (*nqm*) appears only in Psalms 94 and 99 in all of Book IV; in both cases the root is linked with the divine name *ʾēl*. Psalms 95 and 99 likewise share motifs echoing the Mosaic period. Finally, Psalm 96 and 99 are unique in their use of *nwrʾ* to describe YHWH, and (with Psalm 100) in their emphasis on YHWH's name (*šm*). The links between Psalms 99 and 93 and between 99 and 94 are particularly noteworthy, demonstrating that the psalm's placement near the end of the group is particularly appropriate.

## Psalm 100

The crescendo of praise that has been building since Psalm 93 reaches a climax in Psalm 100. For the first time in the section, the unreserved praise of YHWH, who appears as the particular God of Israel and who is associated with the Temple in Jerusalem, is finally manifested. In each previous psalm, this praise is tempered in one way or another, or it is not expressed in specific praise terms. Strikingly, the climax occurs in a very short psalm.[18] The praise and affirmations are expressed succinctly, and they are not repeated.

Psalm 100 is called a 'psalm' (*mzmwr*), echoing Psalm 98, but Psalm 100 has no strong lexical links with Psalm 99. This is the only instance in the group where there is no apparent concatenation of terms between

18. In an analogous way, the entire Psalter ends with a short, concentrated, climactic burst of praise in Psalm 150.

consecutive psalms. However, the particular emphasis on YHWH's relationship with his people in Ps 99:4, 6–8 is echoed strongly in 100:3, and the emphasis on Zion in 99:2, 5, and 9 is echoed in 100:4.[19]

Psalm 100 is primarily linked to Psalm 95, and these links have already been enumerated above. Psalm 100 functions well in bringing Psalms 95–100 to a close. It summarizes the praise motifs and affirms that YHWH has not rejected his people the way he did the early wilderness generation in Psalm 95. It particularly echoes Psalm 96 by sharing a large amount of praise vocabulary.

The cycle of praise begun in Psalm 93 is now complete. The central affirmations of YHWH's kingship and sovereignty have been reiterated numerous times. Likewise, YHWH's activities on behalf of his people and activities against the nations are displayed prominently, though the nations themselves are called in Psalm 96. The message of the section is that YHWH can be trusted, even in the face of adversity (Psalm 94). There is hope for his people. Psalm 100, in its brief compass, affirms this trust in YHWH, the worldwide scope of his sovereignty, the particular relationship he has established with Israel, and Zion, the place where all this is centered.

## Psalms 101–6

Since the primary focus in this work has been the internal structure of Psalms 93–100 and the secondary interest was how the group fits into a consecutive reading of the Psalter,[20] the following comments are necessarily briefer than any previous comments. Further development must await another treatment.

The principle of concatenation of terms continues to be evident in the relationship between Psalms 100 and 101. The term *ḥsd* occurs in 100:5 and 101:1. Both psalms are *mzmwr*s. In fact, Psalm 100, though the last in the 93–100 section, also looks forward to the following section by virtue of its superscription: the next three psalms all bear one as well.

Psalm 101 is generally classified as a royal psalm, following Gunkel (1933: 140). It describes the way a king, as leader of his people, should walk. It does so, however, in sapiential terms and therefore echoes portions of earlier psalms, especially Psalms 92 and 94. Psalm 101 furnishes a

19. Zenger has recently pointed out that Psalms 93–100 cohere as a unified grouping, based on a 7 + 1 pattern, with Psalm 100 functioning as the climax of the group (as I have argued here). The 7 + 1 pattern can be seen in such varied texts as Amos 1:1–2:16; Exod 22:30 [MT 29]; Lev 9:1–4; 1 Sam 16:10–11, 17:12. See Zenger 1991: 240–42 and n. 25. This would explain the looser ties that Psalms 99 and 100 have with each other.

20. This accounts for the more extended discussions above of Psalms 90–92.

prime example of the merging of the wisdom and royal traditions discussed in appendix 4, as Kenik has already pointed out (1976). She showed in some detail (pp. 399–403) how the standards of conduct expected of the nobility in Proverbs are reflected in this psalm. She suggested (p. 402) that "the Israelite traditions of covenant and wisdom attain a point of contact in the royal leader" and went on to say,

> The royal theology contained in Psalm 101 draws upon the sacred covenant tradition on which Israel was founded and the inherited sapiential tradition that flourished and was nurtured by the scribes attached to the royal court. Thus, the wisdom teachings became integrated with the essential faith traditions and supplied the content for the statement about the king's rule (p. 403).

While Psalm 101 echoes Psalms 92 and 94, Psalms 102 and 103 echo Psalms 90 and 91, particularly Psalm 90 (see Wilson 1985a: 218–19). The transience of human life is again a theme in 102 and 103, in contrast to God's eternality. YHWH's anger is seen again, and yet his forgiving nature and his commitment to his people remain.

Book IV ends with three lengthy psalms, each ending with *hllw-yh.* These cohere as a relatively self-contained grouping, and the pattern of inclusios seen earlier in the Psalms 90/94 and Psalms 95/100 pairings is not as evident in the Psalm 101/106 pairing. Rather, Psalms 104–6 function as a concluding group of their own.

Psalm 104 begins as 103 ends: *brky npšy ᵓt-YHWH* 'bless YHWH, O my soul!' As a creation hymn, it echoes many of the motifs in Psalms 93–100. Psalms 105 and 106, two "historical" psalms, tell the story of YHWH's acts in history from two different perspectives: Psalm 105 reviews Israel's history from the perspective of YHWH, who is faithful to his people at all times, whereas Psalm 106 surveys the history of Israel's rebellious unfaithfulness. Psalm 106 (and Book IV) ends on a note far removed from the ringing affirmations found in Psalms 93–100, but there are a few reminders. Ps 106:44–46 recalls the confidence in YHWH as One who answers his people that was present in 99:6–8. Ps 106:47 is a plea for deliverance that desires to engage again in the praise seen so abundantly in Psalms 93–100. The psalm closes (v. 48) with a doxology reminiscent of many of the earlier praise motifs.

## Conclusion

Many of the motifs found throughout the Psalm 93–100 section are common to almost all the psalms, and yet many, such as the concentration of YHWH as King motifs, are unique. The echoes of Mosaic and Davidic covenant motifs are common everywhere. The presence of wisdom motifs reflects concerns often found in the Psalter. Indeed, wisdom came to embrace so many divergent traditions and motifs (Torah, creation, the fact that Israel is YHWH's chosen people, the fact that the Davidic king and Zion are central to YHWH's plans),[21] alongside its better-known concerns with a life of piety and the Two Ways, that there are almost no motifs found in Psalms 93–100 (and indeed, the Psalter as a whole) that did not eventually become motifs in the sapiential tradition. This broadening of the sapiential tradition accounts for the fusing of the various motifs, and it shows the continuity of the early and the later traditions that all came to be embodied in the Psalter.

Psalms 93–100 form a logically coherent unit of community psalms, all concerned with YHWH's kingship in one way or another. They probably did not exist as a separate collection after the fashion of Psalms 120–134, but a clear pattern to the thought progression among the psalms is visible. The heart of the section is Psalms 96–99, bounded by Psalms 95 and 100. Within this core section, Psalm 96 functions well as an all-inclusive introduction, and it is echoed by Psalm 98. Psalm 99 brings the core Kingship of YHWH section to a close, echoing Psalm 97. Psalms 95 and 100 bracket this section, with Psalm 95 uniquely suited to its present location as a bridge between Psalms 93–94 and the following psalms, and Psalm 100 well suited as a climax to the section. The section is introduced by Psalm 93, which functions as an appropriate transition between Psalms 90–92 and 94. Psalm 94, while disjunctive in many ways, also displays significant ties with its context. Psalms 93–100 thus stand as the "center" of Book IV, both positionally and thematically.

This study has shown the internal structure of an all-important section of the Psalter. A logical sequence can be followed, with many identifiable contours and echoes between earlier and later psalms in the sequence. The study confirms the judgment of many scholars that the Kingship of YHWH psalms are the climax to which the Psalter builds throughout Books I–III. The soaring, joyful, trusting, and majestic tone of this section is sustained, for the most part, throughout the rest of the Psalter. The Psalter ends with the sustained burst of praise of YHWH in the Psalter's "appendix," Psalms 146–50. Significantly, the final psalm before this appendix is another Kingship of YHWH psalm (Psalm 145). The Psalter indeed affirms, as we should today, that "YHWH reigns!"

21. See further the discussion in appendix 4.

# *Appendix 1*
# *Dates of Psalms 93–100*

As I indicated in chapters 1 and 2, this work is a synchronic study of the structures of Psalms 93–100, both individually and—especially—as a group. As such, the supposed dates of composition of individual psalms have little or no place in the overall discussion. However, since the discussion of individual words (primarily in chapter 3) sometimes involves the issue of their assumed dating, and since the discussion sometimes engages scholarly opinions on the subject, some treatment of the dating of these psalms is necessary.

The primary discussion of dating methods below is presented at Psalm 93. After Psalm 93, the discussions are relatively brief. In most of these discussions, no more precision can be reached than to say that a psalm probably was preexilic or pre–eighth century B.C.E.[1]

## Dating of Psalm 93

The suggested dates for Psalm 93 range from the tenth century B.C.E. (Dahood 1968: 339; Shenkel 1965: 401–2 and 403 n. 1; Craigie 1972: 144) to the preexilic period in general (Mowinckel 1922: 3; Jefferson 1952) to the postexilic period (Buttenwieser 1938: 317–43). Buttenwieser argued for the late date because of parallels between the psalm and the latter half of Isaiah, even going so far as to suggest that Deutero-Isaiah was the author of the psalm (along with Psalms 97, 98, 96). Mowinckel argued on the basis of his reconstructed New Year's Festival, but Jefferson made her case on the basis of Ugaritic parallels. Shenkel advanced Jefferson's case, and cited Lipiński, who also dated the psalm to the tenth century (Shenkel 1965: 401–2).

1. It is interesting to note that here and in recent literature on the psalms, the movement is away from earlier extremes (represented by Buttenwieser [1938], for example), which assigned almost all the psalms to the postexilic period (often the Maccabean period).

The arguments advanced by Jefferson (1952: 155–57) on the overlapping of vocabulary between the psalm and Ugaritic literature are well taken, and links between the two are fairly clear. She claimed that approximately 75% of the vocabulary of Psalm 93 is found in the Ugaritic corpus, whereas only roughly 50% of the vocabulary in the rest of the Psalter is found there. Dahood (1968: 344) lowered Jefferson's number of unattested roots in Ugaritic from 9 to 5, which would raise her percentage for the psalm even more. These data show, if nothing else, that Buttenwieser's arguments, based as they were on the assumption that "advanced" theology as seen in the psalm can only be late, must be treated with skepticism.

Linguistically, several features point to an early date, on balance. First, Andersen and Forbes (1983) and Freedman (1985a) have developed a fairly reliable method for distinguishing poetry from prose, using the relative density of the so-called prose particles (*h*-, *ʾăšer*, and *ʾēt*). This method can also be used with caution to estimate the relative dates of material (see appendix 2 for the data for Psalms 90–106). Poetry, in general, contains fewer of these particles than prose. Andersen and Forbes contend (1983: 167) that the results can be refined by segregating known poetic material from prose within chapters, giving better results. Exodus 15 is a case in point. In their analysis, the chapter has a 5.61% relative density of prose particles, an unexceptional figure. However, when the generally accepted poetic passages (vv. 1–18, 21) are separated from the prose sections, the counts become more dramatic. Freedman notes (private communication) that the poetry in Exodus 15 has a zero count, and that the prose particle count of the prose sections alone is around 12.5%. This is in line with the results of his study (1985a) of ten poems in the Primary History (that is, Genesis–2 Kings), which he compares with the associated or related prose passages from the same material. The results of the prose particle count this time is just under 2% in the poems and approximately 16% in the prose. This is especially noteworthy in light of the same history of transmission for both sets of material, and in light of the later, Masoretic, tendency to insert the definite article by means of *pātaḥ* and *dāgēš*, but not *h*-. The distinction between prose and poetry was vigorously maintained, even when the scribes did not specifically recognize the differences.

Beyond this, however, as I noted, even the relative dating of texts can be estimated using this method (although much more tentatively), since the earlier texts have a lower concentration of these particles than the later ones. It must be emphasized that this is a rough method, and Andersen and Forbes caution (1983: 167) against giving too much weight to this factor for dating, but a legitimate generalization can be made. On this basis, Psalm 93 can be considered early, since it has *no* prose particles (zero percentage). It is the only one among Psalms 93–100 to have such a count; Psalm 91 is the only other one in Book IV to have a zero count.

A second sign of early composition is the complete absence of the conjunction in the psalm (Jefferson 1952: 156). Later ("standard") poetic Hebrew in paired lines (bicolons, or often, tricolons) characteristically has a conjunction joining the second (and third) line(s) with the first.[2] 11QPs[a] does have a *wāw* in v. 1 (*wytʾzr* for the MT *htʾzr*), which agrees with the Old Greek, but this form is likely a secondary development.[3]

A third indication of date is that Psalm 93 is characterized by tricolons rather than bicolons; the former are very common in Ugaritic, which is early relative to most of the biblical material. Furthermore, v. 3 shows another trait that is common in Ugaritic: a type of parallelism in which the second line repeats the first with only one member changed.[4]

Fourth, the use of divine names should be noted. While the use of *ʾĕlōhîm* to refer to God is rare in Book IV (it occurs only in construct, never in an absolute form), the fact that it is completely absent from this psalm, as well as the fact that there is a relatively high percentage of occurrences of *YHWH* (see appendix 3, on divine names and titles) can also be adduced in favor of an early dating for the psalm. Freedman (1976) has studied divine names in some detail, with an eye to using them in dating early poems, and has detected three phases in early poetic development. Phase One includes poems such as Exodus 15 and Judges 5. These poems use *YHWH* almost exclusively, and they date back to the Mosaic period and immediately following. Phase Two includes the Balaam oracles, Genesis 49, and Deuteronomy 33, and Freedman dates them to the 11th century B.C.E. Poems that use *ʾĕlōhîm* to refer to God do not show up until his Phase Three, which he dates to the late 11th–9th centuries B.C.E. These poems include Hannah's Song, Deuteronomy 32, and Psalms 78, 68, and 72.

Finally, the alternation in the psalm of prefixing and suffixing verb forms (the "imperfect" and "perfect"), with little apparent change in meaning or "tense," must be mentioned as another possible factor in dating (see chapter 3, at 93:3 [pp. 38–39]). Robertson (1972: 7–55) studied the use of these forms in Ugaritic, which is early (14th–12th centuries B.C.E.), and in Hebrew poetry that is clearly datable on nonlinguistic grounds to the eighth century or later. He found (p. 14) that

2. Freedman, private communication; see also Cross and Freedman 1953: 17–20.

3. See Sanders 1967: 76–77, and chapter 2 above, on Qumran.

4. See Jefferson 1952: 156 for this phenomenon.

> Ugaritic seems to have a past narrative suff[ix] conj[ugation] resembling the Hebrew suff[ix] conj[ugation] and a past narrative pref[ix] conj[ugation] resembling the Akkadian preterit tense, and to all appearances there is no syntactical difference between them. Reinforcing this impression of syntactical equivalence is that a narrative can be related with the pref[ix] conj[ugation] predominant . . . or with the suff[ix] conj[ugation] predominant . . . or with neither predominant.

Gordon (1967: 68–69) reflected a similar view:

> If *yqtl* had to be called a tense, "universal tense" would be justified inasmuch as it often refers to the past as well as to the present or future. In fact *yqtl* is the regular narrative form and we shall often translate it as a historical present.

In contrast, Robertson found (p. 25) that "in the overwhelmingly predominant use of the suff[ix] and w-pref[ix] conjugations in past narrative, standard poetic Hebrew [post–eighth century] is identical with Hebrew Prose."

However, he concluded that "the pref[ix] conj[ugation] in datable poetry is both a past frequentative *and* the equivalent of a preterit. Which it is in any individual case the context must determine."[5] His support for identifying a preterite was twofold. One argument came from passages where a prefixing form is paralleled by a *wāw*-consecutive with prefixing form and the situation clearly refers to past, punctiliar time: Hos 11:4 (*wʾṭ* 'and I bent down' // *ʾwkyl* 'I fed'); Isa 42:25 (*wtlhṭhw . . . wlʾydʿ* 'and it scorched him . . . but he did not understand' // *wtbʿr-bw wlʾysym* 'and it burned him but he did not place [it upon his heart]'); and Ezek 19:9 (*wytnhw* 'and they put him' // *wybʾhw* 'and they brought him' // *ybʾhw* 'they brought him'). Additional support comes from passages where the interpretation of prefixing forms as past frequentatives is strained, the best example being Hos 12:5, where the forms *ymṣʾnw* 'he found him' and *ydbr ʿm[w]* 'he spoke with [him]' refer to the specific events narrated in Genesis 28.

Robertson gave no examples of early Hebrew poetry datable by nonlinguistic criteria. He only discussed the Ugaritic texts in his section on "Early Poetic Hebrew" (1972: 9–17). However, in his actual study of the texts of "Poems That Resemble Early Poetry,"[6] he dealt inductively with the poems, showing that they indeed resemble Ugaritic poetry in verb

5. Robertson 1972: 27; emphasis mine.

6. Exodus 15, Judges 5, Habakkuk 3, 2 Samuel 18 = Psalm 18, Deuteronomy 32, and several passages in Job and elsewhere (Robertson 1972: 28–43).

usage, particularly in the interchangeability of prefixing and suffixing forms when all the events referred to occurred in the past.

Cross and Freedman (1953: 20) reflected a similar position: "the imperfect (*sic*) form of the verb was the common, generally used form in old Israelite poetry, as in old Canaanite poetry, and . . . its time aspect was determined by the context, not the presence or absence of the conjunction." Cross later (1973: 125) also maintained that "consistently [in Exodus 15] *yaqtul* is used to express narrative past, precisely as in Old Canaanite of the Byblus-Amarna correspondence and in Ugaritic. Thus it stands in parallelism frequently with *qatal* forms." He spoke of the *yaqṭul* form as being "preterit in force" and documented examples of this in Exodus 15 (p. 125 n. 44).

The alternative to interpreting the prefixing and suffixing forms in early Hebrew poetry as completely interchangeable is to consider the prefixing form a past habitual, as is oftentimes clear in Hebrew prose and standard poetic Hebrew,[7] and to conclude that the preterite force survived in Hebrew only in the *wāw*-consecutive construction.[8] Robertson addressed this possibility in each of the texts he considered early, however, and the weight of the evidence he presented (especially in the cases of Exodus 15 and Judges 5) suggests that the preterite force must be allowed in some cases of the Hebrew prefixing form, namely, where it occurs in early Hebrew poetry as a remnant reflecting the Ugaritic usage and the Akkadian preterite,[9] and even in isolated cases in standard Hebrew poetry.

In Psalm 93 (and indeed in all of Psalms 93–100), the alternation of verb forms must not be relied on too much as a tool for dating. Since there are few nonlinguistic factors that give independent evidence for dating, the use of this criterion alone would be unproductive. However, in Psalm 93, the combination of this evidence with the other factors mentioned above suggests that Freedman's method *can* be used here to postulate an early date for the psalm rather than a late one.

It should be noted that Psalm 93 is similar to Exodus 15 (an early poem by almost all accounts) in the complete absence of prose particles, in the use of *YHWH* (and not *ʾĕlōhîm*) as the divine name, and in some of the imagery found in both. YHWH is described as strong and sovereign in both poems, especially over potentially rebellious waters. Furthermore, YHWH's house/sanctuary is mentioned at the end of both poems without any mention of a human king.

7. Robertson 1972: 25, 27; Lambdin 1971: 100 (§91b); Joüon 1947: 302–3; GKC §§107a–e.

8. Moran 1961: 63–64; G. R. Driver, quoted in Weingreen 1959: 252–53.

9. On the latter, see *GAG* §79.

All of the above data, taken together, argue for dating the composition of Psalm 93 to the earliest stages of Hebrew poetic writing, probably the 10th century, possibly earlier, and perhaps as early as the 12th century. It is difficult to be dogmatic with such a short poem, but the evidence points more strongly to an early date than to a late one.

## Dating of Psalm 94

The question of the date of Psalm 94 is especially elusive. Most scholars date it late, but they hesitate to be specific about any historical references. Gunkel merely mentioned its late composition; Briggs placed the final glosses in the Maccabean period; Kraus assigned it to the late postexilic period; Anderson tentatively suggested the late Persian period. The presence of several prose particles (*h*-, vv. 2, 10, 12; *ʾăšer*, v. 12) suggests a later date than for Psalm 93.[10] The presence of *YH* in 94:7 and 12 is evidence of a later date (Freedman 1976: 110).

The case for an early date for this psalm is not as strong as it is for Psalm 93. In 93, the linguistic argument—tentative though it may be—is reinforced by several other lines of argument, whereas in 94, the support is somewhat less pronounced. The verb forms, for instance, are not as helpful in dating 94 as they are in 93. Nonetheless, the case for a preexilic date for the psalm is plausible enough, even if it is far from definitive. Calès suggested preexilic times, as did Dahood. Dahood's case for an early date is based on the phenomenon of prefixing verbs carrying past punctiliar force.[11] He argued that this usage occurs in vv. 5, 6, 12, 16, 18, 19, 21, and 23. Mendenhall dated it even earlier, on the basis of the antiquity of the clause in v. 1b (*ʾl nqmwt hwpyʿ*) and the archaic nature of the ABC/ABD pattern in v. 1 (1973: 73, 85). The points made by Mendenhall about v. 1 are legitimate, but they may only signal the antiquity of the clauses, not of the entire psalm.

Perhaps the most significant fact concerning the date of Psalm 94 is that it is at least a later psalm than Psalm 93. The *terminus a quo* for Psalm 94 would be the 9th century B.C.E. (after Freedman's Phase III) because of the presence of *YH* and because the divine epithet *ṣwr* (v. 22b) does not appear to occur in any of the earlier poetry (Freedman 1976: 114–15). However, even this evidence for an early date must be viewed with caution because of the small size of the corpus of early texts from which the characteristics of early work are drawn.

10. On the other hand, relatively early poems such as the Song of Deborah and David's Lament are sprinkled with *h*-, as well, so the point cannot be pressed.

11. See discussion in chapter 3, at 94:5–7 (p. 46).

## Dating of Psalm 95

Psalm 95 is difficult to date, as several scholars have stated (Delitzsch, Dahood, Anderson, Kraus). Kraus tentatively placed it between the works of the Deuteronomist and the Chronicler. Anderson guessed that it may have been preexilic. Nötscher placed it in the late monarchic period (so Kraus), Oesterley and Leslie in the middle of the fifth century B.C.E.

There are 6 prose particles in this psalm (relative percentage: 6.74), which is one of the higher counts among Psalms 93–100 and, as I have noted above (pp. 184–86), the higher the concentration of prose particles, the later a poem may prove to be. The use of the divine epithet *ṣwr* also shows that the writing does not belong to the earliest phases of Hebrew poetry, according to Freedman (1976: 114–15). The verb forms do not contribute to the discussion in this case. There are connections between Psalm 95 and Isaiah 40–66 that are often adduced as evidence for a late date (e.g., Oesterley, Kraus), but they are not compelling evidence for an exilic or postexilic date, since the Isaiah material may have been dependent on the psalm.[12]

Psalm 95 also has several connections with the Song of Moses in Deuteronomy 32 that have been noted in chapter 3 (see "Form-Critical Genre and Structure," pp. 60–61). Freedman dated the Song to the 10th–9th centuries (1976: 99–102, 118), and there is evidence (noted above, pp. 60–61) that favors dating at least the prophetic oracle of Psalm 95 on the basis of the dating of the Song of Moses. The first part of the psalm is of a type that could have been composed in almost any period. Taking all of these factors into consideration, I conclude that the psalm is most likely preexilic and possibly goes back to the early monarchial period or earlier.

## Dating of Psalm 96

There are few clear indicators of the date of Psalm 96. What are usually considered by scholars to be the clearest indicators of date—its close connections with Isaiah 40–66 and its universal, eschatological outlook (Kraus 1978: 834–35)—are rather subjective criteria. Thus, Anderson (1972: 681) commented that some of the psalm's material may be preexilic and that Isaiah 40–66 may be dependent on the cultic language of the preexilic period. Dahood pointed out further that universalism was by no means a late idea in the ancient Near East and that both the psalmist and the prophet could have been heirs to "a common literary tradition

12. See below, on the dating of Psalm 96, for more on this argument.

long existent in Canaan" (1968: 357). The presence of tricolons (vv. 1–2a, 7–8a) reflects an early literary pattern.[13] The prose particle count of this psalm is the highest of all of the eight psalms being considered, which probably precludes its being placed too early in the poetic tradition.[14] The prefixing verbs are used in the normal manner of standard Hebrew poetry. Divine name usage provides no real clue, since the psalm follows the pattern in Book IV of preferring *YHWH* over *ʾĕlōhîm*. Aside from the extensive use of *YHWH* (11 times), the only other divine epithet is *mʾd* (v. 4a). The most that can be said with confidence is that it is probably preexilic but post–9th century.

## Dating of Psalm 97

The problems of dating this psalm are similar to those of Psalm 96. See the comments there on connections with Isaiah 40–66 and on eschatological motifs. The prose particle count is 7 (all definite articles), and the relative density is 7.37%, the third highest percentage in Psalms 93–100. These statistics argue against a very early date. On the other hand, the verb pattern seems to use prefixing and suffixing forms interchangeably (see chapter 3, at p. 74), a fact that supports a pre–eighth-century date. The most that can be said with certainty is that Psalm 97 was probably preexilic.

## Dating of Psalm 98

The similarities between Psalm 98 and Psalm 96 noted in chapter 4 extend to the question of dating, as well. Many scholars do not deal with the date at all or are noncommittal (e.g., Leslie, Dahood, and Anderson). This is because there are no clear indicators of the date in the psalm. Other scholars characterize it as late, due to universal and eschatological tendencies: Oesterley (1939: 54) dated it to ca. 300 B.C.E. on this basis; Delitzsch, emphasizing connections with Isaiah 40–66, dated it to the exile; Kraus ascribed it to the postexilic cult.

The prose particle count of the psalm is the second highest count of psalms in the group of eight, second only to Psalm 96. This 8% particle count tends to confirm the evidence that the psalm does not belong to the earliest phases of Hebrew poetry. The verb forms are used in the normal fashion of the classical period, and the predominant divine name is *YHWH*, following the pattern in Book IV.

13. See above, on the date of Psalm 93 (p. 186).

14. The particle *ʾăšer* occurs once and *h-* eight times. The relative percentage is 8.04%.

The arguments made at Psalm 96 about the reliability of criteria such as a universal outlook or similarity to Isaiah 40–66 apply here as well. I tentatively prefer a late preexilic date. Freedman (private communication) dates it either to the premonarchic period or to the exile, pointing out the affinities in outlook with Exodus 15 and the fact that the definite article (*h-*) is the most prevalent prose particle here (five of the six occurrences). He contends that, of the three prose particles considered by Andersen and Forbes, the definite article is the least significant in terms of dating, since it also occurs extensively in the Song of Deborah and the Lament of David (poems that are later than Exodus 15). Thus, the poem could conceivably have come from either the premonarchic, the late preexilic, or the exilic period. The same arguments apply to Psalm 96.

## Dating of Psalm 99

There is nothing in Psalm 99 that militates against considering it to be preexilic and dating it to the monarchic period, similar to Psalms 96–98 (so also Anderson and Kraus). The fact that the prose particle count is lower than for Psalms 96–98, and the fact that the divine title *ᶜz* 'the Victorious One' in 99:4 is also possibly found in Exod 15:2 and Ps 29:1, may indicate a date marginally earlier than for Psalms 96–98. On the other hand, this evidence and the reference to Zion (v. 2) also support a monarchic date. Here again, as with the other psalms, this dating must be tentative.

## Dating of Psalm 100

There is little in Psalm 100 to indicate its date of composition. It must have been written when the Temple was standing (see v. 4), but little more can be said. Kraus saw it as postexilic, but he gave no reasons for this. Delitzsch emphasized connections with Isaiah 40–66, and thus he considered it to be exilic or postexilic. Others (Leslie, Anderson, and Dahood) did not discuss the date at all. The prose particle count is 2 (a relative percentage of 2.33). However, since it is such a short psalm, little can be deduced from this fact, and the same is true of the use of divine names. Verb forms do not shed any light on the dating of this psalm. Since the presence of connections with Isaiah 40–66 do not necessarily demand a late date (see above, on the dating of Psalm 96), a preexilic date for Psalm 100 is a reasonable guess.

*Appendix 2*
# *Prose Particle Counts and Percentages in Book IV*

| Psalm | Words | Relative Pronouns | Article[1] | *ʾet* | Total | Relative Pron. % | Article % | *ʾet* % | Total % |
|---|---|---|---|---|---|---|---|---|---|
| 90 | 140 | 0 | 1 | 0 | 1 | 0 | 0.71 | 0 | 0.71 |
| 91 | 112 | 0 | 0 | 0 | 0 | 0 | 0 | 0 | 0 |
| 92 | 112 | 0 | 1 | 1 | 2 | 0 | 0.89 | 0.89 | 1.79 |
| 93 | 45 | 0 | 0 | 0 | 0 | 0 | 0 | 0 | 0 |
| 94 | 169 | 1 | 3 | 1 | 5 | 0.59 | 1.78 | 0.59 | 2.96 |
| 95 | 89 | 4 | 2 | 0 | 6 | 4.49 | 2.25 | 0 | 6.74 |
| 96 | 112 | 1 | 8 | 0 | 9 | 0.89 | 7.14 | 0 | 8.04 |
| 97 | 95 | 0 | 7 | 0 | 7 | 0 | 7.37 | 0 | 7.37 |
| 98 | 75 | 0 | 5 | 1 | 6 | 0 | 6.67 | 1.33 | 8.00 |
| 99 | 83 | 0 | 2 | 0 | 2 | 0 | 2.41 | 0 | 2.41 |
| 100 | 43 | 0 | 1 | 1 | 2 | 0 | 2.33 | 2.33 | 4.65 |
| 101 | 83 | 0 | 0 | 2 | 2 | 0 | 0 | 2.41 | 2.41 |
| 102 | 213[2] | 0 | 4 | 6 | 10 | 0 | 1.88 | 2.82 | 4.70 |
| 103 | 167 | 0 | 7[3] | 5 | 12 | 0 | 4.19 | 2.99 | 7.19 |
| 104 | 271 | 2 | 16 | 2 | 20 | 0.74 | 5.90 | 0.74 | 7.38 |
| 105 | 294 | 3 | 2 | 8 | 13 | 1.02 | 0.68 | 2.72 | 4.42 |
| 106 | 330 | 2 | 7 | 12 | 21 | 0.61 | 2.12 | 3.64 | 6.36 |

*Author's note*: See Andersen and Forbes (1983) for the method, and specifically, pp. 175–76 for the number of prose particles in the Psalms.

1. Andersen and Forbes's "dubious articles" (i.e., those only indicated in MT pointing) are not included here.

2. Andersen and Forbes count 212 words in Psalm 102, reflecting the difference in v. 4 between BHK (which reads *kmwqd*) and BHS (*kmw-qd*).

3. Andersen and Forbes mistakenly counted 6 articles in Psalm 103. Andersen confirms my count above (private communication).

## *Appendix 3*
# *Divine Names and Titles in Psalms 93–100*

### Psalm 93: Divine Name Distribution

I. Names
  A. *YHWH*: vv. 1 [2×], 3, 4, 5
    1. Without parallels: vv. 1 [2×], 3, 4
    2. In parallel with other divine names and titles
      a. *mʾd*: v. 5
II. Titles and Pronouns
  B. *mʾd*: v. 5
    1. In parallel with other divine names and titles
      a. *YHWH*: v. 5
  C. *ʾth*: v. 2

### Psalm 94: Divine Name Distribution

I. Names
  A. *YHWH*: vv. 1, 3, 5, 11, 14, 17, 18, 22, 23
    1. Without parallels: vv. 1, 3, 5, 11, 14, 17, 18, 23
    2. In parallel with other divine names and titles
      a. *ʾlhy*: v. 22
    3. In conjunction with other divine names and titles
      a. *ʾl-nqmwt*: v. 1
      b. *mśgb*: v. 22
      c. *ʾlhynw*: v. 23
  B. *YH*: vv. 7, 12
    1. Without parallels: v. 12
    2. In parallel with other divine names and titles
      a. *ʾlhy yʿqb*: v. 7
  C. *ʾl*: v. 1 [2×] (*ʾl-nqmwt*)
    1. In parallel with other divine names and titles
      a. *špṭ hʾrṣ*: v. 2

2. In conjunction with other divine names and titles
   a. *YHWH*: v. 1

D. *ʾlhym*: vv. 7, 22, 23
   1. Construct chain
      a. *ʾlhy yʿqb*: v. 7
         (1) In parallel with *YH*: v. 7
   2. Suffixed forms
      a. *ʾlhy*: v. 22
         (1) In parallel with *YHWH*: v. 22
         (2) In conjunction with *ʾṣwr mḥsy*: v. 22
      b. *ʾlhynw*: v. 23
         (1) In conjunction with *YHWH*: v. 23

II. Titles and Descriptive Terms

A. *špṭ hʾrṣ*: v. 2
   1. In parallel with other divine names and titles
      a. *ʾl-nqmwt*: v. 1

B. *nṭʿ ʾzn*: v. 9
   1. In parallel with other divine names and titles
      a. *yṣr ʿyn*: v. 9
      b. *ysr gwym*: v. 10
      c. *mlmd ʾdm*: v. 10

C. *yṣr ʿyn*: v. 9
   1. In parallel with other divine names and titles
      a. *nṭʿ ʾzn*: v. 9
      b. *ysr gwym*: v. 10
      c. *mlmd ʾdm*: v. 10

D. *ysr gwym*: v. 10
   1. In parallel with other divine names and titles
      a. *nṭʿ ʾzn*: v. 9
      b. *yṣr ʿyn*: v. 9
      c. *mlmd ʾdm*: v. 10

E. *mlmd ʾdm*: v. 10
   1. In parallel with other divine names and titles
      a. *nṭʿ ʾzn*: v. 9
      b. *yṣr ʿyn*: v. 9
      c. *ysr gwym*: v. 10

F. *ydʿ mḥšbwt ʾdm*: v. 11
   1. In conjunction with other divine names and titles
      a. *YHWH*: v. 11

G. *mśgb*: v. 22
   1. In parallel with other divine names and titles
      a. *ṣwr mḥsy*: v. 22

2. In conjunction with other divine names and titles
   a. *YHWH*: v. 22

H. *ṣwr*: v. 22
   1. Construct chain
      a. *ṣwr mḥsy*: v. 22
         (1) In parallel with *mśgb*: v. 22
         (2) In conjunction with *ʾlhy*: v. 22

## Psalm 95: Divine Name Distribution

I. Names
   A. *YHWH*: vv. 1, 3, 6
      1. Without parallels: vv. 3, 6
      2. In parallel with other divine names and titles
         a. *ṣwr yšʿnw*: v. 1
      3. In conjunction with other divine names and titles
         a. *ʾl gdwl*: v. 3
         b. *mlk gdwl*: v. 3
         c. *ʿśnw*: v. 6
   B. *ʾl*: v. 3 (*ʾl gdwl*)
      1. In parallel with other divine names and titles
         a. *mlk gdwl*: v. 3
      2. In conjunction with other divine names and titles
         a. *YHWH*: v. 3
   C. *ʾlhym*: v. 7
      1. In conjunction with other divine names and titles
         a. *hwʾ*: v. 7

II. Titles, Descriptive Terms, and Pronouns
   A. *ṣwr*: v. 1
      1. Construct chain
         a. *ṣwr yšʿnw*: v. 1
            (1) In parallel with *YHWH*: v. 1
   B. *mlk*: v. 3 (*mlk gdwl*)
      1. In parallel with other divine names and titles
         a. *ʾl gdwl*: v. 3
      2. In conjunction with other divine names and titles
         a. *YHWH*: v. 3
   C. *ʿśnw*: v. 6
      1. In conjunction with other divine names and titles
         a. *YHWH*: v. 6
   D. *hwʾ*: vv. 5, 7
      1. In conjunction with other divine names and titles
         a. *ʾlhym*: v. 7

## Psalm 96: Divine Name Distribution

- I. Names
  - A. *YHWH*: vv. 1 [3×], 4, 5, 7 [2×], 8, 9, 10, 13
    - 1. Without parallels: vv. 5, 9, 10, 13
    - 2. In parallel with other divine names and titles
      - a. *YHWH*: vv. 1 [3×], 7 [2×], 8
      - b. *mʾd*: v. 4
      - c. *hwʾ*: v. 4
- II. Titles and Pronouns
  - A. *mʾd*: v. 4
    - 1. In parallel with other divine names and titles
      - a. *YHWH*: v. 4
      - b. *hwʾ*: v. 4
  - B. *hwʾ*: v. 4
    - 1. In parallel with other divine names and titles
      - a. *YHWH*: v. 4
      - b. *mʾd*: v. 4

## Psalm 97: Divine Name Distribution

- I. Names
  - A. *YHWH*: vv. 1, 5, 8, 9, 10, 12
    - 1. Without parallels: vv. 1, 8, 10, 12
    - 2. In parallel with other divine names and titles
      - a. *ʾdwn kl-hʾrṣ*: v. 5
      - b. *mʾd*: v. 9
    - 3. In conjunction with other divine names and titles
      - a. *ʾth*: v. 9
      - b. *ʿlywn*: v. 9
- II. Titles and Pronouns
  - A. *mʾd*: v. 9
    - 1. In parallel with other divine names and titles
      - a. *YHWH*: v. 9
  - B. *ʾdwn*: v. 5
    - 1. Construct chain
      - a. *ʾdwn kl-hʾrṣ*: v. 5
        - (1) In parallel with *YHWH*: v. 5
  - C. *ʿlywn*: v. 9
    - 1. In conjunction with other divine names and titles
      - a. *YHWH*: v. 9
      - b. *ʾth*: v. 9
  - D. *ʾth*: v. 9

1. In conjunction with other divine names and titles
    a. *YHWH*: v. 9
    b. *ᶜlywn*: v. 9

## Psalm 98: Divine Name Distribution

I. Names
  A. *YHWH*: vv. 1, 2, 4, 5, 6, 9
    1. Without parallels: vv. 1, 2, 4, 5, 6, 9
    2. In conjunction with other divine names and titles
      a. *mlk*: v. 6
  B. *ᵓlhym*: v. 3
    1. Construct chain
      a. *yšwᶜt ᵓlhynw*: v. 3
    2. Suffixed form
      a. *ᵓlhynw*: v. 3
II. Titles
  A. *mlk*: v. 6
    1. In conjunction with other divine names and titles
      a. *YHWH*: v. 6

## Psalm 99: Divine Name Distribution

I. Names
  A. *YHWH*: vv. 1, 2, 5, 6, 8, 9 [2×]
    1. Without parallels: vv. 5, 8, 9 [2×]
    2. In parallel with other referents
      a. *yšb krwbym*: v. 1
      b. *hwᵓ*: v. 2
      c. *šmw*: v. 6
    3. In conjunction with other divine names and titles
      a. *ᵓlhym*: vv. 5, 8, 9 [2×]
  B. *ᵓl*: v. 8
    1. In conjunction with other divine names and titles
      a. *nśᵓ*: v. 8
      b. *nqm*: v. 8
  C. *ᵓlhym*: vv. 5, 8, 9 [2×]
    1. In conjunction with other divine names and titles
      a. *YHWH*: vv. 5, 8, 9 [2×]
II. Titles, Descriptive Terms, and Pronouns
  A. *yšb krwbym*: v. 1

1. In parallel with other divine names and titles
a. *YHWH*: v. 1
B. *gdwl wnwrʾ*: v. 3
C. *ʿz*: v. 4
1. In conjunction with other divine names and titles
a. *mlk*: v. 4
D. *mlk*: v. 4
1. In conjunction with other divine names and titles
a. *ʿz*: v. 4
E. *nśʾ*: v. 8
1. In conjunction with other divine names and titles
a. *ʾl*: v. 8
b. *nqm*: v. 8
F. *nqm*: v. 8
1. In conjunction with other divine names and titles
a. *ʾl*: v. 8
b. *nśʾ*: v. 8
G. *hwʾ*: vv. 2, 5
1. Without parallels: v. 5
2. In parallel with other divine names and titles
a. *YHWH*: v. 2
H. *ʾth*: v. 4 [2×]

## Psalm 100: Divine Name Distribution

I. Names
A. *YHWH*: vv. 1, 2, 3, 5
1. Without parallels: vv. 1, 2, 3, 5
2. In conjunction with other divine names and titles
a. *hwʾ*: v. 3
b. *ʾlhym*: v. 3
B. *ʾlhym*: v. 3
1. In conjunction with other divine names and titles
a. *YHWH*: v. 3
b. *hwʾ*: v. 3
II. Pronouns
A. *hwʾ*: v. 3 [2×]
1. Without parallels: v. 3 [2×]
2. In conjunction with other divine names and titles
a. *YHWH*: v. 3
b. *ʾlhym*: v. 3

# *Appendix 4*
# *Wisdom and Royalist/Zion Traditions in the Psalter*

The focus of this book is limited: it deals with the internal structure of Psalms 93–100. Definitive higher-level conclusions must await further work. However, in this appendix I shall devote a few brief comments to viewpoints that inform our understanding of the final shape of the Psalter. In general, I agree with Wilson and others about the larger contours of the Psalter. However, on one point, their strong deemphasis of the royalist/Zion traditions,[1] I disagree. In this appendix, I wish to deal with problems that result from this deemphasis.

## The Deemphasis of Royalist/Zion Traditions in the Psalter

Most scholars have been in general agreement that the Psalter is a collection heavily laced with traditions or motifs dealing with Jerusalem, Zion, the Temple, and the Davidic covenant alongside motifs that emphasize YHWH's kingship. The locus of the composition of most psalms appears to have been the Temple circles, and the use of most of the psalms appears to have been liturgical (either as individual compositions or as parts of collections that eventually became part of the final Psalter).

However, as I noted in chapter 1, many scholars have argued more specifically that adherents of wisdom traditions were responsible for the *final* form of the Psalter (see especially Brennan, Sheppard, Reindl, Wilson, Ceresko, Seybold). In the process, many scholars have viewed the

1. I am aware of Ollenburger's work (1987), which, among other things, attempts to separate the Zion traditions from the Davidic/royalist ones. However, in their final forms, the psalms do merge Davidic and Zion traditions (see Psalms 2, 78, 132, etc.). In this regard, see, for example, the work of Roberts (1973, 1982, 1987) and Weinfeld (1976; 1985, especially pp. 95–115). In his 1976 work, Weinfeld went so far as to state that "the Davidic dynasty cannot be separated from Zion" (1976: 189).

royal and Zion motifs in the Psalter as subordinate to wisdom motifs. Reindl and Sheppard emphasized the wisdom redaction of the Psalter, as has Wilson.

Wilson has gone further than other scholars by specifically emphasizing the "failure" of the Davidic Covenant (see Wilson 1985a: 209–28, especially 212–14; 1986; 1993b). On the positive side, he gives much weight to the evidence that highlights YHWH's kingship (as opposed to the earthly king exalted in the royal psalms). He also emphasizes the placement, nature, and function of Psalm 1 as signaling a departure from the liturgical and royalist perspective to the wisdom and eschatological perspective. He argues that a final wisdom frame existed, consisting of Psalms 1, 73, 90, 107, and 145 that brackets and thus offsets or negates the influence of the strategically placed royal psalms (Psalms 2, 72, 89, 144) (Wilson 1993b: 80–81). He also points out the large degree of difference between the character of Books I–III (where royal "frame" psalms are more prominent) and the character of Books IV–V.

On the negative side, Wilson highlights the pessimistic notes about the Davidic Covenant, especially in the pivotal Psalm 89 (Wilson 1985a: 212–14). Similarly, McCann (1993a: 98–99) argues that

> an analysis of the final form of Book III reveals an arrangement that serves to assist the community not only to face squarely the disorienting reality of exile, as Wilson would suggest, but also to reach a reorientation based upon the rejection of the Davidic/Zion theology that had formerly been Judah's primary grounds for hope. The canonical juxtaposition of the traditional Davidic/Zion theology with community psalms of lament serves to signal the rejection of this basis for hope.

## A Positive Assessment of Royalist/Zion Traditions in the Psalter

Despite impressive evidence brought to bear by Wilson, McCann, and others, I maintain that the Psalter does not, in the end, speak of the "failure" and "rejection" of the Davidic Covenant. Rather, the Davidic kingdom and YHWH's kingdom coexist in complementary roles throughout the Psalter. Of the two, YHWH's kingdom is clearly the more important and the one from which the Davidic kingdom derives its legitimacy and authority. Yet Zion and the Davidic kingdom are the earthly expressions of YHWH's kingdom in important ways. Furthermore, in my view, the placement of the royal psalms, along with other considerations, are evidence in the Psalter of a continuing hope that is focused on both

Zion and the Davidic Covenant, despite the many flaws of the kings and people who were heirs of that covenant.

## *Psalms 1 and 2 as the Introduction to the Psalter*

Wilson and others have emphasized the nature, placement, and function of Psalm 1 *alone* as an introduction to the Psalter, to the detriment of the nature, placement, and function of Psalm 2. However, rather than functioning as the first psalm of Book I (after the introductory psalm), Psalm 2 more properly should be seen as a companion psalm to Psalm 1, the two in tandem introducing the Psalter.[2] Just as Wilson has (correctly, in my view) identified Psalms 146–50 (and not just Psalm 150) as the concluding "appendix" or climax of praise in the Psalter,[3] so also Book I more properly begins with Psalm 3, and Psalms 1–2 function together as an introduction. Wilson has rightly pointed out the Davidic character of Book I (all of Psalms 3–41 can be shown to be Davidic: Wilson 1985a: 173–76). However, Psalm 2 more properly belongs with Psalm 1 as an opening introduction to the entire Psalter, rather than divorced from it as an introduction solely to Book I.

This is for several reasons.[4] (1) As many scholars have noted, Psalm 1 speaks about the two ways for individuals (the way of the righteous versus the way of the wicked), while Psalm 2 speaks of the two ways for nations. (2) YHWH's anointed king in Psalm 2 functions as the ideal exemplar of a divinely appointed king; he exemplifies in his own person the qualities of the righteous one in Psalm 1. The focus on study of the Torah links Psalm 1 back to the Charter for Kingship in Deut 17:14–20, where the ideal king is instructed to make the study of Torah his all-consuming concern, leaving military and other concerns to YHWH.[5] (3) Psalm 1 begins and Psalm 2 ends with an *ᵓašrê* clause, which further binds the two psalms together. (4) The root *hgh* 'to meditate' is a key word linking both psalms: in Ps 1:2b, the righteous one 'meditates' on YHWH's Torah, whereas in Ps 2:1b, the peoples 'plot' (*hgh*, literally 'meditate') against YHWH and

2. This is not to argue for the single *authorship* of the two psalms (see Willis 1979a), only for their editorial function as a two-part introduction to the Psalter. They *have* been read in various manuscript and literary traditions throughout history as companion psalms (see, e.g., Millard 1994: 9–10)

3. In this way, he shows that Book V actually concludes with the modified doxology in Ps 145:21.

4. Some of the connections between Psalms 1 and 2 were noted in chapter 1, in connection with Sheppard's work (above, p. 7); see also Auffret 1977: 31–34; and, from a different perspective, Brownlee 1971, for discussion and bibliography.

5. See Gerbrandt 1986; Howard 1990.

his anointed one, the Davidic king. (5) The twin motifs of wisdom and Davidic Covenant introduced in Psalms 1–2 are found throughout the Psalter, affirmed, and not (in the case of the Davidic Covenant) merely rejected. The juxtaposition of wisdom and royal psalms noted by Wilson (e.g., Psalms 1 and 2, 72 and 73, 89 and 90, 144 and 145) can just as easily be seen as the Psalter's *affirmation* of both traditions, rather than the subordination or negation of one of them. (6) The untitled nature of Psalm 2 makes it more naturally a companion to Psalm 1 than to the Davidic collection following it.[6] If one compares the Hebrew text of the Psalter with the Old Greek, the relation to Psalm 1 becomes even more striking: whereas 116 of 150 psalms have superscriptions in the MT (131 of 150 if one counts *hllwyh* as a superscription, as Wilson does [see Wilson 1985a: 238–44], and as does the Old Greek version itself), 148 of 150 have them in the Old Greek; the two untitled psalms are Psalms 1 and 2. These data lend credence to the view that the two psalms together are an introduction to the entire work.

Many scholars rightly observe that one of the main emphases of the wisdom portions of the Psalter is an eschatological view of YHWH's kingship that focuses on YHWH as King, not a human king. This is certainly an undisputed focus in Book IV. However, it must be remembered that the human king was a vice-regent for YHWH, that he was YHWH's anointed one, installed and blessed by YHWH to represent him (Ps 2:2, 7; cf. 2 Samuel 7). The royalist outlook in the Psalter and elsewhere was not *inherently* negative, at least in its theoretical underpinnings.[7] Thus, the two views of kingship—divine and human—should be seen as complementing each other, not contradicting. As Mays states (1986a: 155),

> The relation of the Psalms to David brings out and emphasizes the organizing, unifying subject of the psalter, namely, the Kingdom of God. . . . Yet the Davidic connection directs the reader to think of each psalm and the entire psalter as an expression of faith in the reign of the Lord as the sphere in which individual and corporate life is lived. It does so because it is quite impossible to separate David from his identity as king chosen to be the regent and agent on earth of God's reign over God's people and the nations of the world.

6. See Wilson's arguments about the Davidic character of Book I (1985a: 173–76).

7. Many scholars have argued that most biblical texts favor the idea behind the Davidic kingship, which is the earthly complement to YHWH's kingship or the earthly expression of it. See my reviews of much of this literature (Howard 1988, 1990).

Mays has developed this idea further in a recent work, in which he states that "the declaration '*YHWH malak*' involves a vision of reality that is the theological centre of the Psalter" (1994b: 245). An integral part of this is that "YHWH has a special person. The person is called his king, his anointed, his son, his chosen, David his servant" (1994b: 241). He develops this more fully in his 1991 essay, in which he shows that the expectation of a Messiah was part of the warp and woof of the Psalter, the downbeat nature of Psalm 89 notwithstanding. As for Psalm 2, Mays states (1991: 2) that "Psalm 2 is the second panel of the introduction to the Book of Psalms. . . . Together Psalms 1 and 2 introduce major topics and terms that are woven throughout the texture of the entire book."

Seen in this way, the introduction to the Psalter (Psalms 1–2) states that what follows is indeed Torah, to be studied (Psalm 1), that YHWH is king (Psalm 2), and that he has vested a human king with kingly authority (Psalm 2).[8]

Miller's 1993 essay focuses especially on the role of Psalms 1 and 2 as an introduction. However, his emphasis in this essay (and in his 1994 essay, as well) is primarily on their function in signaling a royalist interest in Book I. In both essays, however, he suggests that the two psalms may indeed go beyond being a "royalist" introduction to Book I to being a "royalist" introduction to the entire Psalter. For example, he states that "Psalms 1 and 2 were to be read together as an *entrée* into the Psalter" (1993: 85), and he concludes his later essay by stating (1994: 141):

> It almost seems as if we are once more before the Deuteronomistic theology of kingship. It may be that all of this in fact reflects a Deuteronomistic influence on the redaction of the Psalter. I do not know. If it does, then we are made even more aware of the centrality of that particular stream in biblical theology and its influence on the theology of kingship and the royal idea.

However, Miller also emphasizes Wilson's point that Psalm 89 marks the "failure" of the Davidic Covenant (1994: 140–41) so much that he does not follow his own suggestions to what should be their logical conclusion, which is the point I am arguing here, that a royalist outlook can be traced throughout the *entire* Psalter, not just Book I (or Books I–III).

There is a delicate interplay between trust in and focus on the human king (seen in the royal psalms) and trust in and focus on YHWH

8. See now also Zenger's 1993 essay, which argues for Psalms 1 *and* 2 as the editorial introduction to the Psalter. Shepherd (1995: 443–44) argues the same point (see the comments on both essays above, in chapter 1, pp. 17, 18–19).

the King (seen in the Kingship of YHWH psalms). The transition from Book III to Book IV emphasizes that, if God's people relied too heavily on a human institution for salvation (the Davidic monarchy), then they were bound to be disappointed (see the discussion of Psalms 88–92 above, chapter 5, pp. 167–70). However, the point in the Psalter is not that the Davidic Covenant itself has failed; it is a gift from YHWH to David and to his own people Israel. Rather, YHWH's *people* have failed, and thus the Davidic Covenant has of necessity taken a back seat historically (and in the Psalter) for a time. In the Psalter, focus on this covenant yields, after Psalm 89, to a focus on YHWH's infinitely greater kingship, but it does not completely disappear (see, e.g., Psalms 132, 144).

We should remember that there is another biblical work that is indisputably postexilic (as is the Psalter in its final form), 1–2 Chronicles, a work that is overwhelmingly positive about the Davidic kingship.[9] Thus, just because Judah had experienced exile does not mean that it had abandoned all hope in the promises and benefits of the Davidic Covenant.

The eight concluding psalms of David in Book V of the Psalter (Psalms 138–45) serve as a reminder that, despite the pessimism of Psalm 89, David still was an important figure in the outlook of the book.[10] The juxtaposition of a royal psalm (Psalm 144) with a Kingship of YHWH psalm (Psalm 145) to conclude the book serves the same purpose that the juxtaposition of Psalm 1 and Psalm 2 does: human and divine kingship are *both* important in the Psalter. If the two themes were to be weighed, obviously YHWH's kingship is, in the end, infinitely more important,[11] but its superiority does not negate the significance of the ideal expression of the human kingship.[12]

## *The Merging of Wisdom and Royalist/Zion Motifs*

Another proof that the Psalter does not in the end reject the royalist views contained in it is that wisdom and royal perspectives have much in common, despite obvious differences. The tension between the two is eased somewhat, for example, by the viewpoint advanced in Psalm 15, that the one who lives a life in accordance with precepts commonly found

9. See Howard 1988: 26–30 and bibliography there.

10. The fact that in the Psalter 73 of 150 psalms are attributed to David also shows David's importance.

11. See Millard's point, cited above, p. 18. His point is not necessarily that David or royal motifs are *insignificant* in the Psalter, but only that YHWH's kingship is indisputably greater than any human kingship.

12. See especially Howard 1990.

in the Torah—and advanced in the wisdom literature at large—is the one who will dwell on YHWH's holy hill, Zion. Zion was the site of the earthly expression of YHWH's heavenly kingdom, and it was there that human and divine kingship met. Psalm 101—a royal psalm—also brings together the two perspectives, by couching the king's responsibilities in sapiential terms.[13] Furthermore, there is a late passage, Sir 24:8–12, that also unambiguously brings the Zion and wisdom motifs together, this time in the intertestamental period.[14] In this text, Dame Wisdom finds a locus for her dwelling on earth in Israel, specifically in Jerusalem, on Zion.

## *Royalist/Zion Motifs in Book IV*

Wilson (1985a: 187–88, 215) and Goulder (1975: 274–75) have correctly observed that Mosaic and Exodus motifs are most concentrated in Book IV. I have pointed out in the course of this book the presence of extensive wisdom motifs, as well.[15] However, despite these valid observations, we must heed the indications that Zion, Temple, and royalist perspectives were also important in Book IV. My focus here is primarily on Psalms 93–100 in Book IV.

Zion and YHWH's holy mountain are important in Ps 97:8 and, especially, Psalm 99 (vv. 2, 5, 9).[16] Zion is YHWH's footstool (99:5). The reference to YHWH's holy mountain in 99:9 can only be Zion, because of the reference in v. 2.

References to the Temple include Ps 93:5 ("your house, [your] holy habitation"),[17] Ps 95:11b ("my rest"),[18] and Ps 100:4 ("his gates . . . his courts"). Again, Psalm 99 emerges as an important passage on this theme. Not only are Zion and YHWH's holy mountain mentioned (vv. 2, 9), but the material of vv. 6–8 serves to bring early motifs from the Mosaic period down into the time and perspective of the monarchy. As I noted in chapter 3 (p. 89), the reference to Samuel alongside Moses and Aaron in v. 6 serves to loosen the ties with the period of Moses and to link the perspective of the psalm to a later period. Since Samuel was the inaugurator of the period of the monarchy and since Psalm 99 otherwise fo-

13. See the discussion of Psalm 101 in chapter 5 (pp. 181–82).

14. Gese has made this point as part of a wide-ranging essay (1981: 32–35).

15. See the summary above in chapter 5, pp. 167–73.

16. They are also prominent in Ps 102:14, 17, 22[13, 16, 21].

17. Despite the early parallel with Exod 15:13; see the discussion in chapter 3 at 93:5b (p. 41).

18. See the discussion in chapter 3 on this understanding, p. 57.

cuses on Zion, its outlook (along with Psalm 100's) is firmly rooted in Temple worship on Zion.

Furthermore, in Psalms 97 and 99, the references to the theophanic cloud (*ᶜnn*: 97:2, 99:7) also serve to bring the reader's attention away from the Mosaic period exclusively. In 99:6, the reference to Moses and Aaron in conjunction with a reference to the cloud obviously refers back to the wilderness cloud; however, the references to Samuel in v. 6 and Zion in v. 2 broaden the meaning of the *ᶜnn*. As noted in the discussion of the "Key-Word Links" between Psalms 97 and 99 in chapter 4 (pp. 158–59), *ᶜnn* is used in Biblical Hebrew to refer to more than just YHWH's appearance in the Mosaic period.

Psalm 95 is also important in bridging the gap between Mosaic and later periods. I have mentioned (in chapter 3 above, p. 57) Braulik's contention (1987) that the reference in 95:11b to "my rest" points beyond the land of the inheritance to the Temple, where YHWH's presence and true rest are to be found, an argument that is well taken.

Thus, despite many obvious Mosaic motifs in the original forms of individual psalms among Psalms 93–100, the psalms as they now stand focus much more on Zion and traditions associated with the monarchy than many scholars have allowed.[19]

## Conclusion

I conclude, then, with Mays (1986a: 155), that the organizing principle of the Psalter ultimately has to do with the reign of God as King. This theme manifests itself in the dual expressions of YHWH's divine kingship and the Davidic kings' human kingship, both of which find their earthly expression at Zion. The Zion, royal, and Davidic traditions displayed prominently and placed strategically throughout the Psalter take their place alongside the traditions of YHWH as King to portray the fact that YHWH's rule extends everywhere: to the nations, the cosmos, nature, and even Israel. Its expression in Israel is through the Davidic kingship, which is centered at Zion, and it is focused on YHWH through worship at Zion. The faithful reader of the Psalter will do as the king is supposed to do: study and meditate on YHWH's disclosure of himself in both the Torah *and* the Psalter (Deut 17:18–19, Psalm 1). The final wisdom editing of the Psalter does not obliterate these important components of the Psalter's message.

19. If my analysis were extended beyond Psalms 93–100, this emphasis would certainly be found elsewhere in Book IV (and Book V), as well.

# *Select Bibliography*


Achtemeier, P. J., editor

1980 *Society of Biblical Literature 1980: Seminar Papers.* Society of Biblical Literature Seminar Papers 19. Missoula, Montana: Scholars Press.

Ackroyd, P. R.

1966 The Interpretation of הַדְרַת קֹדֶשׁ. *Journal of Theological Studies* 17: 393–96.

Alden, R. L.

1974 Chiastic Psalms: A Study in the Mechanics of Semitic Poetry in Psalms 1–50. *Journal of the Evangelical Theological Society* 17: 11–28.

1976 Chiastic Psalms (II): A Study in the Mechanics of Semitic Poetry in Psalms 51–100. *Journal of the Evangelical Theological Society* 19: 191–200.

1978 Chiastic Psalms (III): A Study in the Mechanics of Semitic Poetry in Psalms 101–50. *Journal of the Evangelical Theological Society* 21: 199–210.

Alexander, J. A.

1865 *The Psalms.* 6th edition. 3 volumes. New York: Scribner's.

Allen, L. C.

1982 Psalm 73: An Analysis. *Tyndale Bulletin* 33: 93–118.

1983 *Psalms 101–150.* Word Biblical Commentary 21. Waco, Texas: Word.

1986 David as Exemplar of Spirituality: The Redactional Function of Psalm 19. *Biblica* 67: 544–46.

Alter, R.

1981 *The Art of Biblical Narrative.* New York: Basic Books.

1985 *The Art of Biblical Poetry.* New York: Basic Books.

Andersen, F. I.

1974 *The Sentence in Biblical Hebrew.* The Hague: Mouton.

Andersen, F. I., and Forbes, A. D.

1983 "Prose Particle" Counts of the Hebrew Bible. Pp. 165–83 in C. L. Meyers and M. O'Connor, editors, *The Word of the Lord Shall Go Forth: Essays in Honor of David Noel Freedman in Celebration of His Sixtieth Birthday.* Winona Lake, Indiana: Eisenbrauns.

Andersen, F. I., and Freedman, D. N.

1980 *Hosea.* Anchor Bible 24. Garden City, New York: Doubleday.

Anderson, A. A.

1972 *The Book of Psalms.* 2 volumes. New Century Bible Commentary. Grand Rapids, Michigan: Eerdmans.

Anderson, R. D. Jr.

1994 The Division and Order of the Psalms. *Westminster Theological Journal* 56: 219–41.

Auffret, P.

1977 *The Literary Structure of Psalm 2.* Translated by D. J. A. Clines. Journal for the Study of the Old Testament Supplement Series 3. Sheffield: JSOT Press.

1978 Essai sur la structure littéraire du psaume 1. *Biblische Zeitschrift* 22: 26–45.

1982 *La sagesse a bâti sa maison: Études de structures littéraires dans l'Ancient Testament et specialement dans les psaumes.* Orbis biblicus et orientalis 49. Fribourg: Editions Universitaires.

1984 Essai sur la structure littéraire du Psaume 94. *Biblische Notizen* 24: 44–72.

1986 Complements sur la structure littéraire du Ps 2 et son rapport au Ps 1. *Biblische Notizen* 35: 7–13.

1988 "Allez, fils, entendez-moi": Étude structurelle du Psaume 34 et son rapport au Psaume 33. *Église et Théologie* 19: 5–31.

1992 *Quatre psaumes et un cinquième: Étude structurelle des Psaumes 7 à 10 et 35.* Paris: Letouzey & Ané.

1993 *Voyez de vos yeux: Étude structurelle de vingt psaumes, dont le Psaume 119.* Vetus Testamentum Supplements 48. Leiden: Brill.

Auwers, J.-M.

1994 *Le psautier hébraique et ses éditeurs: Recherches sur une forme canonique du livre des Psaumes.* Ph.D. Dissertation, University of Louvain.

Bar-Efrat, S.

1980 Some Observations on the Analysis of Structure in Biblical Narrative. *Vetus Testamentum* 30: 154–73.

Barré, L. M

1983 *Halĕlû yāh*: A Broken Inclusion. *Catholic Biblical Quarterly* 45: 195–200.

Barth, C.

1976 Concatenatio im Ersten Buch des Psalters. Pp. 30–40 in B. Benzing, O. Böcher, and G. Mayer, editors, *Wort und Wirklichkeit: Studien zur afrikanistik und orientalistik.* E. L. Rapp Festschrift. Meisenheim am Glan: Hain.

Beckwith, R.

1985 *The Old Testament Canon of the New Testament Church and Its Background in Early Judaism.* Grand Rapids, Michigan: Eerdmans.

1995 The Early History of the Psalter. *Tyndale Bulletin* 46: 1–28.

Berlin, A.

1985 *The Dynamics of Biblical Parallelism.* Bloomington: Indiana University Press.

Boys, T.

1825 *Key to the Book of Psalms.* London: Seeley.

Braude, W. G., translator

1959 *The Midrash on Psalms.* 2 volumes. New Haven: Yale University Press.

Braulik, G.

1987 Gottes Ruhe—Das Land oder der Tempel? Zu Psalm 95,11. Pp. 33–44 in E. Haag and F.-L. Hossfeld, editors, *Freude an der Weisung des Herrn: Beiträge zur Theologie der Psalmen.* H. Groß Festschrift. Stuttgart: Katholisches Bibelwerk.

Brennan, J. P.

1976 Some Hidden Harmonies in the Fifth Book of Psalms. Pp. 126–58 in R. F. McNamara, editor, *Essays in Honor of Joseph P. Brennan.* Rochester, New York: St. Bernard's Seminary.

1980 Psalms 1–8: Some Hidden Harmonies. *Biblical Theology Bulletin* 10: 25–29.

Brettler, M. Z.

1989 *God Is King: Understanding an Israelite Metaphor.* Journal for the Study of the Old Testament Supplement Series 76. Sheffield: Sheffield Academic Press.

Briggs, C. A.

1906 *A Critical and Exegetical Commentary on the Book of Psalms.* 2 volumes. International Critical Commentary. Edinburgh: T. & T. Clark.

Brown, F.; Driver, S. R.; and Briggs, C. A.

1907 *A Hebrew and English Lexicon of the Old Testament.* Oxford: Clarendon.

Brownlee, W. H.

1971 Psalms 1–2 as a Coronation Liturgy. *Biblica* 52: 321–36.

Brueggemann, W.

1991 Bounded by Obedience and Praise: The Psalms as Canon. *Journal for the Study of the Old Testament* 50: 63–92.

1993 Response to James L. Mays, "The Question of Context." Pp. 29–41 in J. C. McCann, editor, *The Shape and Shaping of the Psalter.* Journal for the Study of the Old Testament Supplement Series 159. Sheffield: JSOT Press.

Brunert, G.

1996 *Psalm 102 im Kontext des vierten Psalmenbuches.* Stuttgarter biblische Beiträge 30. Stuttgart: Katholisches Bibelwerk.

Buber, M.

1953 *Good and Evil: Two Interpretations.* New York: Scribner's.

Bullinger, E. W.

1898 *Figures of Speech Used in the Bible: Explained and Illustrated.* London: Eyre & Spottiswoode.

Buttenwieser, M.

1938 *The Psalms: Chronologically Treated with a New Translation.* Chicago: University of Chicago Press.

Calès, J.

1936 *Le livre des Psaumes.* 5th edition. 2 volumes. Paris: Beauchesne.

Calvin, J.

1949 *Commentary on the Book of Psalms.* 5 volumes. Translated by J. Anderson. Grand Rapids, Michigan: Eerdmans.

Casanowicz, I. M.

1896 The Emphatic Particle ל in the Old Testament. *Journal of the American Oriental Society* 16: clxvi–clxxi.

Cassuto, U.

1947 The Sequence and Arrangement of the Biblical Sections. Paper read at World Congress of Jewish Studies. Reprinted. Pp. 1–6 in his *Biblical and Oriental Studies, Volume 1: Bible.* Translated by I. Abrahams. Jerusalem: Magnes (1973).

Ceresko, A. R.

1990 The Sage in the Psalms. Pp. 217–30 in J. G. Gammie and L. G. Perdue, editors, *The Sage in Israel and the Ancient Near East.* Winona Lake, Indiana: Eisenbrauns.

Cheyne, T. K.

1891 *The Origin and Religious Contents of the Psalter in the Light of Old Testament Criticism and the History of Religions.* New York: Whittaker.

1904 *The Book of Psalms.* 2 volumes. London: Kegan, Paul, Touch.

Childs, B. S.

1976 Reflections on the Modern Study of the Psalms. Pp. 377–88 in F. M. Cross, W. E. Lemke, and P. D. Miller, editors, *Magnalia Dei: The Mighty Acts of God—Essays on the Bible and Archaeology in Memory of G. Ernest Wright.* Garden City, New York: Doubleday.

1979 *Introduction to the Old Testament as Scripture.* Philadelphia: Fortress.

Cohen, A.

1945 *The Psalms.* Soncino Books of the Bible. London: Soncino.

Collins, T.

1987 Decoding the Psalms: A Structural Approach to the Psalter. *Journal for the Study of the Old Testament* 37: 41–60.

Combs, A. E.

1963 *The Creation Motif in the "Enthronement Psalms."* Ph.D. Dissertation, Columbia University.

Craigie, P. C.

1972 Psalm XXIX in the Hebrew Poetic Tradition. *Vetus Testamentum* 22: 143–51.

1983 *Psalms 1–50.* Word Biblical Commentary 19. Waco, Texas: Word.

Creach, J. F. D.

1996a *The Choice of Yahweh's Refuge in the Editing of the Psalter.* Journal for the Study of the Old Testament Supplement Series 217. Sheffield: Sheffield Academic Press.

1996b The Shape of Book Four of the Psalter and the Shape of Second Isaiah. Paper delivered at the 1996 Society of Biblical Literature Meetings, New Orleans, Book of Psalms Section.

Crenshaw, J. L.

1969 Method in Determining Wisdom Influence upon "Historical" Literature. *Journal of Biblical Literature* 88: 129–42.

1974 Wisdom. Pp. 225–64 in J. H. Hayes, editor, *Old Testament Form Criticism.* San Antonio: Trinity University Press.

1976a Studies in Ancient Israelite Wisdom: Prolegomenon. Pp. 1–60 in *Studies in Ancient Israelite Wisdom.* New York: KTAV.

1976b Wisdom in the Old Testament. Pp. 952–56 in K. Crim, editor, *The Interpreter's Dictionary of the Bible: Supplement.* Nashville: Abingdon.

1985 The Wisdom Literature. Pp. 369–407 in D. A. Knight and G. M. Tucker, editors, *The Hebrew Bible and Its Modern Interpreters.* Philadelphia: Fortress / Chico, California: Scholars Press.

Crenshaw, J. L., editor

1976 *Studies in Ancient Israelite Wisdom.* New York: KTAV.

Crim, K. R.

1959 *Israelite Kingship and the Royal Psalms.* Th.D. Dissertation, Union Theological Seminary.

1962 *The Royal Psalms.* Richmond: John Knox.

Cross, F. M. Jr.

1950 Notes on a Canaanite Psalm in the Old Testament. *Bulletin of the American Schools of Oriental Research* 117: 19–21.

1973 *Canaanite Myth and Hebrew Epic.* Cambridge: Harvard University Press.

Cross, F. M. Jr., and Freedman, D. N.
1953 A Royal Song of Thanksgiving: II Samuel 22 = Psalm 18. *Journal of Biblical Literature* 72: 15–34.
1975 *Studies in Ancient Yahwistic Poetry.* Society of Biblical Literature Dissertation Series 21. Missoula, Montana: Scholars Press.

Culley, R. C.
1967 *Oral Formulaic Language in the Biblical Psalms.* Toronto: University of Toronto Press.

Dahood, M. J.
1952 The *Lāmedh* of Reinforcement. *Biblica* 33: 192–94.
1966 *Psalms I.* 2d edition. Anchor Bible 16. Garden City, New York: Doubleday.
1968 *Psalms II.* 3d edition. Anchor Bible 17. Garden City, New York: Doubleday.
1970 *Psalms III.* Anchor Bible 17A. Garden City, New York: Doubleday.

Davies, G. H.
1973 Psalm 95. *Zeitschrift für die Alttestamentliche Wissenschaft* 85: 183–95.

Davis, B. C.
1996 *A Contextual Analysis of Psalms 107–118.* Ph.D. Dissertation, Trinity Evangelical Divinity School.

Delitzsch, F.
1846 *Symbolae ad Psalmos illustrandos isagogicae.* Leipzig.
1881 *Biblical Commentary on the Psalms.* 3 volumes. Translated by Francis Bolton. Grand Rapids, Michigan: Eerdmans.

DeMeyer, F.
1981 La sagesse psalmique et le psaume 94. *Bijdragen* 42: 22–45.

Dever, W. G.
1984 Asherah, Consort of Yahweh? New Evidence from Kuntillet Ajrud. *Bulletin of the American Schools of Oriental Research* 255: 21–37.

Donner, H.
1967 Ugaritismen in der Psalmenforschung. *Zeitschrift für die Alttestamentliche Wissenschaft* 79: 322–50.

Drijvers, P.
1964 *The Psalms: Their Structure and Meaning.* New York: Herder & Herder.

Eaton, J. H.
1967 *Psalms.* Torch Bible Commentaries. London: SCM.
1968 Proposals in Psalms XCIX and CXIX. *Vetus Testamentum* 18: 555–58.
1979 The Psalms and Israelite Worship. Pp. 238–73 in G. W. Anderson, editor, *Tradition and Interpretation.* Oxford: Clarendon.
1986 *Kingship and the Psalms.* 2d edition. Sheffield: JSOT Press.

Elliger, K., and Rudolph, W., editors
1977 *Biblia Hebraica Stuttgartensia.* Stuttgart: Deutsche Bibelstiftung.

Emerton, J. A.
1982 New Light on Israelite Religion: The Implications of the Inscriptions from Kuntillet ᶜAjrud. *Zeitschrift für die Alttestamentliche Wissenschaft* 94: 2–20.

Even-Shoshan, A., editor
1981 *A New Concordance of the Bible.* Jerusalem: Kiryat Sepher.

Ewald, G. H. A. V.
1880 *Commentary on the Psalms.* 2 volumes. Translated by E. Johnson. London: Williams and Norgate.

Fabry, H.-J.
1987 11QPs[a] und die Kanonizität des Psalters. Pp. 45–67 in E. Haag and F.-L. Hossfeld, editors, *Freude an der Weisung des Herrn: Beiträge zur Theologie der Psalmen.* H. Groß Festschrift. Stuttgart: Katholisches Bibelwerk.

Fischer, B.
1987 Eine Predigt John Henry Newmans aus dem Jahre 1840 zur Frage des christlichen Psalmen verständnisses. Pp. 69–79 in E. Haag and F.-L. Hossfeld, editors, *Freude an der Weisung des Herrn: Beiträge zur Theologie der Psalmen.* H. Groß Festschrift. Stuttgart: Katholisches Bibelwerk.

Fitzmyer, J. A.
1967 *The Aramaic Inscriptions of Sefîre.* Biblica et Orientalia 19. Rome: Pontifical Biblical Institute.

Flint, P.
1996 *The Dead Sea Psalms Scrolls and the Book of Psalms.* Studies on the Texts of the Desert of Judah 17. Leiden: Brill.

Franke, C.
1994 *Isaiah 46, 47, and 48: A New Literary-Critical Reading.* University of California, San Diego Biblical and Judaic Studies 3. Winona Lake, Indiana: Eisenbrauns.

Freedman, D. N.
1971 The Structure of Psalm 137. Pp. 187–205 in Hans Goedicke, editor, *Near Eastern Studies in Honor of William Foxwell Albright.* Baltimore: Johns Hopkins University Press. Reprinted. Pp. 303–21 in *Pottery, Poetry, and Prophecy* (1980a).

1972a Prolegomena. Pp. VIII–XLVI in G. B. Gray, *The Forms of Hebrew Poetry*: New York: KTAV.

1972b Acrostics and Metrics in Hebrew Poetry. *Harvard Theological Review* 65: 367–92. Reprinted. Pp. 51–76 in *Pottery, Poetry, and Prophecy* (1980a).

1972c The Refrain in David's Lament over Saul and Jonathan. Pp. 115–26 in volume 1 of *Ex Orbe Religionum: Studia Geo Widengren Oblata.* Leiden: Brill. Reprinted. Pp. 263–72 in *Pottery, Poetry, and Prophecy* (1980a).

1972d The Broken Contruct Chain. *Biblica* 53: 534–36. Reprinted. Pp. 51–76 in *Pottery, Poetry, and Prophecy* (1980a).

1973 God Almighty in Psalm 78,59. *Biblica* 54: 268. Reprinted. P. 347 in *Pottery, Poetry, and Prophecy* (1980a).

1975a Early Israelite History in the Light of Early Israelite Poetry. Pp. 3–35 in H. Goedicke and J. J. M. Roberts, editors, *Unity and Diversity.* Baltimore: Johns Hopkins University Press. Reprinted. Pp. 131–78 in *Pottery, Poetry, and Prophecy* (1980a).

1975b Psalm 113 and the Song of Hannah. *Eretz-Israel* 14 (H. L. Ginsberg Volume): 56–70. Reprinted. Pp. 243–61 in *Pottery, Poetry, and Prophecy* (1980a).

1976 Divine Names and Titles in Early Hebrew Poetry. Pp. 55–107 in F. M. Cross, W. E. Lemke, and P. D. Miller, editors, *Magnalia Dei: The Mighty Acts of God—Essays on the Bible and Archaeology in Memory of G. Ernest Wright.* Garden City, New York: Doubleday. Reprinted. Pp. 77–129 in *Pottery, Poetry, and Prophecy* (1980a).

1977 Pottery, Poetry, and Prophecy. *Journal of Biblical Literature* 96: 5–26. Reprinted. Pp. 1–22 in *Pottery, Poetry, and Prophecy* (1980a).

1980a *Pottery, Poetry, and Prophecy: Studies in Early Hebrew Poetry.* Winona Lake, Indiana: Eisenbrauns.

1980b The Broken Construct Chain. *Biblica* 53: 534–36. Reprinted. Pp. 339–41 in *Pottery, Poetry, and Prophecy* (1980a).

1985a Prose Particles in the Poetry of the Primary History. Pp. 49–62 in A. Kort and S. Morschauser, editors, *Biblical and Related Studies Presented to Samuel Iwry.* Winona Lake, Indiana: Eisenbrauns.

1985b Acrostic Poems in the Hebrew Bible: Alphabetic and Otherwise. *Catholic Biblical Quarterly* 47: 624–42.

1987 Another Look at Biblical Hebrew Poetry. Pp. 11–28 in E. Follis, editor, *Directions in Biblical Hebrew Poetry.* Journal for the Study of the Old Testament Supplement Series 40. Sheffield: JSOT Press.

1991 *The Unity of the Hebrew Bible.* Ann Arbor: The University of Michigan Press.

Freedman, D. N., and Franke Hyland, C.

1973 Psalm 29: A Structural Analysis. *Harvard Theological Review* 66: 237–56.

Gelston, A.

1966 A Note on יהוה מלך. *Vetus Testamentum* 16: 507–12.

Gerbrandt, G. E.

1986 *Kingship according to the Deuteronomistic History.* Society of Biblical Literature Dissertation Series 87. Atlanta: Scholars Press.

Gerstenberger, E. S.

1974 Psalms. Pp. 179–223 in J. H. Hayes, editor, *Old Testament Form Criticism.* San Antonio: Trinity University Press.

1988 *Psalms: Part I with an Introduction to Cultic Poetry.* The Forms of the Old Testament Literature 14. Grand Rapids: Eerdmans.

1994 Der Psalter als Buch und als Sammlung. Pp. 3–13 in K. Seybold and E. Zenger, editors, *Neue Wege der Psalmenforschung: Für Walter Beyerlin.* Herders biblische Studien 1. Freiburg: Herder.

Gese, H.

1972 Die Enstehung der Büchereinteilung des Psalters. Pp. 57–64 in volume 2 of J. Schreiner, editor, *Wort, Lied und Gottesspruch: Beiträge zu Psalmen und Propheten.* J. Ziegler Festschrift. Würzburg/Stuttgart: Echter.

1981 Wisdom, Son of Man, and the Origins of Christology: The Consistent Development of Biblical Theology. *Horizons in Biblical Theology* 3: 23–57.

Girard, M.

1981 Analyse structurelle du Psaume 95. *Science et Esprit* 33: 179–89.

Glueck, N.

1967 *Ḥesed in the Bible.* Cincinnati: Hebrew Union College Press.

Goldingay, J. E.

1977 Repetition and Variation in the Psalms. *Jewish Quarterly Review* 68: 146–51.

Gordon, C. H.

1967 *Ugaritic Textbook.* Rome: Pontifical Biblical Institute.

1977 Poetic Legends and Myths from Ugarit. *Berytus* 25: 5–133.

Gottwald, N. K.

1979 *The Tribes of Yahweh: A Sociology of the Religion of Liberated Israel, 1250–1050 B.C.E.* Maryknoll, New York: Orbis.

Goulder, M. D.

1975 The Fourth Book of the Psalter. *Journal of Theological Studies* 26: 269–89.

1982 *The Psalms of the Sons of Korah.* Journal for the Study of the Old Testament Supplement Series 20. Sheffield: JSOT Press.

Gray, J.
1956 Hebrew Conception of the Kingship of God. *Vetus Testamentum* 6: 268–85.

Grol, H. W. M. van
1983 Paired Tricola in the Psalms, Isaiah, and Jeremiah. *Journal for the Study of the Old Testament* 25: 55–73.

Gros Louis, K. R. R.
1982 Some Methodological Considerations. Pp. 13–24 in Gros Louis and Ackerman, editors, *Literary Interpretations of Biblical Narratives, II.* Nashville: Abingdon.

Gros Louis, K. R. R., and Ackerman, J. S., editors
1982 *Literary Interpretations of Biblical Narratives, II.* Nashville: Abingdon.

Gros Louis, K. R. R.; Ackerman, J. S.; and Warshaw, T. S., editors
1974 *Literary Interpretations of Biblical Narratives, I.* New York: Abingdon.

Grossberg, D.
1989 *Centripetal and Centrifugal Structures in Biblical Poetry.* Society of Biblical Literature Monograph Series 39. Atlanta: Scholars Press.

Gunkel, H.
1926 *Die Psalmen.* 4th edition. Göttinger Handkommentar zum Alten Testament. Göttingen: Vandenhoeck & Ruprecht.
1933 *Einleitung in Die Psalmen.* 2d edition. Edited by J. Begrich. Göttingen: Vandenhoeck & Ruprecht.
1967 *The Psalms: A Form-Critical Introduction.* Translated by T. M. Horner. Philadelphia: Fortress.

Haag, E., and Hossfeld, F.-L., editors
1987 *Freude an der Weisung des Herrn: Beiträge zur Theologie de Psalmen.* H. Groß Festschrift. Stuttgart: Katholisches Bibelwerk.

Hallo, W. W.
1976 Toward a History of Sumerian Literature. Pp. 181–203 in *Sumerological Studies in Honor of Thorkild Jacobsen.* Assyriological Studies 20. Chicago: University of Chicago Press.

Haran, M.
1992 11QPs[a] and the Composition of the Book of Psalms [Hebrew]. Pp. 123*–28* in M. Fishbane, E. Tov, and W. W. Fields, editors, *"Sha<sup>c</sup>arei Talmon": Studies in the Bible, Qumran, and the Ancient Near East Presented to Shemaryahu Talmon.* Winona Lake, Indiana: Eisenbrauns. [English summary: pp. xxi–xxii.]
1993 11QPs[a] and the Canonical Book of Psalms. Pp. 193–201 in M. Brettler and M. Fishbane, editors, *Minḥah le-Naḥum.* Nahum M. Sarna Festschrift. Journal for the Study of the Old Testament Supplement Series 154. Sheffield: JSOT Press.

Haupt, P.
1905–1906 The Hebrew Stem Naḥal, to Rest. *American Journal of Semitic Languages and Literatures* 22: 195–206.

Held, M.
1962 The YQTL-QTL (QTL-YQTL) Sequence of Identical Verbs in Biblical Hebrew and Ugaritic. Pp. 281–90 in M. Ben-Horim et al., editors, *Studies and Essays in Honor of Abraham A. Neuman.* Leiden: Brill.

Hengstenberg, E. W.
1860–1969 *Commentary on the Psalms.* 4th edition. 3 volumes. Edinburgh: T. & T. Clark.
Henn, T. R.
1970 *The Bible as Literature.* New York: Oxford University Press.
Hermisson, H.-J.
1978 Observations on the Creation Theology in Wisdom. Pp. 43–57 in J. G. Gammie et al., editors, *Israelite Wisdom.* Missoula, Montana: Scholars Press.
Hirsch, S. R.
1960–1966 *The Psalms.* 2 volumes. Translated by G. Hirschler. New York: Feldheim.
Holladay, W. L.
1993 *The Psalms through Three Thousand Years: Prayerbook of a Cloud of Witnesses.* Minneapolis: Fortress.
Hossfeld, F.-L.
1994 Psalm 95: Gattungsgeschichtliche, kompositionskritische und bibeltheologische Anfragen. Pp. 29–44 in K. Seybold and E. Zenger, editors, *Neue Wege der Psalmenforschung: Für Walter Beyerlin.* Herders biblische Studien 1. Freiburg: Herder.
Hossfeld, F.-L., and Zenger, E.
1993 *Die Psalmen I: Psalms 1–50.* Die Neue Echter Bibel. Würzburg/Stuttgart: Echter.
Howard, D. M. Jr.
1988 The Case for Kingship in the Old Testament Narrative Books and the Psalms. *Trinity Journal* 9: 19–35.
1989 Editorial Activity in the Psalter: A State-of-the-Field Survey. *Word and World* 9: 274–85.
1990 The Case for Kingship in Deuteronomy and the Former Prophets. *Westminster Theological Journal* 52: 101–15.
1992 David. Pp. 40–49 in volume 2 of D. N. Freedman, editor, *Anchor Bible Dictionary.* New York: Doubleday.
1993a Editorial Activity in the Psalter: A State-of-the-Field Survey. Pp. 52–70 in J. C. McCann, editor, *The Shape and Shaping of the Psalter.* Journal for the Study of the Old Testament Supplement Series 159. Sheffield: JSOT Press.
1993b A Contextual Reading of Psalms 90–94. Pp. 108–23 in J. C. McCann, editor, *The Shape and Shaping of the Psalter.* Journal for the Study of the Old Testament Supplement Series 159. Sheffield: JSOT Press.
1994 Rhetorical Criticism in Old Testament Studies. *Bulletin for Biblical Research* 4: 87–104.
1995 Psalm 94 among the Kingship of YHWH Psalms. Paper delivered at the 1995 Society of Biblical Literature Meetings, Philadelphia, Book of Psalms Group (21 pp.).
Hummel, H. D.
1957 Enclitic *mem* in Early Northwest Semitic, Especially Hebrew. *Journal of Biblical Literature* 76: 83–107.
Jefferson, H. G.
1952 Psalm 93. *Journal of Biblical Literature* 71: 155–60.

Jepsen, A.
1977 אָמַן ʾā-man. Pp. 292–323 in G. J. Botterweck and H. Ringgren, editors, *Theological Dictionary of the Old Testament*. Revised edition. Translated by J. T. Willis. Grand Rapids, Michigan: Eerdmans.
Jeremias, J.
1987 *Das Königtum Gottes in den Psalmen: Israels Begegnun mit dem kanaanäischen Mythos in den Jahwe-König-Psalmen*. Forschungen zur Religion und Literatur des Alten und Neuen Testaments 141. Göttingen: Vandenhoeck & Ruprecht.
Johnson, A. R.
1951 The Psalms. Pp. 162–209 in H. H. Rowley, editor, *The Old Testament and Modern Study*. Oxford: Clarendon.
1967 *Sacral Kingship in Ancient Israel*. 2d edition. Cardiff: University of Wales Press.
Joüon, P.
1947 *Grammaire de l'Hebreu biblique*. 2d edition. Rome: Pontifical Biblical Institute.
1991 *A Grammar of Biblical Hebrew*. 2 volumes. Translated and revised by T. Muraoka. Subsidia Biblica 14/1. Rome: Pontifical Biblical Institute.
Kautzsch, E., editor
1910 *Gesenius' Hebrew Grammar*. 2d English edition. Translated by A. E. Cowley. Oxford: Clarendon.
Keet, C. C.
1969 *A Study of the Psalms of Ascents*. London: Mitre.
Kenik, H. A.
1976 Code of Conduct for a King: Psalm 101. *Journal of Biblical Literature* 95: 391–403.
Kessler, M. J.
1978 Inclusio in the Hebrew Bible. *Semitics* 6: 44–49.
Khanjian, J.
1975 Wisdom. Pp. 371–400 in L. Fisher, editor, *Ras Shamra Parallels, II*. Analecta Orientalia 50. Rome: Pontifical Biblical Institute.
Kidner, D.
1973 *Psalms 1–72*. Tyndale Old Testament Commentary. Downers Grove, Illinois: InterVarsity.
1975 *Psalms 73–150*. Tyndale Old Testament Commentary. Downers Grove, Illinois: InterVarsity.
Kirkpatrick, A. F.
1901 *The Book of Psalms*. Cambridge: Cambridge University Press.
Kissane, M. E. J.
1954 *The Book of Psalms*. 2 volumes. Dublin: Richview.
Kitchen, K. A.
1966 *Ancient Orient and Old Testament*. Downers Grove, Illinois: InterVarsity.
Kittel, R., editor
1937 *Biblia Hebraica*. 3d edition. Stuttgart: Würtembergische Bibelanstalt.
Kleer, M.
1996 *"Der liebliche Sänger der Psalmen Israels": Untersuchungen zu David als Dichter und Beter der Psalmen*. Bonner biblische Beiträge 108. Weinheim: Beltz Athenäum.

Koch, K.
1994 Der Psalter und seine Redaktionsgeschichte. Pp. 243–77 in K. Seybold and E. Zenger, editors, *Neue Wege der Psalmenforschung: Für Walter Beyerlin.* Herders biblische Studien 1. Freiburg: Herder.
Koehler, L.
1953 *Jahwäh Mālāk. Vetus Testamentum* 3: 188–89.
Koehler, L., and Baumgartner, W.
1958 *Lexikon in Veteris Testamenti Libros.* 2d edition, including Supplement. Leiden: Brill.
1967–1991 *Hebräisches und aramäisches Lexikon zum Alten Testament.* 3d edition. 4 volumes. Leiden: Brill.
Kraus, H.-J.
1951 *Die Königsherrschaft Gottes im Alten Testament.* Tübingen: Mohr.
1966 *Worship in Israel: A Cultic History of the Old Testament.* Translated by G. Buswell. Richmond, Virginia: John Knox.
1978 *Psalmen.* 5th edition. 2 volumes. Biblischer Kommentar Altes Testament 15/1–2. Neukirchen-Vluyn: Neukirkener Verlag.
1986 *Theology of the Psalms.* Translated by K. Crim. Minneapolis: Augsburg.
1988 *Psalms 1–59: A Commentary.* Translated by H. C. Oswald. Minneapolis: Augsburg.
1989 *Psalms 60–150: A Commentary.* Translated by H. C. Oswald. Minneapolis: Augsburg.
Kselman, J. S.
1980 Design and Structure in Hebrew Poetry. Pp. 1–16 in P. J. Achtemeier, editor, *Society of Biblical Literature 1980: Seminar Papers.* Society of Biblical Literature Seminar Papers 19. Missoula, Montana: Scholars Press.
Kuntz, J. K.
1974 The Canonical Wisdom Psalms of Ancient Israel: Their Rhetorical, Thematic, and Formal Dimensions. Pp. 186–222 in J. J. Jackson and M. J. Kessler, editors, *Rhetorical Criticism: Essays in Honor of James Muilenburg.* Pittsburgh Theological Monograph Series 1. Pittsburgh: Pickwick.
1977 The Retribution Motif in Psalmic Wisdom. *Zeitschrift für die Alttestamentliche Wissenschaft* 89: 223–33.
1986 King Triumphant: A Rhetorical Study of Psalms 20 and 21. *Hebrew Annual Review* 10: 157–76.
1992 Wisdom Psalms and the Shaping of the Hebrew Psalter. Paper delivered at the 1992 Society of Biblical Literature Meetings, San Francisco, Book of Psalms Group (25 pp.).
Labuschagne, C. J.
1982 The Pattern of the Divine Speech Formulas in the Pentateuch. *Vetus Testamentum* 32: 268–96.
Lambdin, T. O.
1971 *Introduction to Biblical Hebrew.* New York: Scribner's.
Leeuwen, C. van
1979 עֵד *ʿēd* Zeuge. Columns 209–21 in E. Jenni and C. Westermann, editors, *Theologisches Handwörterbuch zum Alten Testament.* 2 volumes. Munich: Chr. Kaiser.

Leiman, S. Z.
1976 *The Canonization of Hebrew Scripture: The Talmudic and Midrashic Evidence.* Transactions of the Connecticut Academy of Arts and Sciences 47. Hamden, Connecticut: Archon.

Leslie, E. A.
1949 *The Psalms: Translated and Interpreted in the Light of Hebrew Life and Worship.* New York: Abingdon.

Lewis, J. O.
1967 An Asseverative לא in Psalm 100[3]? *Journal of Biblical Literature* 86: 216.

Liebreich, L. J.
1955– The Compilation of the Book of Isaiah. *Jewish Quarterly Review* 46: 259–77.
1956 Psalms 34 and 145 in the Light of Their Key Words. *Hebrew Union College Annual* 27: 181–92.
1956– The Compilation of the Book of Isaiah. *Jewish Quarterly Review* 47: 114–38.
1957

Lipiński, E.
1968 *La royauté de Yahwé dans la poésie et le culte de l'ancien Israël.* 2d edition. Brussels: Academie voor Wetenschappen, Letteren en Schone Kunsten van Belgie.

Lisowsky, G.
1981 *Konkordanz zum Hebräischen Alten Testament.* 2d edition. Stuttgart: Deutsche Bibelgesellschaft.

Lohfink, N., and Zenger, E.
1994 *Der Gott Israels und die Völker: Untersuchungen zum Jesajabuch und zu den Psalmen.* Stuttgarter Bibelstudien 154. Stuttgart: Katholisches Bibelwerk.

Longman, T.
1984 Psalm 98: A Divine Warrior Victory Song. *Journal of the Evangelical Theological Society* 27: 257–66.

Loretz, O.
1974a Psalmenstudien III. *Ugarit-Forschungen* 6: 175–210.
1974b Stichometrische und textologische Probleme in den Thronbesteigungspsalmen: Psalmenstudien (IV). *Ugarit Forschungen* 6: 211–40.
1974c Die Umpunktierung von *mʾd* zu *māʾēd* in den Psalmen. *Ugarit-Forschungen* 6: 481–84.

Lund, N. W.
1930 The Presence of Chiasmus in the Old Testament. *American Journal of Semitic Languages and Literatures* 46: 104–20.
1933 Chiasmus in the Psalms. *American Journal of Semitic Languages and Literatures* 49: 281–312.

Lyons, J.
1969 *Introduction to Theoretical Linguistics.* Cambridge: Cambridge University Press.

McCann, J. C. Jr.
1992 The Psalms as Instruction. *Interpretation* 46: 117–28.
1993a Books I–III and the Editorial Purpose of the Hebrew Psalter. Pp. 93–107 in McCann, editor, *The Shape and Shaping of the Psalter* (1993b).
1993b *A Theological Introduction to the Book of Psalms: The Psalms as Torah.* Nashville: Abingdon.

1996 "The Book of Psalms: Introduction, Commentary, and Reflections." Pp. 639–1280 in volume 4 of L. Keck et al., editors, *The New Interpreter's Bible.* Nashville: Abingdon.

McCann, J. C. Jr., editor

1993 *The Shape and Shaping of the Psalter.* Journal for the Study of the Old Testament Supplement Series 159. Sheffield: JSOT Press.

McCarter, P. K. Jr.

1984 *II Samuel.* Anchor Bible 9. New York: Doubleday.

McCullough, W. S.

1956 The "Enthronement of Yahweh" Psalms. Pp. 53–61 in E. C. Hobbs, editor, *A Stubborn Faith.* Dallas: Southern Methodist University Press.

McCullough, W. S., and Taylor, W. R.

1955 Introduction and Exegesis to the Book of Psalms. Pp. 3–763 in volume 4 of G. A. Buttrick, editor, *The Interpreter's Bible.* New York: Abingdon.

McFall, L.

1982 *The Enigma of the Hebrew Verbal System: Solutions from Ewald to the Present Day.* Historic Texts and Interpreters 2. Sheffield: Almond.

McKenzie, J. L.

1967 Reflections on Wisdom. *Journal of Biblical Literature* 86: 1–9.

Magne, J.

1958 Repetitions de mots et exégèse dans quelques psaumes et le Pater. *Biblica* 39: 177–97.

Marcus, D.

1974 Ugaritic Evidence for "The Almighty / The Grand One"? *Biblica* 55: 404–7.

Massouh, S.

1983 Exegetical Notes: Psalm 95. *Trinity Journal* 4: 84–88.

May, H. G.

1955 Some Cosmic Implications of *Mayim Rabbim*, "Many Waters." *Journal of Biblical Literature* 74: 9–21.

Mays, J. L.

1969 Worship, World, and Power: An Interpretation of Psalm 100. *Interpretation* 23: 315–30.

1986a The David of the Psalms. *Interpretation* 40: 143–55.

1986b The Place of Torah-Psalms in the Psalter. *Journal of Biblical Literature* 106: 3–12.

1991 "In a Vision": The Portrayal of the Messiah in the Psalms. *Ex Auditu* 7: 1–8.

1993 The Question of Context in Psalm Interpretation. Pp. 14–20 in J. C. McCann, editor, *The Shape and Shaping of the Psalter.* Journal for the Study of the Old Testament Supplement Series 159. Sheffield: JSOT Press.

1994a *Psalms.* Interpretation. Louisville: John Knox.

1994b The Centre of the Psalms. Pp. 231–46 in S. E. Balentine and J. Barton, editors, *Language, Theology, and the Bible: Essays in Honor of James Barr.* Oxford: Clarendon.

Mendenhall, G. E.

1954a Ancient Oriental and Biblical Law. *The Biblical Archaeologist* 17: 26–46.

1954b Covenant Forms in Israelite Tradition. *The Biblical Archaeologist* 17: 50–76.

1973 The "Vengeance" of Yahweh. Pp. 70–104 in *The Tenth Generation: The Origins of the Biblical Tradition.* Baltimore: Johns Hopkins University Press.

Mendenhall, G. E., and Herion, G. A.

1992 Covenant. Pp. 1179–202 in volume 1 of D. N. Freedman, editor, *Anchor Bible Dictionary.* Garden City, New York: Doubleday.

Meyers, C. L., and O'Connor, M., editors

1983 *The Word of the Lord Shall Go Forth: Essays in Honor of David Noel Freedman in Celebration of His Sixtieth Birthday.* Winona Lake, Indiana: Eisenbrauns / Philadelphia: American Schools of Oriental Research.

Michel, D.

1956 Studien zu den sogenannten Thronbesteigungspsalmen. *Vetus Testamentum* 6: 40–68.

Millard, A. R.

1970 "Scriptio Continua" in Early Hebrew: Ancient Practice or Modern Surmise? *Journal of Semitic Studies* 15: 2–15.

Millard, M.

1994 *Die Komposition des Psalters: Ein formgeschichtlicher Ansatz.* Forschungen Alten Testament 9. Tübingen: Mohr, Siebeck.

Miller, P. D. Jr.

1980 Synonymous-Sequential Parallelism in the Psalms. *Biblica* 61: 256–60.

1983 Trouble and Woe: Interpreting Biblical Laments. *Interpretation* 37: 32–45.

1985 Current Issues in Psalms Studies. *Word and World* 5: 132–43.

1993 The Beginning of the Psalter. Pp. 83–92 in J. C. McCann, editor, *The Shape and Shaping of the Psalter.* Journal for the Study of the Old Testament Supplement Series 159. Sheffield: JSOT Press.

1994 Kingship, Torah Obedience, and Prayer: The Theology of Psalms 15–24. Pp. 127–42 in K. Seybold and E. Zenger, editors, *Neue Wege der Psalmenforschung: Für Walter Beyerlin.* Herders biblische Studien 1. Freiburg: Herder.

Moll, C. B., and Conant, T. J.

1872 *The Psalms.* Lange's Bible Commentary 11. New York: Scribner, Armstrong.

Moran, W. L.

1961 The Hebrew Language in Its Northwest Semitic Background. Pp. 54–72 in G. E. Wright, editor, *The Bible and the Ancient Near East: Essays in Honor of William Foxwell Albright.* New York: Doubleday. Reprinted. Winona Lake, Indiana: Eisenbrauns (1979).

Mowinckel, S. O. P.

1922 *Psalmenstudien II: Das Thronbesteigungfest Jahwäs und der Ursprung der Eschatologie.* Kristiania (Oslo): Jacob Dybwad.

1962 *The Psalms in Israel's Worship.* 2 volumes. Translated by D. R. Ap-Thomas. Nashville: Abingdon.

Muilenburg, J.

1961 The Linguistic and Rhetorical Usages of the Particle כי in the Old Testament. *Hebrew Union College Annual* 32: 135–60.

Murphy, R. E.

1963 A Consideration of the Classification, "Wisdom Psalms." Pp. 156–67 in *Congress Volume: Bonn, 1962.* Vetus Testamentum Supplements 9. Leiden: Brill.

1981 Hebrew Wisdom. *Journal of the American Oriental Society* 101: 21–34.

1993 Reflections on Contextual Interpretation of the Psalms. Pp. 21–28 in J. C. McCann, editor, *The Shape and Shaping of the Psalter.* Journal for the Study of the Old Testament Supplement Series 159. Sheffield: JSOT Press.

Neale, J. M., and Littledale, R. F.

1874–79 *A Commentary on the Psalms: From Primitive and Medieval Writers.* 3d edi-
1979 tion. 4 volumes. London: Joseph Masters.

Niemeyer, C. T.

1950 *Het probleem van de rangschikking der Psalmen.* Leiden: Luctor et Emergo.

Nötscher, F.

1947 *Die Psalmen.* Echter Bibel. Würzburg: Echter.

1953 Zum emphatischen *Lamed. Vetus Testamentum* 3: 372–80.

O'Connor, M.

1980 *Hebrew Verse Structure.* Winona Lake, Indiana: Eisenbrauns.

Oesterley, W. O. E.

1910 *The Psalms in the Jewish Church.* London: Skeffington.

1937 *A Fresh Approach to the Psalms.* New York: Scribner's.

1939 *The Psalms: Translated with Text-Critical and Exegetical Notes.* London: SPCK.

Ollenburger, B. C.

1987 *Zion, The City of the Great King: A Theological Symbol of the Jerusalem Cult.* Journal for the Study of the Old Testament Supplement Series 41. Sheffield: JSOT Press.

Parunak, H. V. D.

1983 Transitional Techniques in the Bible. *Journal of Biblical Literature* 102: 525–48.

Perowne, J. J. S.

1890 *The Book of Psalms.* 7th edition. 2 volumes. Andover: Warren F. Draper.

Porter, J. R.

1963 The Pentateuch and the Triennial Lectionary Cycle: An Exam-ination of a Recent Theory. Pp. 163–74 in F. F. Bruce, editor, *Promise and Fulfillment.* S. H. Hooke Festschrift. Edinburgh: T. & T. Clark.

Raabe, P. R.

1990 *Psalms Structures: A Study of Psalms with Refrains.* Journal for the Study of the Old Testament Supplement Series 104. Sheffield: JSOT Press.

Rad, G. von

1972 *Wisdom in Israel.* Nashville: Abingdon.

Rahlfs, A., editor

1935 *Septuaginta.* 2 volumes. Stuttgart: Deutsche Bibelgesellschaft.

Reindl, J.

1979 Psalm 1 und der Sitz im Leben des Psalters. *Theologisches Jahrbuch*: 39–50.

1981 Weisheitliche Bearbeitung von Psalmen: Ein Beitrag zum Verständnis der Sammlung des Psalters. Pp. 333–56 in *Congress Volume: Vienna 1980.* Vetus Testamentum Supplements 32. Leiden: Brill.

Rendtorff, R.

1986 *The Old Testament: An Introduction.* Philadelphia: Fortress.

Richardson, H. N.

1966 A Critical Note on Amos 7:14. *Journal of Biblical Literature* 85: 89.

Ridderbos, J.
1953 *Jahwäh Malak. Vetus Testamentum* 4: 87–89.
Ridderbos, N. H.
1963 The Psalms: Style-Figures and Structure. *Oudtestamentische Studien* 13: 43–76.
Riding, C. B.
1976 Psalm 95:1–7c as a Large Chiasm. *Zeitschrift für die Alttestamentlich Wissenschaft* 88: 418.
Ringgren, H.
1962 Enthronement Festival or Covenant Renewal? *Biblical Research* 7: 45–48.
Roberts, J. J. M.
1973 The Davidic Origin of the Zion Tradition. *Journal of Biblical Literature* 92: 329–44.
1982 Zion in the Theology of the Davidic-Solomonic Empire. Pp. 93–108 in T. Ishida, editor, *Studies in the Period of David and Solomon and Other Essays.* Winona Lake, Indiana: Eisenbrauns.
1987 In Defense of the Monarchy: The Contribution of Israelite Kingship to Biblical Theology. Pp. 377–96 in P. D. Miller Jr., P. D. Hanson, S. D. McBride, editors, *Ancient Israelite Religion: Essays in Honor of Frank Moore Cross.* Philadelphia: Fortress.
Robertson, D. A.
1972 *Linguistic Evidence in Dating Early Hebrew Poetry.* Society of Biblical Literature Dissertation Series 3. Missoula, Montana: Society of Biblical Literature.
Rosenberg, R. A.
1966 Yahweh Becomes King. *Journal of Biblical Literature* 85: 297–307.
Sabourin, L.
1969 *The Psalms: Their Origin and Meaning.* 2 volumes. Staten Island, New York: Alba House.
Sakenfeld, K. D.
1978 *The Meaning of Ḥesed in the Hebrew Bible: A New Inquiry.* Harvard Semitic Monographs 17. Missoula, Montana: Scholars Press.
Sanders, J. A.
1967 *The Dead Sea Psalms Scroll.* Ithaca, New York: Cornell University Press.
1972 *Torah and Canon.* Philadelphia: Fortress.
1984 *Canon and Community: A Guide to Canonical Criticism.* Guides to Biblical Scholarship. Philadelphia: Fortress.
1992 The Dead Sea Scrolls and Biblical Studies. Pp. 323–36 in M. Fishbane, E. Tov, and W. W. Fields, editors, *"Shaᶜarei Talmon": Studies in the Bible, Qumran, and the Ancient Near East Presented to Shemaryahu Talmon.* Winona Lake, Indiana: Eisenbrauns.
Schmidt, H.
1934 *Die Psalmen.* Handbuch zum Alten Testament 15. Tübingen: Mohr, Siebeck.
Schreiner, J., editor
1972 *Wort, Lied und Gottesspruch: Beiträge zu Psalmen und Propheten.* 2 volumes. J. Ziegler Festschrift. Würzburg/Stuttgart: Echter.

Scott, R. B. Y.
1971 *The Way of Wisdom in the Old Testament.* New York: Macmillan.

Seybold, K.
1978 *Die Wallfahrtpsalmen: Studien zur Entstehungsgeschichte von Psalm 120–134.* Biblische-Theologische Studien 3. Neukirchen-Vluyn: Neukirchener Verlag.
1979 Die Redaktion der Wallfahrtspsalmen. *Zeitschrift für die Alttestamentliche Wissenschaft* 91: 247–68.
1990 *Introducing the Psalms.* Translated by R. G. Dunphy. Edinburgh: T. & T. Clark.

Seybold, K., and Zenger, E., editors
1994 *Neue Wege der Psalmenforschung: Für Walter Beyerlin.* Herders biblische Studien 1. Freiburg: Herder.

Sharrock, G. E.
1983 Psalm 74: A Literary-Structural Analysis. *Andrews University Seminary Studies* 21: 211–23.

Shenkel, J. D.
1965 An Interpretation of Psalm 93,5. *Biblica* 46: 401–16.

Shepherd, J. E.
1995 *The Book of Psalms as the Book of Christ: The Application of the Christo-Canonical Method to the Book of Psalms.* Ph.D. Dissertation, Westminster Theological Seminary.

Sheppard, G. T.
1980 *Wisdom as a Hermeneutical Construct: A Study in the Sapientializing of the Old Testament.* Beiheft zur Zeitschrift für die alttestamentliche Wissenschaft 151. Berlin: de Gruyter.
1988 "Blessed Are Those Who Take Refuge in Him" (Psa 2:11): Biblical Criticism and Deconstruction. *Religion and Intellectual Life* 5: 57–66.
1991 The Role of the Canonical Context in the Interpretation of the Solomonic Wisdom Books. Pp. 67–107 in G. T. Sheppard, editor, *Solomon's Divine Arts: Joseph Hall's Representation of Proverbs, Ecclesiastes, and the Song of Songs (1609).* Cleveland: Pilgrim.
1992 Theology and the Book of Psalms. *Interpretation* 46: 143–55.

Sinclair, L. A.
1990 11QPs[a], a Psalms Scroll from Qumran: Text and Canon. Pp. 109–15 in J. C. Knight and L. A. Sinclair, editors, *The Psalms and Other Studies on the Old Testament Presented to Joseph I. Hunt.* Nashotah, Wisconsin: Nashotah House Seminary.

Skehan, P. W.
1964 A Psalm Manuscript from Qumran (4QPs[b]). *Catholic Biblical Quarterly* 26: 313–22.
1971 The Seven Columns of Wisdom's House in Proverbs 1–9. Pp. 9–14 in *Studies in Israelite Poetry and Wisdom.* Catholic Biblical Quarterly Monograph Series I. Washington: Catholic Biblical Association.
1979 Structures in Poems on Wisdom: Proverbs 8 and Sirach 24. *Catholic Biblical Quarterly* 41: 365–79.

Smith, H. P.
1905 The Emphatic ל or לא. *Journal of Biblical Literature* 24: 80.
Smith, M. S.
1992a The Psalms as a Book for Pilgrims. *Interpretation* 46: 156–66.
1992b The Theology of the Redaction of the Psalter: Some Observations. *Zeitschrift für die Alttestamentliche Wissenschaft* 104: 408–12.
Soden, W. von
1969 *Grundriss der Akkadischen Grammatik, samt Ergänzungsheft.* Analecta Orientalia 33, 47. Rome: Pontifical Biblical Institute.
Stek, J. H.
1974 The Stylistics of Hebrew Poetry: A (Re)New(ed) Focus of Study. *Calvin Theological Journal* 9: 15–30.
Sternberg, M.
1985 *The Poetics of Biblical Narrative.* Bloomington: Indiana University Press.
Tate, M. E.
1990 *Psalms 51–100.* Word Biblical Commentary 20. Waco, Texas: Word.
1995 Psalms. Pp. 431–526 in W. E. Mills and R. F. Wilson, editors, *Mercer Commentary on the Bible.* Macon, Georgia: Mercer University Press.
Tur-Sinai, N. H.
1950 The Literary Character of the Book of Psalms. *Oudtestamentische Studien* 8: 263–81.
Vogels, W.
1979 A Structural Analysis of Psalm 1. *Biblica* 60: 410–16.
Waltke, B. K.
1981 A Canonical Process Approach to the Psalms. Pp. 3–18 in J. S. and P. D. Feinberg, editors, *Tradition and Testament.* C. L. Feinberg Festschrift. Chicago: Moody.
Walton, J. H.
1991 Psalms: A Cantata about the Davidic Covenant. *Journal of the Evangelical Theological Society* 34: 21–31.
Watson, W. G. E.
1969 Shared Consonants in Northwest Semitic. *Biblica* 50: 525–33.
1984 *Classical Hebrew Poetry: A Guide to Its Techniques.* Journal for the Study of the Old Testament Supplement Series 26. Sheffield: JSOT Press.
Watters, W. R.
1976 *Formula Criticism and the Poetry of the Old Testament.* Beiheft zur Zeitschrift für die Alttestamentliche Wissenschaft 138. Berlin: de Gruyter.
Watts, J. D. W.
1965 *Yahweh Mālak* Psalms. *Theologische Zeitschrift* 21: 341–48.
Weinfeld, M.
1976 Covenant, Davidic. Pp. 188–92 in K. Crim, editor, *Interpreter's Dictionary of the Bible: Supplement.* Nashville: Abingdon.
1985 Zion and Jerusalem as Religious and Political Capital: Ideology and Utopia. Pp. 75–115 in R. E. Friedman, editor, *The Poet and the Historian: Essays in Literary and Historical Biblical Criticism.* Harvard Semitic Studies. Chico, California: Scholars Press.

Weingreen, J.
1959 *A Practical Grammar for Classical Hebrew.* 2d edition. Oxford: Oxford University Press.
Weiser, A.
1962 *The Psalms.* Old Testament Library. Translated by H. Hartwell. Philadelphia: Westminster.
Welch, J. W., editor
1981 *Chiasmus in Antiquity: Structures, Analyses, Exegesis.* Hildesheim: Gerstenberg.
Wellhausen, J.
1898 *The Book of Psalms.* Polychrome Bible. London: James Clark.
Welten, P.
1982 Königsherrschaft Jahwes und Thronbesteigung: Bemerkungen zu unerledigten Fragen. *Vetus Testamentum* 32: 297–310.
Westermann, C.
1962 Zur Sammlung des Psalters. *Theologia Viatorum* 8: 278–84.
1980 *The Psalms: Structure, Content and Message.* Minneapolis: Augsburg.
1981a *Praise and Lament in the Psalms.* Translated by K. R. Crim and R. N. Soulen. Atlanta: John Knox.
1981b The Formation of the Psalter. Translated by R. N. Soulen. Pp. 250–58 in *Praise and Lament in the Psalms* (1981a).
Westhuizen, J. P. van der
1978 Hendiadys in Biblical Hymns of Praise. *Semitics* 6: 50–57.
Whitley, C. F.
1973 Psalm 99 8. *Zeitschrift für die Alttestamentliche Wissenschaft* 85: 227–30.
Whybray, R. N.
1969 "Their Wrongdoings" in Psalm 99. *Zeitschrift für die Alttestamentliche Wissenschaft* 81: 237–39.
1996 *Reading the Psalms as a Book.* Journal for the Study of the Old Testament Supplement Series 222. Sheffield: Sheffield Academic Press.
Williams, W. G.
1957 Liturgical Aspects in Enthronement Psalms. *Journal of Bible and Religion* 25: 118–22.
Willis, J. T.
1979a Psalm 1: An Entity. *Zeitschrift für die Alttestamentliche Wissenschaft* 91: 381–401.
1979b The Juxtaposition of Synonymous and Chiastic Parallelism in Tricola in Old Testament Hebrew Psalms Poetry. *Vetus Testamentum* 29: 465–80.
Wilson, G. H.
1983 The Qumran Psalms Manuscripts and the Consecutive Arrangement of Psalms in the Hebrew Psalter. *Catholic Biblical Quarterly* 45: 377–88.
1984 Evidence of Editorial Divisions in the Hebrew Psalter. *Vetus Testamentum* 34: 337–52.
1985a *The Editing of the Hebrew Psalter.* Society of Biblical Literature Dissertation Series 76. Chico, California: Scholars Press.
1985b The Qumran Psalms Scroll Reconsidered: Analysis of the Debate. *Catholic Biblical Quarterly* 47: 624–42.

1985c The Use of "Untitled" Psalms in the Hebrew Psalter. *Zeitschrift für die Alttestamentliche Wissenschaft* 97: 404–13.

1986 The Use of Royal Psalms at the "Seams" of the Hebrew Psalter. *Journal for the Study of the Old Testament* 35: 85–94.

1990 A First-Century CE Date for the Closing of the Hebrew Psalter? Pp. 136–43 in J. J. Adler and B. Z. Luria, editors, *Haim M. I. Gevaryahu Memorial Volume.* Jerusalem: World Jewish Bible Center.

1992 The Shape of the Book of Psalms. *Interpretation* 46: 129–42.

1993a Understanding the Purposeful Arrangement of Psalms in the Psalter: Pitfalls and Promise. Pp. 42–51 in J. C. McCann, editor, *The Shape and Shaping of the Psalter.* Journal for the Study of the Old Testament Supplement Series 159. Sheffield: JSOT Press.

1993b Shaping the Psalter: A Consideration of Editorial Linkage in the Book of Psalms. Pp. 72–82 in J. C. McCann, editor, *The Shape and Shaping of the Psalter.* Journal for the Study of the Old Testament Supplement Series 159. Sheffield: JSOT Press.

Yeivin, I.

1969 The Division into Sections in the Book of Psalms. *Textus* 7: 76–102.

Zenger, E.

1991 Israel und Kirche im gemeinsamen Gottesbund: Beobachtungen zum theologischen Programm des 4. Psalmenbuchs (Ps 90–106). Pp. 236–54 in M. Marcus, E. W. Stegemann, E. Zenger, editors, *Israel und Kirche heute: Beiträge zum christlich-jüdischen Dialog—Für Ernst Ludwig Ehrlich.* Freiburg: Herder.

1993 Der Psalter als Wegweiser und Wegbegleiter: Ps 1–2 als Proömium des Psalmenbuchs. Pp. 29–47 in A. Angenendt and H. Vorgrimler, editors, *Sie wandern von Kraft zu Kraft: Aufbrüche, Wege, Begegnungen—Festgabe für Bischof Reinhard Lettman.* Kevelaer: Butzon & Bercker.

1994a Das Weltenkönigtum des Gottes Israels (Ps 90–106). Pp. 151–78 in N. Lohfink and E. Zenger, *Der Gott Israels und die Völker: Untersuchungen zum Jesajabuch und zu den Psalmen.* Stuttgarter Bibelstudien 154. Stuttgart: Katholisches Bibelwerk.

1994b New Approaches to the Study of the Psalter. *Proceedings of the Irish Biblical Association* 17: 37–54.

Zimmerli, W.

1972 Zwillingspsalmen. Pp. 105–13 in volume 2 of J. Schreiner, editor, *Wort, Lied und Gottesspruch: Beiträge zu Psalmen und Propheten.* J. Ziegler Festschrift. Würzburg/Stuttgart: Echter.

# *Index of Authors*